HISTORY OF
ANCIENT CIVILIZATION

HISTORY OF
ANCIENT CIVILIZATION

By

CHARLES SEIGNOBOS

TRANSLATED AND EDITED BY

ARTHUR HERBERT WILDE

WITH AN INTRODUCTION BY

JAMES ALTON JAMES, Ph.D.

GYAN

Published by

GYAN

Gyan Publishing House
5, Ansari Road
Daryaganj, New Delhi-110002
Phone: 011-47034999, 9811692060
E-mail: books@gyanbooks.com

Distribution Network
gyanbooks.com
India, USA, Canada, UK, Australia, France

ISBN : 978-81-212-6484-6 (PB)
First Published, 1906

2nd Impression 2022

Printed at: Gyan Press, Delhi.

HISTORY OF ANCIENT CIVILIZATION
Author: CHARLES SEIGNOBOS

HISTORY OF
ANCIENT CIVILIZATION

BY

CHARLES SEIGNOBOS

TRANSLATED AND EDITED BY

ARTHUR HERBERT WILDE

WITH AN INTRODUCTION BY

JAMES ALTON JAMES, Ph.D.

1906

INTRODUCTORY NOTE

DURING the year 1900, the "Histoire de la Civilisation" by M. Charles Seignobos appeared as three volumes in the third edition and as two volumes in the sixth edition. It seemed that a work so meritorious and so widely used, especially in the secondary schools of France, would be of value to teachers and pupils in American schools. The ability of the author to select significant events in the political and social history of the various nations is notable. Professor Seignobos willingly gave his consent to having the translation made.

It was thought best to select material from both the three volumes and the two volumes in so far as the one supplemented the other. Ordinarily, the original three-volume edition has been used.

In some particulars the work is not merely a translation. Phrases here and there not regarded as essential to an understanding of the text have been omitted. The tables of contents have been made more usable. An index has been added to each volume, and a general bibliography has been prepared for each period.

It is believed desirable to give American readers the following brief notice of Professor Seignobos. He was born in Lamastre, France, in the year 1854.

After a course of study in the "École Normale Supérieure," he spent two years in the universities of Germany, making a study of their courses in history. In 1879 he was elected Professor of History in the University of Dijon. He was called to a professorship in the Sorbonne in 1883, and in 1890 was made Maître des Conférences at the Sorbonne, and is now Maître des Conférences in the "Faculté des Lettres" of Paris. Professor Seignobos occupies a place of prominence among modern French historians and is also a leader in the cause of secondary education.

In addition to the "Histoire de la Civilisation" he is the author of numerous historical works. Among the more important are: "Le régime féodal en Bourgogne"; "Histoire narrative et descriptive des anciens peuples de l'Orient"; "Scènes et épisodes de l'histoire nationale"; "Histoire politique de l'Europe contemporaine." He is joint author with M. Langlois of "Introduction aux études historiques."

JAMES ALTON JAMES.

NORTHWESTERN UNIVERSITY, *April* 20, 1906.

EDITOR'S PREFACE

In preparing this volume, I have used both the three-volume edition and the two-volume edition of the "Histoire de la Civilisation." I have usually preferred the order of topics of the two-volume edition, but have supplemented the material therein with other matter drawn from the three-volume edition.

A few corrections to the text have been given in foot-notes. These notes are always clearly distinguished from the elucidations of the author.

I have had the benefit of a critical reading of the manuscript by my colleague, Professor James Alton James, at whose suggestion the work of translation was undertaken.

Arthur H. Wilde,
Northwestern University.

Evanston, Ill., *April* 20, 1906.

CONTENTS

CHAPTER I

CHAPTER II

CHAPTER III

CHAPTER IV

CHAPTER V

CHAPTER VI

CHAPTER VII

CHAPTER XII

CHAPTER XIII

CHAPTER XIV

CHAPTER XV

CHAPTER XVI

CHAPTER XVII

CHAPTER XVIII

CHAPTER XIX

CHAPTER XX

CHAPTER XXV

CHAPTER XXVI

CHAPTER XXVII

CHAPTER I

THE ORIGINS OF CIVILIZATION

PREHISTORIC ARCHÆOLOGY

Prehistoric Remains.—One often finds buried in the earth, weapons, implements, human skeletons, débris of every kind left by men of whom we have no direct knowledge. These are dug up by the thousand in all the provinces of France, in Switzerland, in England, in all Europe; they are found even in Asia and Africa. It is probable that they exist in all parts of the world.

These remains are called prehistoric because they are more ancient than written history. For about fifty years men have been engaged in recovering and studying them. Today most museums have a hall, or at least, some cases filled with these relics. A museum at Saint-German-en-Laye, near Paris, is entirely given up to prehistoric remains. In Denmark is a collection of more than 30,000 objects. Every day adds to the discoveries as excavations are made, houses built, and cuts made for railroads.

These objects are not found on the surface of the ground, but ordinarily buried deeply where the earth has not been disturbed. They are recovered from a stratum of gravel or clay which has been deposited gradually and has fixed them in place safe from the air, a sure proof that they have been there for a long time.

Prehistoric Science.—Scholars have examined the débris and have asked themselves what men have left them. From their skeletons, they have tried to construct their physical appearance; from their tools, the kind of life they led. They have determined that these instruments resemble those used by certain savages today. The study of all these objects constitutes a new science, Prehistoric Archæology.[1]

The Four Ages.—Prehistoric remains come down to us from very diverse races of men; they have been deposited in the soil at widely different epochs since the time when the mammoth lived in western Europe, a sort of gigantic elephant with woolly hide and curved tusks. This long lapse of time may be divided into four periods, called Ages:

1. The Rough Stone Age.
2. The Polished Stone Age.
3. The Bronze Age.
4. The Iron Age.

The periods take their names from the materials used in the manufacture of the tools,—stone, bronze, iron. These epochs, however, are of very unequal length. It may be that the Rough Stone Age was ten times as long as the Age of Iron.

THE ROUGH STONE AGE

Gravel Débris.—The oldest remains of the Stone Age have been found in the gravels. A French scholar found between 1841 and 1853, in the valley of the Somme, certain sharp instruments made of flint. They

[1] It originated especially with French, Swiss, and Danish scholars.

were buried to a depth of six metres in gravel under three layers of clay, gravel, and marl which had never been broken up. In the same place they discovered bones of cattle, deer, and elephants. For a long time people made light of this discovery. They said that the chipping of the flints was due to chance. At last, in 1860, several scholars came to study the remains in the valley of the Somme and recognized that the flints had certainly been cut by men. Since then there have been found more than 5,000 similar flints in strata of the same order either in the valley of the Seine or in England, and some of them by the side of human bones. There is no longer any doubt that men were living at the epoch when the gravel strata were in process of formation. If the strata that cover these remains have always been deposited as slowly as they are today, these men whose bones and tools we unearth must have lived more than 200,000 years ago.

The Cave Men.—Remains are also found in caverns cut in rock, often above a river. The most noted are those on the banks of the Vézère, but they exist in many other places. Sometimes they have been used as habitations and even as graves for men. Skeletons, weapons, and tools are found here together. There are axes, knives, scrapers, lance-points of flint; arrows, harpoon-points, needles of bone like those used by certain savages to this day. The soil is strewn with the bones of animals which these men, untidy like all savages, threw into a corner after they had eaten the meat; they even split the bones to extract the marrow just as savages do now. Among the animals are found not only the hare, the deer, the ox, the horse, the salmon, but also the rhinoceros, the cave-bear, the mammoth, the elk, the bison, the reindeer, which are all extinct or have long disappeared from France. Some designs have been discovered engraved on the bone of a reindeer or on the tusk of a mammoth. One of these represents a combat of reindeer; another a mammoth with woolly hide and curved tusks. Doubtless these men were the contemporaries of the mammoth and the reindeer. They were, like the Esquimaux of our day, a race of hunters and fishermen, knowing how to work in flint and to kindle fires.

POLISHED STONE AGE

Lake Dwellings.—In 1854, Lake Zurich being very low on account of the unusual dryness of the summer, dwellers on the shore of the lake found, in the mud, wooden piles which had been much eaten away, also some rude utensils. These were the remains of an ancient village built over the water. Since this time more than 200 similar villages have been found in the lakes of Switzerland. They have been called Lake Villages. The piles on which they rest are trunks of trees, pointed and driven into the lake-bottom to a depth of several yards. Every village required 30,000 to 40,000 of these.

A wooden platform was supported by the pile work and on this were built wooden houses covered with turf. Objects found by the hundred among the piles reveal the character of the life of the former inhabitants. They ate animals killed in the chase—the deer, the boar, and the elk. But they were already acquainted with such domestic animals as the ox, the goat, the sheep, and the dog. They knew how to till the ground, to reap, and to grind their grain; for in the ruins of their villages are to be found grains of wheat and even fragments of bread, or rather unleavend cakes. They wore coarse cloths of hemp and sewed them into garments with needles of bone. They made pottery but were very awkward in its manufacture. Their vases were poorly burned, turned by hand, and adorned with but few lines. Like the cave-men, they used knives and arrows of flint; but they made their axes of a very hard stone which they had learned to polish. This is why we call their epoch the Polished Stone Age. They are much later than the cave-men, for they know neither the mammoth nor the rhinoceros, but still are acquainted with the elk and the reindeer.[1]

Megalithic Monuments.—Megalith is the name given to a monument formed of enormous blocks of rough stone. Sometimes the rock is bare, sometimes covered with a mass of earth. The buried monument is called a *Tumulus* on account of its resemblance to a hill. When it is opened, one finds within a chamber of rock, sometimes paved with flag-stones. The monuments whose stone is above ground are of various sorts. The *Dolmen,* or table of rock, is formed of a long stone laid flat over other stones set in the ground. The *Cromlech,* or stone-circle, consists of massive rocks arranged in a circle. The *Menhir* is a block of stone standing on its end. Frequently several menhirs are ranged in line. At Carnac in Brittany four thousand

[1] According to Lubbock (Prehistoric Times, N. Y., 1890, p. 212) the reindeer was not known to the Second Stone Age.—Ed.

menhirs in eleven rows are still standing. Probably there were once ten thousand of these in this locality. Megalithic monuments appear by hundreds in western France, especially in Brittany; almost every hill in England has them; the Orkney Islands alone contain more than two thousand. Denmark and North Germany are studded with them; the people of the country call the tumuli the tombs of the giants.

Megalithic monuments are encountered outside of Europe—in India, and on the African coast. No one knows what people possessed the power to quarry such masses and then transport and erect them. For a long time it was believed that the people were the ancient Gauls, or Celts, whence the name Celtic Monuments. But why are like remains found in Africa and in India?

When one of these tumuli still intact is opened, one always sees a skeleton, often several, either sitting or reclining; these monuments, therefore, were used as tombs. Arms, vases, and ornaments are placed at the side of the dead. In the oldest of these tombs the weapons are axes of polished stone; the ornaments are shells, pearls, necklaces of bone or ivory; the vases are very simple, without handle or neck, decorated only with lines or with points. Calcined bones of animals lie about on the ground, the relics of a funeral repast laid in the tomb by the friends of the dead. Amidst these bones we no longer find those of the reindeer, a fact which proves that these monuments were constructed after the disappearance of this animal from western Europe, and therefore at a time subsequent to that of the lake villages.

THE AGE OF BRONZE

Bronze Age.—As soon as men learned to smelt metals, they preferred these to stone in the manufacture of weapons. The metal first to be used was copper, easier to extract because found free, and easier to manipulate since it is malleable without the application of heat. Pure copper, however, was not employed, as weapons made of it were too fragile; but a little tin was mixed with it to give it more resistance. It is this alloy of copper and tin that we call bronze.

Bronze Utensils.—Bronze was used in the manufacture of ordinary tools—knives, hammers, saws, needles, fish-hooks; in the fabrication of ornaments—bracelets, brooches, ear-rings; and especially in the making of arms—daggers, lance-points, axes, and swords. These objects are found by thousands throughout Europe in the mounds, under the more recent dolmens, in the turf-pits of Denmark, and in rock-tombs. Near these objects of bronze, ornaments of gold are often seen and, now and then, the remains of a woollen garment. It cannot be due to chance that all implements of bronze are similar and all are made according to the same alloy. Doubtless they revert to the same period of time and are anterior to the coming of the Romans into Gaul, for they are never discovered in the midst of débris of the Roman period. But what men used them? What people invented bronze? Nobody knows.

THE IRON AGE

Iron.—As iron was harder to smelt and work than bronze, it was later that men learned how to use it. As soon as it was appreciated that iron was harder and cut better than bronze, men preferred it in the manufacture of arms. In Homer's time iron is still a precious metal reserved for swords, bronze being retained for other purposes. It is for this reason that many tombs contain confused remains of utensils of bronze and weapons of iron.

Iron Weapons.—These arms are axes, swords, daggers, and bucklers. They are ordinarily found by the side of a skeleton in a coffin of stone or wood, for warriors had their arms buried with them. But they are found also scattered on ancient battle-fields or lost at the bottom of a marsh which later became a turf-pit. There were found in a turf-pit in Schleswig in one day 100 swords, 500 lances, 30 axes, 460 daggers, 80 knives, 40 stilettos—and all of iron. Not far from there in the bed of an ancient lake was discovered a great boat 66 feet long, fully equipped with axes, swords, lances, and knives.

It is impossible to enumerate the iron implements thus found. They have not been so well preserved as the bronze, as iron is rapidly eaten away by rust. At the first glance, therefore, they appear the older, but in reality are more recent.

Epoch of the Iron Age.—The inhabitants of northern Europe knew iron before the coming of the Romans, the first century before Christ. In an old cemetery near the salt mines of Hallstadt in Austria they have opened 980 tombs filled with instruments of iron and bronze without finding a single piece of Roman money. But the Iron Age continued under the Romans. Almost always iron objects are found accompanied by ornaments of gold and silver, by Roman pottery, funeral urns, inscriptions, and Roman coins bearing the effigy of the emperor. The warriors whom we find lying near their sword and their buckler lived for the most part in a period quite close to ours, many under the Merovingians, some even at the time of Charlemagne. The Iron Age is no longer a prehistoric age.

CONCLUSIONS

How the Four Ages are to be Conceived.—The inhabitants of one and the same country have successively made use of rough stone, polished stone, bronze, and iron. But all countries have not lived in the same age at the same time. Iron was employed by the Egyptians while yet the Greeks were in their bronze age and the barbarians of Denmark were using stone. The conclusion of the polished stone age in America came only with the arrival of Europeans. In our own time the savages of Australia are still in the rough stone age. In their settlements may be found only implements of bone and stone similar to those used by the cave-men. The four ages, therefore, do not mark periods in the life of humanity, but only epochs in the civilization of each country.

Uncertainties.—Prehistoric archæology is yet a very young science. We have learned something of primitive men through certain remains preserved and discovered by chance. A recent accident, a trench, a landslip, a drought may effect a new discovery any day. Who knows what is still under ground? The finds are already innumerable. But these rarely tell us what we wish to know. How long was each of the four ages? When did each begin and end in the various parts of the world? Who planned the caverns, the lake villages, the mounds, the dolmens? When a country passes from polished stone to bronze, is it the same people changing implements, or is it a new people come on the scene? When one thinks one has found the solution, a new discovery often confounds the archæologists. It was thought that the Celts originated the dolmens, but these have been found in sections which could never have been traversed by Celts.

What has been determined.—Three conclusions, however, seem certain:

1.—Man has lived long on the earth, familiar as he was with the mammoth and the cave-bear; he lived at least as early as the geological period known as the Quaternary.

2.—Man has emerged from the savage state to civilized life; he has gradually perfected his tools and his ornaments from the awkward axe of flint and the necklace of bears' teeth to iron swords and jewels of gold. The roughest instruments are the oldest.

3.—Man has made more and more rapid progress. Each age has been shorter than its predecessor.

CHAPTER II

HISTORY AND THE RECORDS

HISTORY

Legends.—The most ancient records of people and their doings are transmitted by oral tradition. They are recited long before they are written down and are much mixed with fable. The Greeks told how their heroes of the oldest times had exterminated monsters, fought with giants, and battled against the gods. The Romans had Romulus nourished by a wolf and raised to heaven. Almost all peoples relate such stories of their infancy. But no confidence is to be placed in these legends.

History.—History has its true beginning only with authentic accounts, that is to say, accounts written by men who were well informed. This moment is not the same with all peoples. The history of Egypt commences more than 3,000 years before Christ; that of the Greeks ascends scarcely to 800 years before Christ; Germany has had a history only since the first century of our era; Russia dates back only to the ninth century; certain savage tribes even yet have no history.

Great Divisions of History.—The history of civilization begins with the oldest civilized people and continues to the present time. Antiquity is the most remote period, Modern Times the era in which we live.

Ancient History.—Ancient History begins with the

oldest known nations, the Egyptians and Chaldeans (about 3,000 years before our era), and surveys the peoples of the Orient, the Hindoos, Persians, Phœnicians, Jews, Greeks, and last of all the Romans. It terminates about the fifth century A.D., when the Roman empire of the west is extinguished.

Modern History.—Modern History starts with the end of the fifteenth century, with the invention of printing, the discovery of America and of the Indies, the Renaissance of the sciences and arts. It concerns itself especially with peoples of the West, of Spain, Italy, France, Germany, Russia, and America.

The Middle Age.—Between Antiquity and Modern Times about ten centuries elapse which belong neither to ancient times (for the civilization of Antiquity has perished) nor to modern (since modern civilization does not yet exist). This period we call the Middle Age.

SOURCES OF INFORMATION FOR THE HISTORY OF ANCIENT PEOPLES

The Sources.—The Assyrians, Greeks, and Romans are no longer with us; all the peoples of antiquity have passed away. To know their religion, their customs, and arts we have to seek for instruction in the remains they have left us. These are books, monuments, inscriptions, and languages, and these are our means for the study of ancient civilizations. We term these *sources* because we draw our knowledge from them. Ancient History flows from these sources.

Books.—Ancient peoples have left written records

behind them. Some of these peoples had sacred books —for example, the Hindoos, the Persians, and the Jews; the Greeks and Romans have handed down to us histories, poems, speeches, philosophical treatises. But books are very far from furnishing all the information that we require. We do not possess a single Assyrian or Phœnician book. Other peoples have transmitted very few books to us. The ancients wrote less than we, and so they had a smaller literature to leave behind them; and as it was necessary to transcribe all of this by hand, there was but a small number of copies of books. Further, most of these manuscripts have been destroyed or have been lost, and those which remain to us are difficult to read. The art of deciphering them is called Palæography.

The Monuments.—Ancient peoples, like ourselves, built monuments of different sorts: palaces for their kings, tombs for the dead, fortresses, bridges, aqueducts, triumphal arches. Of these monuments many have fallen into ruin, have been razed, shattered by the enemy or by the people themselves. But some of them survive, either because there was no desire to destroy them, or because men could not. They still stand in ruins like the old castles, for repairs are no longer made; but enough is preserved to enable us to comprehend their former condition. Some of them are still above ground, like the pyramids, the temples of Thebes and of the island of Philæ, the palace of Persepolis in Persia, the Parthenon in Greece, the Colosseum in Rome, and the Maison Carrée and Pont du Gard in France. Like any modern monument, these are visible to the traveller. But the majority of these monuments have been recovered from the earth, from sand, from river deposits, and from débris. One must disengage them from this thick covering, and excavate the soil, often to a great depth. Assyrian palaces may be reached only by cutting into the hills. A trench of forty feet is necessary to penetrate to the tombs of the kings of Mycenæ. Time is not the only agency for covering these ruins; men have aided it. When the ancients wished to build, they did not, as we do, take the trouble to level off the space, nor to clear the site. Instead of removing the débris, they heaped it together and built above it. The new edifice in turn fell into ruins and its débris was added to that of more remote time; thus there were formed several strata of remains. When Schliemann excavated the site of Troy, he had passed through five beds of débris; these were five ruined villages one above another, the oldest at a depth of fifty feet.

By accident one town has been preserved to us in its entirety. In 79 A.D. the volcano of Vesuvius belched forth a torrent of liquid lava and a rain of ashes, and two Roman cities were suddenly buried, Herculaneum by lava, and Pompeii by ashes; the lava burnt the objects it touched, while the ashes enveloped them, preserving them from the air and keeping them intact. As we remove the ashes, Pompeii reappears to us just as it was eighteen centuries ago. One still sees the wheel-ruts in the pavement, the designs traced on the walls with charcoal; in the houses, the pictures, the utensils, the furniture, even the bread, the nuts, and olives, and here and there the skeleton of an inhabitant surprised by the catastrophe. Monuments teach us much about the ancient peoples. The science of monuments is called Archæology.

Inscriptions.—By inscriptions one means all writings other than books. Inscriptions are for the most part cut in stone, but some are on plates of bronze. At Pompeii they have been found traced on the walls in colors or with charcoal. Some have the character of commemorative inscriptions just as these are now attached to our statues and edifices; thus in the monument of Ancyra the emperor Augustus publishes the story of his life.

The greatest number of inscriptions are epitaphs graven on tombs. Certain others fill the function of our placards, containing, as they do, a law or a regulation that was to be made public. The science of inscriptions is called Epigraphy.

Languages.—The languages also which ancient peoples spoke throw light on their history. Comparing the words of two different languages, we perceive that the two have a common origin—an evidence that the peoples who spoke them were descended from the same stock. The science of languages is called Linguistics.

Lacunæ.—It is not to be supposed that books, monuments, inscriptions, and languages are sufficient to give complete knowledge of the history of antiquity. They present many details which we could well afford to lose, but often what we care most to know escapes us. Scholars continue to dig and to decipher; each year new discoveries of inscriptions and monuments are made; but there remain still many gaps in our knowledge and probably some of these will always exist.

RACES AND PEOPLES

Anthropology.—The men who people the earth do not possess exact resemblances, some differing from others in stature, the form of the limbs and the head, the features of the face, the color of the hair and eyes. Other differences are found in language, intelligence, and sentiments. These variations permit us to separate the inhabitants of the earth into several groups which we call races. A *race* is the aggregate of those men who resemble one another and are distinguished from all others. The common traits of a race—its characteristics—constitute the type of the race. For example, the type of the negro race is marked by black skin, frizzly hair, white teeth, flat nose, projecting lips, and prominent jaw. That part of Anthropology which concerns itself with races and their sub-divisions is called Ethnology.[1] This science is yet in its early development on account of its complete novelty, and is very complex since types of men are very numerous and often very difficult to differentiate.

The Races.—The principal races are:

1.—The White race, which inhabits Europe, the north of Africa, and western Asia.

2.—The Yellow race in eastern Asia to which belong the Chinese, the Mongols, Turks, and Hungarians, who invaded Europe as conquerors. They have yellow skin, small regular eyes, prominent cheek-bones, and thin beard.

[1] Ethnography is the study of races from the point of view of their objects and customs.

3.—The Black race, in central Africa. These are the Negroes, of black skin, flat nose, woolly hair.

4.—The Red race, in America. These are the Indians, with copper-colored skin and flat heads.

Civilized Peoples.—Almost all civilized peoples belong to the white race. The peoples of the other races have remained savage or barbarian, like the men of prehistoric times.[1]

It is within the limits of Asia and Africa that the first civilized peoples had their development—the Egyptians in the Nile valley, the Chaldeans in the plain of the Euphrates. They were peoples of sedentary and peaceful pursuits. Their skin was dark, the hair short and thick, the lips strong. Nobody knows their origin with exactness and scholars are not agreed on the name to give them (some terming them Cushites, others Hamites). Later, between the twentieth and twenty-fifth centuries B.C. came bands of martial shepherds who had spread over all Europe and the west of Asia —the Aryans and the Semites.

The Aryans and the Semites.—There is no clearly marked external difference between the Aryans and the Semites. Both are of the white race, having the oval face, regular features, clear skin, abundant hair, large eyes, thin lips, and straight nose. Both peoples were originally nomad shepherds, fond of war. We do not know whence they came, nor is there agreement whether the Aryans came from the mountain region

[1] The Chinese only of the yellow race have elaborated among themselves an industry, a regular government, a polite society. But placed at the extremity of Asia they have had no influence on other civilized peoples. [The Japanese should be included. —ED.]

in the northwest of the Himalayas or from the plains of Russia. What distinguishes them is their spiritual bent and especially their language, sometimes also their religion. Scholars by common consent call those peoples Aryan who speak an Aryan language: in Asia, the Hindoos and Persians; in Europe, the Greeks, Italians, Spaniards, Germans, Scandinavians, Slavs (Russians, Poles, Serfs), and Celts.[1]

Similarly, we call Semites those peoples who speak a Semitic language: Arabs, Jews and Syrians. But a people may speak an Aryan or a Semitic language and yet not be of Aryan or Semitic race; a negro may speak English without being of English stock. Many of the Europeans whom we classify among the Aryans are perhaps the descendants of an ancient race conquered by the Aryans and who have adopted their language, just as the Egyptians received the language of the Arabs, their conquerors.

These two names (Aryan and Semite), then, signify today rather two groups of peoples than two distinct races. But even if we use the terms in this sense, one may say that all the greater peoples of the world have been Semites or Aryans. The Semitic family included the Phœnicians, the people of commerce; the Jews, the people of religion; the Arabs, the people of war. The Aryans, some finding their homes in India, others in Europe, have produced the nations which have been, and still are, foremost in the world—in antiquity, the Hindoos, a people of great philosophical and religious ideas; the Greeks, creators of art and of

[1] The English and French are mixtures of Celtic and German blood.

science; the Persians and Romans, the founders, the former in the East, the latter in the West, of the greatest empires of antiquity; in modern times, the Italians, French, Germans, Dutch, Russians, English and Americans.

The history of civilization begins with the Egyptians and the Chaldeans; but from the fifteenth century before our era, history concerns itself only with the Aryan and Semitic peoples.

CHAPTER III

ANCIENT HISTORY OF THE EAST

THE EGYPTIANS

The Land of Egypt.—Egypt is only the valley of the Nile, a narrow strip of fertile soil stretching along both banks of the stream and shut in by mountains on either side, somewhat over 700[1] miles in length and 15 in width. Where the hills fall away, the Delta begins, a vast plain cut by the arms of the Nile and by canals. As Herodotus says, Egypt is wholly the gift of the Nile.

The Nile.—Every year at the summer solstice the Nile, swollen by the melted snows of Abyssinia, overflows the parched soil of Egypt. It rises to a height of twenty-six or twenty-seven feet, sometimes even to thirty-three feet. The whole country becomes a lake from which the villages, built on eminences, emerge like little islands. The water recedes in September; by December it has returned to its proper channel. Everywhere has been left a fertile, alluvial bed which serves the purpose of fertilization. On the softened earth the peasant sows his crop with almost no labor. The Nile, then, brings both water and soil to Egypt; if the river should fail, Egypt would revert, like the land

[1] Following the curves of the stream.—Ed.

[2] In some localities, *e.g.* Thebes, the flood is even higher.—Ed.

on either side of it, to a desert of sterile sand where the rain never falls. The Egyptians are conscious of their debt to their stream. A song in its honor runs as follows: "Greeting to thee, O Nile, who hast revealed thyself throughout the land, who comest in peace to give life to Egypt. Does it rise? The land is filled with joy, every heart exults, every being receives its food, every mouth is full. It brings bounties that are full of delight, it creates all good things, it makes the grass to spring up for the beasts."

Fertility of the Country.—Egypt is truly an oasis in the midst of the desert of Africa. It produces in abundance wheat, beans, lentils, and all leguminous foods; palms rear themselves in forests. On the pastures irrigated by the Nile graze herds of cattle and goats, and flocks of geese. With a territory hardly equal to that of Belgium, Egypt still supports 5,500,000 inhabitants. No country in Europe is so thickly populated, and Egypt in antiquity was more densely thronged than it is today.

The Accounts of Herodotus.—Egypt was better known to the Greeks than the rest of the Orient. Herodotus had visited it in the fifth century B.C. He describes in his History the inundations of the Nile, the manners, costume, and religion of the people; he recounts events of their history and tales which his guides had told him. Diodorus and Strabo also speak of Egypt. But all had seen the country in its decadence and had no knowledge of the ancient Egyptians.

Champollion.—The French expedition to Egypt (1798-1801) opened the country to scholars. They made a close examination of the Pyramids and ruins of Thebes, and collected drawings and inscriptions. But no one could decipher the hieroglyphs, the Egyptian writing. It was an erroneous impression that every sign in this writing must each represent a word. In 1821 a French scholar, Champollion, experimented with another system. An official had reported that there was an inscription at Rosetta in three forms of writing—parallel with the hieroglyphs was a translation in Greek. The name of King Ptolemy, was surrounded with a cartouche.[1] Champollion succeeded in finding in this name the letters P, T, O, L, M, I, S. Comparing these with other names of kings similarly enclosed, he found the whole alphabet. He then read the hieroglyphs and found that they were written in a language like the Coptic, the language spoken in Egypt at the time of the Romans, and which was already known to scholars.

Egyptologists.—Since Champollion, many scholars have travelled over Egypt and have ransacked it thoroughly. We call these students Egyptologists, and they are to be found in every country of Europe. A French Egyptologist, Mariette (1821-1881), made some excavations for the Viceroy of Egypt and created the museum of Boulak. France has established in Cairo a school of Egyptology, directed by Maspero.

Discoveries.—Not every country yields such rich discoveries as does Egypt. The Egyptians constructed their tombs like houses, and laid in them objects of every kind for the use of the dead—furniture, gar-

[1] An enclosing case.

ments, arms, and edibles. The whole country was filled with tombs similarly furnished. Under this extraordinarily dry climate everything has been preserved; objects come to light intact after a burial of 4,000 or 5,000 years. No people of antiquity have left so many traces of themselves as the Egyptians; none is better known to us.

THE EGYPTIAN EMPIRE

Antiquity of the Egyptian People.—An Egyptian priest said to Herodotus, "You Greeks are only children." The Egyptians considered themselves the oldest people of the world. Down to the Persian conquest (520[1] B.C.) there were twenty-six dynasties of kings. The first ran back 4,000 years,[2] and during these forty centuries Egypt had been an empire. The capital down to the tenth dynasty (the period of the Old Empire) was at Memphis in Lower Egypt, later, in the New Empire, at Thebes in Upper Egypt.

Memphis and the Pyramids.—Memphis, built by the first king of Egypt, was protected by an enormous dike. The village has existed for more than five thousand years; but since the thirteenth century the inhabitants have taken the stones of its ruins to build the houses of Cairo; what these people left the Nile recaptured. The Pyramids, not far from Memphis, are contemporaneous with the old empire; they are

[1] 525 B.C.—ED.

[2] The chronology of early Egyptian history is uncertain. Civilization existed in this land much earlier than was formerly supposed.—ED.

the tombs of three kings of the fourth dynasty. The greatest of the pyramids, 480 feet high, required the labor of 100,000 men for thirty years.[1] To raise the stones for it they built gradually ascending platforms which were removed when the structure was completed.

Egyptian Civilization.—The statues, paintings, and instruments which are taken from the tombs of this epoch give evidence of an already civilized people. When all the other eminent nations of antiquity—the Hindoos, Persians, Jews, Greeks, Romans—were still in a savage state, 3,500 years before our era, the Egyptians had known for a long time how to cultivate the soil, to weave cloths, to work metals, to paint, sculpture, and to write; they had an organized religion, a king, and an administration.

Thebes.—At the eleventh dynasty Thebes succeeds Memphis as capital. The ruins of Thebes are still standing. They are marvellous, extending as they do on both banks of the Nile, with a circuit of about seven miles. On the left bank there is a series of palaces and temples which lead to vast cemeteries. On the right bank two villages, Luxor and Karnak, distant a half-hour one from the other, are built in the midst of the ruins. They are united by a double row of sphinxes, which must have once included more than 1,000 of these monuments. Among these temples in ruins the greatest was the temple of Ammon at Karnak. It was surrounded by a wall of over one and one-third miles in length; the famous Hall of Columns, the great-

[1] According to Petrie ("History of Egypt," New York, 1895, i., 40) *twenty* years were consumed.—Ed.

est in the world, had a length of 334 feet, a width of 174 feet,[1] and was supported by 134 columns; twelve of these are over 65 feet high. Thebes was for 1,500 years the capital and sacred city, the residence of kings and the dwelling-place of the priests.

The Pharaoh.—The king of Egypt, called Pharaoh, was esteemed as the son of the Sun-god and his incarnation on earth; divinity was ascribed to him also. We may see in a picture King Rameses II standing in adoration before the divine Rameses who is sitting between two gods. The king as man adores himself as god. Being god, the Pharaoh has absolute power over men; as master, he gives his orders to his great nobles at court, to his warriors, to all his subjects. But the priests, though adoring him, surround and watch him; their head, the high priest of the god Ammon, at last becomes more powerful than the king; he often governs under the name of the king and in his stead.

The Subjects of Pharaoh.—The king, the priests, the warriors, the nobles, are proprietors of all Egypt; all the other people are simply their peasants who cultivate the land for them. Scribes in the service of the king watch them and collect the farm-dues, often with blows of the staff. One of these functionaries writes as follows to a friend, "Have you ever pictured to yourself the existence of the peasant who tills the soil. The tax-collector is on the platform busily seizing the tithe of the harvest. He has his men with him armed with staves, his negroes provided with strips of palm. All cry, 'Come, give us grain.' If the peasant hasn't

[1] Perrot and Chipiez ("History of Ancient Egyptian Art," London. 1883, i., 365) give 340 feet by 170.—Ed.

it, they throw him full length on the earth, bind him, draw him to the canal, and hurl him in head foremost."

Despotism.—The Egyptian people has always been, and still is, gay, careless, gentle, docile as an infant, always ready to submit to tyranny. In this country the cudgel was the instrument of education and of government. "The young man," said the scribes, "has a back to be beaten; he hears when he is struck." "One day," says a French traveller, "finding myself before the ruins of Thebes, I exclaimed, 'But how did they do all this?' My guide burst out laughing, touched me on the arm and, showing me a palm, said to me, 'Here is what they used to accomplish all this. You know, sir, with 100,000 branches of palms split on the backs of those who always have their shoulders bare, you can build many a palace and some temples to boot."

Isolation of the Egyptians.—The Egyptians moved but little beyond their borders. As the sea inspired them with terror, they had no commerce and did not trade with other peoples. They were not at all a military nation. Their kings, it is true, often went on expeditions at the head of mercenaries either against the negroes of Ethiopia or against the tribes of Syria. They gained victories which they had painted on the walls of their palaces, they brought back troops of captives whom they used in building monuments; but they never made great conquests. Foreigners came more to Egypt than Egyptians went abroad.

Religion of the Egyptians.—"The Egyptians," said Herodotus, "are the most religious of all men." We do not know any people so devout; almost all their paintings represent men in prayer before a god; almost all their manuscripts are religious books.

Egyptian Gods.—The principal deity is a Sun-god, creator, beneficent, "who knows all things, who exists from the beginning." This god has a divine wife and son. All the Egyptians adored this trinity; but not all gave it the same name. Each region gave a different name to these three gods. At Memphis they called the father Phtah, the mother Sekhet, the son Imouthes; at Abydos they called them Osiris, Isis, and Horus; at Thebes, Ammon, Mouth, and Chons. Then, too, the people of one province adopted the gods of other provinces. Further, they made other gods emanate from each god of the trinity. Thus the number of gods was increased and religion was complicated.

Osiris.—These gods have their history; it is that of the sun; for the sun appeared to the Egyptians, as to most of the primitive peoples, the mightiest of beings, and consequently a god. Osiris, the sun, is slain by Set, god of the night; Isis, the moon, his wife, bewails and buries him; Horus, his son, the rising sun, avenges him by killing his murderer.

Ammon-râ.—Ammon-râ, god of Thebes, is represented as traversing heaven each day in a bark ("the good bark of millions of years"); the shades of the dead propel it with long oars; the god stands at the prow to strike the enemy with his lance. The hymn which they chanted in his honor is as follows: "Homage to thee; thou watchest favoringly, thou watchest truly, O master of the two horizons. . . . . Thou treadest the heavens on high, thine enemies are laid low. The heaven is glad, the earth is joyful, the gods unite in festal cheer to render glory to Râ when they see him rising in his bark after he has overwhelmed his enemies. O Râ, give abounding life to Pharaoh, bestow bread for his hunger (belly), water for his throat, perfumes for his hair."

Animal-Headed Gods.—The Egyptians often represented their gods with human form, but more frequently under the form of a beast. Each god has his animal: Phtah incarnates himself in the beetle, Horus in the hawk, Osiris in the bull. The two figures often unite in a man with the head of an animal or an animal with the head of a man. Every god may be figured in four forms: Horus, for example, as a man, a hawk, as man with the head of a hawk, as a hawk with the head of a man.

Sacred Animals.— What did the Egyptians wish to designate by this symbol? One hardly knows. They, themselves, came to regard as sacred the animals which served to represent the gods to them: the bull, the beetle, the ibis, the hawk, the cat, the crocodile. They cared for them and protected them. A century before the Christian era a Roman citizen killed a cat at Alexandria; the people rose in riot, seized him, and, notwithstanding the entreaties of the king, murdered him, although at the same time they had great fear of the Romans. There was in each temple a sacred animal which was adored. The traveller Strabo records a visit to a sacred crocodile of Thebes: "The beast," said he, "lay on the edge of a pond, the priests drew near, two of them opened his mouth, a third thrust in cakes, grilled fish, and a drink made with meal."

The Bull Apis.—Of these animal gods the most venerated was the bull Apis. It represented at once Osiris and Phtah and lived at Memphis in a chapel served by the priests. After its death it became an Osiris (Osar-hapi), it was embalmed, and its mummy deposited in a vault. The sepulchres of the "Osar-hapi" constituted a gigantic monument, the Serapeum, discovered in 1851 by Mariette.

Cult of the Dead.—The Egyptians adored also the spirits of the dead. They seem to have believed at first that every man had a "double" (Kâ), and that when the man was dead his double still survived. Many savage peoples believe this to this day. The Egyptian tomb in the time of the Old Empire was termed "House of the Double." It was a low room arranged like a chamber, where for the service of the double there were placed all that he required, chairs, tables, beds, chests, linen, closets, garments, toilet utensils, weapons, sometimes a war-chariot; for the entertainment of the double, statues, paintings, books; for his sustenance, grain and foods. And then they set there a double of the dead in the form of a statue in wood or stone carved in his likeness. At last the opening to the vault was sealed; the double was enclosed, but the living still provided for him. They brought him foods or they might beseech a god that he supply them to the spirit, as in this inscription, "An offering to Osiris that he may confer on the Kâ of the deceased N. bread, drink, meat, geese, milk, wine, beer, clothing, perfumes—all good things and pure on which the god (*i.e.* the Kâ) subsists.

Judgment of the Soul.—Later, originating with the

eleventh dynasty, the Egyptians believed that the soul flew away from the body and sought Osiris under the earth, the realm into which the sun seemed every day to sink. There Osiris sits on his tribunal, surrounded by forty-two judges; the soul appears before these to give account of his past life. His actions are weighed in the balance of truth, his "heart" is called to witness. "O heart," cries the dead, "O heart, the issue of my mother, my heart when I was on earth, offer not thyself as witness, charge me not before the great god." The soul found on examination to be bad is tormented for centuries and at last annihilated. The good soul springs up across the firmament; after many tests it rejoins the company of the gods and is absorbed into them.

Mummies.—During this pilgrimage the soul may wish to re-enter the body to rest there. The body must therefore be kept intact, and so the Egyptians learned to embalm it. The corpse was filled with spices, drenched in a bath of natron, wound with bandages and thus transformed into a mummy. The mummy encased in a coffin of wood or plaster was laid in the tomb with every provision necessary to its life.

Book of the Dead.—A book was deposited with the mummy, the Book of the Dead, which explains what the soul ought to say in the other world when it makes its defence before the tribunal of Osiris: "I have never committed fraud; . . . I have never vexed the widow; . . . I have never committed any forbidden act; . . . I have never been an idler; . . . I have never taken the slave from his master; . . . I never stole the bread from the temples; . . . I never removed the provisions or the bandages of the dead; I never altered the grain measure; . . . I never hunted sacred beasts; I never caught sacred fish; . . . I am pure; . . . I have given bread to the hungry, water to the thirsty, clothing to the naked; I have sacrificed to the gods, and offered funeral feasts to the dead." Here we see Egyptian morality: observance of ceremonies, respect for everything pertaining to the gods, sincerity, honesty, and beneficence.

THE ARTS

Industry.—The Egyptians were the first to practise the arts necessary to a civilized people. From the first dynasty, 3,000[1] years B.C., paintings on the tombs exhibit men working, sowing, harvesting, beating and winnowing grain; we have representations of herds of cattle, sheep, geese, swine; of persons richly clothed, processions, feasts where the harp is played—almost the same life that we behold 3,000 years later. As early as this time the Egyptians knew how to manipulate gold, silver, bronze; to manufacture arms and jewels, glass, pottery, and enamel; they wove garments of linen and wool, and cloths, transparent or embroidered with gold.

Architecture.—They were the oldest artists of the world. They constructed enormous monuments which appear to be eternal, for down to the present, time has not been able to destroy them. They never built, as we do, for the living, but for the gods and

[1] Probably much earlier than this.—ED.

for the dead, *i.e.*, temples and tombs. Only a slight amount of débris is left of their houses, and even the palaces of their kings in comparison with the tombs appear, in the language of the Greeks, to be only inns. The house was to serve only for a lifetime, the tomb for eternity.

Tombs.—The Great Pyramid is a royal tomb. Ancient tombs ordinarily had this form. In Lower Egypt there still remain pyramids arranged in rows or scattered about, some larger, others smaller. These are the tombs of kings and nobles. Later the tombs are constructed underground, some under earth, others cut into the granite of the hills. Each generation needs new ones, and therefore near the town of living people is built the richer and greater city of the dead (necropolis).

Temples.—The gods also required eternal and splendid habitations. Their temples include a magnificent sanctuary, the dwelling of the god, surrounded with courts, gardens, chambers where the priests lodge, wardrobes for his jewels, utensils, and vestments. This combination of edifices, the work of many generations is encircled with a wall. The temple of Ammon at Thebes had the labors of the kings of all the dynasties from the twelfth to the last. Ordinarily in front of the temple a great gate-way is erected, with inclined faces—the pylone. On either side of the entrance is an obelisk, a needle of rock with gilded point, or perhaps a colossus in stone representing a sitting giant. Often the approach to the temple is by a long avenue rimmed with sphinxes.

Pyramids, pylones, colossi, sphinxes, and obelisks

characterize this architecture. Everything is massive, compact, and, above all, immense. Hence these monuments appear clumsy but indestructible.

Sculpture.—Egyptian sculptors began with imitating nature. The oldest statues are impressive for their life and freshness, and are doubtless portraits of the dead. Of this sort is the famous squatting scribe of the Louvre.[1] But beginning with the eleventh dynasty the sculptor is no longer free to represent the human body as he sees it, but must follow conventional rules fixed by religion. And so all the statues resemble one another—parallel legs, the feet joined, arms crossed on the breast, the figure motionless; the statues are often majestic, but always stiff and monotonous. Art has ceased to reproduce nature and is become a conventional symbol.

Painting.—The Egyptians used very solid colors; after 5,000 years they are still fresh and bright. But they were ignorant of coloring designs; they knew neither tints, shadows, nor perspective. Painting, like sculpture, was subject to religious rules and was therefore monotonous. If fifty persons were to be represented, the artist made them all alike.

Literature.—The literature of the Egyptians is found in the tombs—not only books of medicine, of magic and of piety, but also poems, letters, accounts of travels, and even romances.

Destiny of the Egyptian Civilization.—The Egyptians conserved their customs, religion, and arts even after the fall of their empire. Subjects of the Per-

[1] The Louvre Museum in Paris has an excellent collection of Egyptian subjects.

sians, then the Greeks, and at last of the Romans, they kept their old usages, their hieroglyphics, their mummies and sacred animals. At last between the third and second centuries A.D., Egyptian civilization was slowly extinguished.

CHAPTER IV

ASSYRIANS AND BABYLONIANS

CHALDEA

The Land.—From the high and snowy mountains of Armenia flow two deep and rapid rivers, the Tigris to the east, the Euphrates to the west. At first in close proximity, they separate as they reach the plain. The Tigris makes a straight course, the Euphrates a great détour towards the sandy deserts; then they unite before emptying into the sea. The country which they embrace is Chaldea. It is an immense plain of extraordinarily fertile soil; rain is rare and the heat is overwhelming. But the streams furnish water and this clayey soil when irrigated by canals becomes the most fertile in the world. Wheat and barley produce 200-fold; in good years the returns are 300-fold. Palms constitute the forests and from these the people make their wine, meal and flour.[1]

The People.—For many centuries, perhaps as long as Egypt, Chaldea has been the abode of civilized peoples. Many races from various lands have met and mingled in these great plains. There were Turanians of the yellow race, similar to the Chinese, who came from the north-east; Cushites, deep brown in color, related to the Egyptians, came from the east; Semites,

[1] A Persian song enumerates 360 different uses of the palm.

of the white race, of the same stock as the Arabs, descended from the north.[1] The Chaldean people had its origin in this mixture of races.

The Cities.—Chaldean priests related that their kings had ruled for 150,000 years. While this is a fable, they were right in ascribing great antiquity to the Chaldean empire. The soil of Chaldea is everywhere studded with hills and each of these is a mass of débris, the residue of a ruined city. Many of these have been excavated and many cities brought to view. (Our, Larsam, Bal-ilou), and some inscriptions recovered. De Sarsec, a Frenchman, has discovered the ruins of an entire city, overwhelmed by the invader and its palace destroyed by fire. These ancient peoples are still little known to us; many sites remain to be excavated when it is hoped new inscriptions will be found. Their empire was destroyed about 2,300 B.C.; it may then have been very old.[2]

THE ASSYRIANS

Assyria.—The country back of Chaldea on the Tigris is Assyria. It also is fertile, but cut with hills and rocks. Situated near the mountains, it experiences snow in winter and severe storms in summer.

Origins.—Chaldea had for a long time been covered with towns while yet the Assyrians lived an obscure life in their mountains. About the thirteenth century B.C. their kings leading great armies began to invade the plains and founded a mighty empire whose capital was Nineveh.

[1] Or perhaps from the east (Arabia).—ED.

[2] Recent discoveries confirm the view of a very ancient civilization.—ED.

Ancient Accounts.—Until about forty years ago we knew almost nothing of the Assyrians—only a legend recounted by the Greek Diodorus Siculus. Ninus, according to the story, had founded Nineveh and conquered all Asia Minor; his wife, Semiramis, daughter of a goddess, had subjected Egypt, after which she was changed into the form of a dove. Incapable kings had succeeded this royal pair for the space of 1,300 years; the last, Sardanapalus, besieged in his capital, was burnt with his wives. This romance has not a word of truth in it.

Modern Discoveries.—In 1843, Botta, the French consul at Mossoul, discovered under a hillock near the Tigris, at Khorsabad, the palace of an Assyrian king. Here for the first time one could view the productions of Assyrian art; the winged bulls cut in stone, placed at the gate of the palace were found intact and removed to the Louvre Museum in Paris. The excavations of Botta drew the attention of Europe, so that many expeditions were sent out, especially by the English; Place and Layard investigated other mounds and discovered other palaces. These ruins had been well preserved, protected by the dryness of the climate and by a covering of earth. They found walls adorned with bas-reliefs and paintings; statues and inscriptions were discovered in great number. It was now possible to study on the ground the plan of the structures and to publish reproductions of the monuments and inscriptions.

The palace first discovered, that of Khorsabad, had been built by King Sargon at Nineveh, the site of the capital of the Assyrian kings. The city was built on several eminences, and was encircled by a wall 25 to 30 miles[1] in length, in the form of a quadrilateral. The wall was composed of bricks on the exterior and of earth within. The dwellings of the city have disappeared leaving no traces, but we have recovered many palaces constructed by various kings of Assyria. Nineveh remained the residence of the kings down to the time that the Assyrian empire was destroyed by the Medes and Chaldeans.

Inscriptions on the Bricks.—In these inscriptions every character is formed of a combination of signs shaped like an arrow or wedge, and this is the reason that this style of writing is termed cuneiform (Latin *cuneus* and *forma*). To trace these signs the writer used a stylus with a triangular point; he pressed it into a tablet of soft clay which was afterwards baked to harden it and to make the impression permanent. In the palace of Assurbanipal a complete library of brick tablets has been found in which brick serves the purpose of paper.

Cuneiform Writing.—For many years the cuneiform writing has occupied the labors of many scholars impatient to decipher it. It has been exceedingly difficult to read, for, in the first place, it served as the writing medium of five different languages—Assyrian, Susian, Mede, Chaldean, and Armenian, without counting the Old Persian—and there was no knowledge of these five languages. Then, too, it is very complicated, for several reasons:

1. It is composed at the same time of symbolic

[1] Somewhat exaggerated. See Perrot and Chipiez, "History of Art in Assyria and Chaldea," ii., 60; and Maspero, "Passing of the Empires," p. 468.—Ed.

signs, each of which represents a word (sun, god, fish), and of syllabic signs, each of which represents a syllable.

2. There are nearly two hundred syllabic signs, much alike and easy to confuse.

3. The same sign is often the representation of a word and a syllable.

4. Often (and this is the hardest condition) the same sign is used to represent different syllables. Thus the same sign is sometimes read "ilou," and sometimes "an." This writing was difficult even for those who executed it. "A good half of the cuneiform monuments which we possess comprises guides (grammars, dictionaries, pictures), which enable us to decipher the other half, and which we consult just as Assyrian scholars did 2,500 years ago."[1]

Cuneiform inscriptions have been solved in the same manner as the Egyptian hieroglyphics—there was an inscription in three languages—Assyrian, Mede, and Persian. The last gave the key to the other two.

The Assyrian People.—The Assyrians were a race of hunters and soldiers. Their bas-reliefs ordinarily represent them armed with bow and lance, often on horseback. They were good knights—alert, brave, clever in skirmish and battle; also bombastic, deceitful, and sanguinary. For six centuries they harassed Asia, issuing from their mountains to hurl themselves on their neighbors, and returning with entire peoples reduced to slavery. They apparently made war for the mere pleasure of slaying, ravaging, and pillaging. No people ever exhibited greater ferocity.

[1] Lenormant, "Ancient History."

The King.—Following Asiatic usage they regarded their king as the representative of God on earth and gave him blind obedience. He was absolute master of all his subjects, he led them in battle, and at their head fought against other peoples of Asia. On his return he recorded his exploits on the walls of his palace in a long inscription in which he told of his victories, the booty which he had taken, the cities burned, the captives beheaded or flayed alive. We present some passages from these stories of campaigns:

Assurnazir-hapal in 882 says, "I built a wall before the great gates of the city; I flayed the chiefs of the revolt and with their skins I covered this wall. Some were immured alive in the masonry, others were crucified or impaled along the wall. I had some of them flayed in my presence and had the wall hung with their skins. I arranged their heads like crowns and their transfixed bodies in the form of garlands."

In 745 Tiglath-Pilezer II writes, "I shut up the king in his royal city. I raised mountains of bodies before his gates. All his villages I destroyed, desolated, burnt. I made the country desert, I changed it into hills and mounds of débris."

In the seventh century Sennacherib wrote: "I passed like a hurricane of desolation. On the drenched earth the armor and arms swam in the blood of the enemy as in a river. I heaped up the bodies of their soldiers like trophies and I cut off their extremities. I mutilated those whom I took alive like blades of straw; as punishment I cut off their hands." In a bas-relief which shows the town of Susa surrendering to Assurbanipal one sees the chiefs of the conquered tortured by the Assyrians; some have their ears cut off, the eyes of others are put out, the beard torn out, while some are flayed alive. Evidently these kings took delight in burnings, massacres, and tortures.

Ruin of the Assyrian Empire.—The Assyrian régime began with the capture of Babylon (about 1270). From the ninth century the Assyrians, always at war, subjected or ravaged Babylonia, Syria, Palestine, and even Egypt. The conquered always revolted, and the massacres were repeated. At last the Assyrians were exhausted. The Babylonians and Medes made an alliance and destroyed their empire. In 625 their capital, Nineveh, "the lair of lions, the bloody city, the city gorged with prey," as the Jewish prophets call it, was taken and destroyed forever. "Nineveh is laid waste," says the prophet Nahum, "who will bemoan her?"

THE BABYLONIANS

The Second Chaldean Empire.—In the place of the fallen Assyrian empire there arose a new power—in ancient Chaldea. This has received the name Babylonian Empire or the Second Chaldean Empire. A Jewish prophet makes one say to Jehovah, "I raise up the Chaldeans, that bitter and hasty nation which shall march through the breadth of the land to possess dwelling places that are not theirs. Their horses are swifter than leopards. Their horsemen spread themselves; (their horsemen) shall fly as the eagle that hasteth to eat." They were a people of knights, martial and victorious, like the Assyrians. They subjected Susiana, Mesopotamia, Syria, and Jordan. But their régime was short: founded in 625, the Babylonian Empire was overthrown by the Persians in 538.

Babylon.—The mightiest of its kings, Nebuchadrezzar (or Nebuchadnezzar), 604-561, who destroyed Jerusalem and carried the Jews into captivity, built many temples and places in Babylon, his capital. These monuments were in crude brick as the plain of the Euphrates has no supply of stone; in the process of decay they have left only enormous masses of earth and débris. And yet it has been possible on the site of Babylon to recover some inscriptions and to restore the plan of the city. The Greek Herodotus who had visited Babylon in the fifth century B.C., describes it in detail. The city was surrounded by a square wall cut by the Euphrates; it covered about 185 square miles, or seven times the extent of Paris. This immense space was not filled with houses; much of it was occupied with fields to be cultivated for the maintenance of the people in the event of a siege. Babylon was less a city than a fortified camp. The walls equipped with towers and pierced by a hundred gates of brass were so thick that a chariot might be driven on them. All around the wall was a large, deep ditch full of water, with its sides lined with brick. The houses of the city were constructed of three or four stories. The streets intersected at right angles. The bridge and docks of the Euphrates excited admiration; the fortified palace also, and the hanging gardens, one of the seven wonders of the world. These gardens were terraces planted with trees, supported by pillars and rows of arches.

Tower of Babylon.—Hard by the city Nebuchadnezzar had aimed to rebuild the town of Babel. "For the admiration of men," he says in an inscription: "I rebuilt and renovated the wonder of Borsippa, the temple of the seven spheres of the world. I laid the foundations and built it according to its ancient plan." This temple, in the form of a square, comprised seven square towers raised one above another, each tower being dedicated to one of the seven planets and painted with the color attributed by religion to this planet. They were, beginning with the lowest: Saturn (black), Venus (white), Jupiter (purple), Mercury (blue), Mars (vermilion), the moon (silver), the sun (gold). The highest tower contained a chapel with a table of gold and magnificent couch whereon a priestess kept watch continually.

CUSTOMS AND RELIGION

Customs.—We know almost nothing of these peoples apart from the testimony of their monuments, and nearly all of these refer to the achievements of their kings. The Assyrians are always represented at war, hunting, or in the performance of ceremonies; their women never appear on the bas-reliefs; they were confined in a harem and never went into public life. The Chaldeans on the contrary, were a race of laborers and merchants, but of their life we know nothing. Herodotus relates that once a year in their towns they assembled all the girls to give them in marriage; they sold the prettiest, and the profits of the sale of these became a dower for the marriage of the plainest. "According to my view," he adds, "this is the wisest of all their laws."

Religion.—The religion of the Assyrians and Chaldeans was the same, for the former had adopted that of the latter. It is very obscure to us, since it originated, like that of the Chaldean people, in a confusion of religions very differently mingled. The Turanians, like the present yellow race of Siberia, imagined the world full of demons (plague, fever, phantoms, vampires), engaged in prowling around men to do them harm; sorcerers were invoked to banish these demons by magical formulas. The Cushites adored a pair of gods, the male deity of force and the female of matter. The Chaldean priests, united in a powerful guild, confused the two religions into a single one.

The Gods.—The supreme god at Babylon is Ilou; in Assyria, Assur. No temple was raised to him. Three gods proceed from him: Anou, the "lord of darkness," under the figure of a man with the head of a fish and the tail of an eagle; Bel, the "sovereign of spirits," represented as a king on the throne; Nouah, the "master of the visible world," under the form of a genius with four extended wings. Each has a feminine counterpart who symbolizes fruitfulness. Below these gods are the Sun, the Moon, and the five planets, for in the transparent atmosphere of Chaldea the stars shine with a brilliancy which is strange to us; they gleam like deities. To these the Chaldeans raised temples, veritable observatories in which men who adored them could follow all their motions.

Astrology.—The priests believed that these stars, being powerful deities, had determining influence on the lives of men. Every man comes into the world under the influence of a planet and this moment decides his destiny; one may foretell one's fortune if the star under which one is born is known. This is the origin of the horoscope. What occurs in heaven is indicative of what will come to pass on earth; a comet, for example, announces a revolution. By observing the heavens the Chaldean priests believed they could predict events. This is the origin of Astrology.

Sorcery.—The Chaldeans had also magical words; these were uttered to banish spirits or to cause their appearance. This custom, a relic of the Turanian religion, is the origin of sorcery. From Chaldea astrology and sorcery were diffused over the Roman empire, and later over all Europe. In the formulas of sorcery of the sixteenth century corrupted Assyrian words may still be detected.[1]

Sciences.—On the other hand it is in Chaldea that we have the beginning of astronomy. From this land have come down to us the zodiac, the week of seven days in honor of the seven planets; the division of the year into twelve months, of the day into twenty-four hours, of the hour into sixty minutes, of the minute into sixty seconds. Here originated, too, the system of weights and measures reckoned on the unit of length, a system adopted by all the ancient peoples.

ARTS

Architecture.—We do not have direct knowledge of the art of the Chaldeans, since their monuments have fallen to ruin. But the Assyrian artists whose works we possess imitated those of Chaldea, and so we may

[1] For exampie, hilka, hilka, bescha, bescha (begone! begone! bad! bad!)

form a judgment at the same time of the two countries. The Assyrians like the Chaldeans built with crude, sun-dried brick, but they faced the exterior of the wall with stone.

Palaces.—They constructed their palaces[1] on artificial mounds, making these low and flat like great terraces. The crude brick was not adapted to broad and high arches. Halls must therefore be straight and low, but in compensation they were very long. An Assyrian palace, then, resembled a succession of galleries; the roofs were flat terraces provided with battlements. At the gate stood gigantic winged bulls. Within, the walls were covered now with panelling in precious woods, now with enamelled bricks, now with plates of sculptural alabaster. Sometimes the chambers were painted, and even richly encrusted marbles were used.

Sculpture.—The sculpture of the Assyrian palaces is especially admirable. Statues, truly, are rare and coarse; sculptors preferred to execute bas-reliefs similar to pictures on great slabs of alabaster. They represented scenes which were often very complicated —battles, chases, sieges of towns, ceremonies in which the king appeared with a great retinue. Every detail is scrupulously done; one sees the files of servants in charge of the feast of the king, the troops of workmen who built his palace, the gardens, the fields, the ponds, the fish in the water, the birds perched over their nests or flitting from tree to tree. Persons are exhibited in profile, doubtless because the artist could

[1] The temples were pyramidal, of stories or terraces similar to the tower of Borsippa.

not depict the face; but they possess dignity and life. Animals often appeared, especially in hunting scenes; they are ordinarily made with a startling fidelity. The Assyrians observed nature and faithfully reproduced it; hence the merit of their art.

The Greeks themselves learned in this school, by imitating the Assyrian bas-reliefs. They have excelled them, but no people, not even the Greeks, has better known how to represent animals.

CHAPTER V

THE ARYANS OF INDIA

THE ARYANS

Aryan Languages.—The races which in our day inhabit Europe—Greeks and Italians to the south, Slavs in Russia, Teutons in Germany, Celts in Ireland—speak very different languages. When, however, one studies these languages closely, it is perceived that all possess a stock of common words, or at least certain roots. The same roots occur in Sanscrit, the ancient language of the Hindoos, and also in Zend, the ancient tongue of the Persians. Thus,

Father—père (French), pitar (Sanscrit), pater (Greek and Latin). It is the same word pronounced in various ways. From this (and other such examples) it has been concluded that all—Hindoos, Persians, Greeks, Latins, Celts, Germans, Slavs—once spoke the same language, and consequently were one people.

The Aryan People.—These peoples then called themselves Aryans and lived to the north-west of India, either in the mountains of Pamir, or in the steppes of Turkestan or Russia; from this centre they dispersed in all directions. The majority of the people—Greeks, Latins, Germans, Slavs—forgot their origin; but the sacred books of the Hindoos and the Persians preserve the tradition. Effort has been made[1] to reconstruct the life of our Aryan ancestors in their mountain home before the dispersion. It was a race of shepherds; they did not till the soil, but subsisted from their herds of cattle and sheep, though they already had houses and even villages.

It was a fighting race; they knew the lance, the javelin, and shield. Government was patriarchal; a man had but one wife; as head of the family he was for his wife, his children, and his servants at once priest, judge, and king. In all the countries settled by the Aryans they have followed this type of life—patriarchal, martial, and pastoral.

PRIMITIVE RELIGION OF THE HINDOOS

The Aryans on the Indus.—About 2,000 years before our era some Aryan tribes traversed the passes of the Hindu-Kush and swarmed into India. They found the fertile plains of the Indus inhabited by a people of dark skin, with flat heads, industrious and wealthy; they called these aborigines Dasyous (the enemy). They made war on them for centuries and ended by exterminating or subjecting them; they then gradually took possession of all the Indus valley (the region of the five rivers).[2] They then called themselves Hindoos.

The Vedas.—These people were accustomed in their ceremonies to chant hymns (vedas) in honor of their

[1] The process is as follows: when a word (or rather a root) is found in several Aryan languages at once, it is admitted that this was in use before the dispersion occurred, and therefore the people knew the object designated by the word.

[2] The Punjab.—Ed.

gods. These chants constituted a vast compilation which has been preserved to the present time. They were collected, perhaps, about the fourteenth century B.C. when the Aryans had not yet passed the Indus. The hymns present to us the oldest religion of the Hindoos.

The Gods.—The Hindoo calls his gods devas (the resplendent). Everything that shines is a divinity—the heavens, the dawn, the clouds, the stars—but especially the sun (Indra) and fire (Agni).

Indra.—The sun, Indra, the mighty one, "king of the world and master of creatures," bright and warm, traverses the heavens on a car drawn by azure steeds; he it is who hurls the thunderbolt, sends the rain, and banishes the clouds. India is a country of violent tempests; the Hindoo struck with this phenomenon explained it in his own fashion. He conceived the black cloud as an envelope in which were contained the waters of heaven; these beneficent waters he called the gleaming cows of Indra. When the storm is gathering, an evil genius, Vritra, a three-headed serpent, has driven away the cows and enclosed them in the black cavern whence their bellowings are heard (the far-away rumblings of thunder). Indra applies himself to the task of finding them; he strikes the cavern with his club, the strokes of which are heard (the thunderbolt), and the forked tongue of the serpent (the lightning) darts forth. At last the serpent is vanquished, the cave is opened, the waters released fall on the earth, Indra the victor appears in glory.

Agni.—Fire (Agni, the tireless) is regarded as another form of the sun. The Hindoo, who produces it by rapidly rubbing two pieces of wood together, imagines that the fire comes from the wood and that the rain has placed it there. He conceives it then as the fire of heaven descended to earth; in fact, when one places it on the hearth, it springs up as if it would ascend toward heaven. Agni dissipates darkness, warms mankind, and cooks his food; it is the benefactor and the protector of the house. It is also "the internal fire," the soul of the world; even the ancestor of the human race is the "son of lightning." Thus, heat and light, sources of all life, are the deities of the Hindoo.

Worship.—To adore his gods he strives to reproduce what he sees in heaven. He ignites a terrestrial fire by rubbing sticks, he nourishes it by depositing on the hearth, butter, milk, and soma, a fermented drink. To delight the gods he makes offerings to them of fruits and cakes; he even sacrifices to them cattle, rams and horses; he then invokes them, chanting hymns to their praise. "When thou art bidden by us to quaff the soma, come with thy sombre steeds, thou deity whose darts are stones. Our celebrant is seated according to prescription, the sacred green is spread, in the morning stones have been gathered together. Take thy seat on the holy sward; taste, O hero, our offering to thee. Delight thyself in our libations and our chants, vanquisher of Vritra, thou who art honored in these ceremonies of ours, O Indra."

The Hindoo thinks that the gods, felicitated by his offerings and homage, will in their turn make him happy. He says naïvely, "Give sacrifice to the gods for their profit, and they will requite you. Just as men traffic by the discussion of prices, let us exchange force and vigor, O Indra. Give to me and I will give to you; bring to me and I will bring to you."

Ancestor Worship.—At the same time the Hindoo adores his ancestors who have become gods, and perhaps this cult is the oldest of all. It is the basis of the family. The father who has transmitted the "fire of life" to his children makes offering every day at his hearth-fire, which must never be extinguished, the sacrifice to gods and ancestors, and utters the prayers. Here it is seen that among Hindoos, as among other Aryans, the father is at once a priest and a sovereign.

THE BRAHMANIC SOCIETY

The Hindoos on the Ganges.—The Hindoos passing beyond the region of the Indus, between the fourteenth and tenth century B.C. conquered all the immense plains of the Ganges. Once settled in this fertile country, under a burning climate, in the midst of a people of slaves, they gradually changed customs and religion. And so the Brahmanic society was established. Many works in Sanscrit are preserved from this time, which, with the Vedas, form the sacred literature of the Hindoos. The principal are the great epic poems, the Mahabarata, which has more than 200,000 verses; the Ramayana with 50,000, and the laws of Manou, the sacred code of India.

Caste.—In this new society there were no longer, as in the time of the Vedas, poets who chanted hymns to the gods. The men who know the prayers and the ceremonies are become theologians by profession; the people revere and obey them. The following is their conception of the structure of society: the supreme god, Brahma, has produced four kinds of men to each of whom he has assigned a mission. From his mouth he drew the Brahmans, who are, of course, the theologians; their mission is to study, to teach the hymns, to perform the sacrifices. The Kchatrias have come from his arms; these are the warriors who are charged with the protection of the people. The Vaïcyas proceed from the thigh; they must raise cattle, till the earth, loan money at interest, and engage in commerce. The Soudras issue from his foot; their only mission is to serve all the others.

There were already in the Aryan people theologians, warriors, artisans, and below them aborigines reduced to slavery. These were classes which one could enter and from which one could withdraw. But the Brahmans determined that every man should be attached to the condition in which he was born, he and his descendants for all time. The son of a workman could never become a warrior, nor the son of a warrior a theologian. Thus each is chained to his own state. Society is divided into four hereditary and closed castes.

The Unclean.—Whoever is not included in one of the four castes is unclean, excluded from society and religion. The Brahmans reckoned forty-four grades of outcasts: the last and the lowest is that of the pariahs; their very name is an insult. The outcasts may not practise any honorable trade nor approach other men. They may possess only dogs and asses, for these are unclean beasts. "They must have for their clothing the garments of the dead; for plates, broken pots; ornaments of iron; they must be ceaselessly on the move from one place to another."

The Brahmans.—In the organization of society the Brahmans were assigned the first place. "Men are the first among intelligent beings; the Brahmans are the first among men. They are higher than warriors, than kings, even. As between a Brahman of ten years of age and a Kchatria of one hundred years, the Brahman is to be regarded as the father." These are not priests as in Egypt and Chaldea, but only men who know religion, and pass their time in reading and meditating on the sacred books; they live from presents made to them by other men. To this day they are the dominating class of India. As they marry only among themselves, better than the other Hindoos they have preserved the Aryan type and have a clearer resemblance to Europeans.

The New Religion of Brahma.—The Brahmans did not discard the ancient gods of the Vedas, they continued to adore them. But by sheer ingenuity they invented a new god. When prayers are addressed to the gods, the deities are made to comply with the demands made on them, as if they thought that prayer was more powerful than the gods. And so prayer (Brahma) has become the highest of all deities. He is invoked with awe:[1] "O god, I behold in thy body all the gods and the multitudes of living beings. I am powerless to regard thee in thine entirety, for thou shinest like the fire and the sun in thine immensity. Thou art the Invisible, thou art the supreme Intelligence, thou art the sovereign treasure of the universe,

[1] Prayer of the Mahabarata cited by Lenormant.

without beginning, middle, or end; equipped with infinite might. Thine arms are without limit, thine eyes are like the moon and the sun, thy mouth hath the brightness of the sacred fire. With thyself alone thou fillest all the space between heaven and earth, and thou permeatest all the universe." Brahma is not only supreme god; he is the soul of the universe. All beings are born from Brahma, all issue naturally from him, not as a product comes from the hands of an artisan, but "as the tree from the seed, as the web from the spider." Brahma is not a deity who has created the world; he is the very substance of the world.

Transmigration of Souls.—There is, then, a soul, a part of the soul of Brahma, in every being, in gods, in men, in animals, in the very plants and stones. But these souls pass from one body into another; this is the transmigration of souls. When a man dies, his soul is tested; if it is good, it passes into the heaven of Indra there to enjoy felicity; if it is bad, it falls into one of the twenty-eight hells, where it is devoured by ravens, compelled to swallow burning cakes, and is tormented by demons. But souls do not remain forever in heaven or in the hells; they part from these to begin a new life in another body. The good soul rises, entering the body of a saint, perhaps that of a god; the evil soul descends, taking its abode in some impure animal —in a dog, an ass, even in a plant. In this new state it may rise or fall. And this journey from one body to another continues until the soul by degrees comes to the highest sphere. From lowest to highest in the scale, say the Brahmans, twenty-four millions of years elapse. At last perfect, the soul returns to the level of Brahma from which it descends and is absorbed into it.

Character of this Religion.—The religion of the Aryans, simple and happy, was that of a young and vigorous people. This is complicated and barren; it takes shape among men who are not engaged in practical life; it is enervated by the heat and vexations of life.

Rites.—The practice of the religion is much more complicated. Hymns and sacrifices are still offered to the gods, but the Brahmans have gradually invented thousands of minute customs so that one's life is completely engaged with them. For all the ceremonies of the religious life there are prayers, offerings, vows, libations, ablutions. Some of the religious requirements attach themselves to dress, ornaments, etiquette, drinking, eating, mode of walking, of lying down, of sleeping, of dressing, of undressing, of bathing. It is ordered: "That a Brahman shall not step over a rope to which a calf is attached; that he shall not run when it rains; that he shall not drink water in the hollow of his hand; that he shall not scratch his head with both his hands. The man who breaks clods of earth, who cuts grass with his nails or who bites his nails is, like the outcast, speedily hurried to his doom." An animal must not be killed, for a human soul may perhaps be dwelling in the body; one must not eat it on penalty of being devoured in another life by the animals which one has eaten.

All these rites have a magical virtue; he who observes them all is a saint; he who neglects any of them is impious and destined to pass into the body of an animal.

Purity.—The principal duty is keeping one's self pure; for every stain is a sin and opens one to the attack of evil spirits. But the Brahmans are very scrupulous concerning purity: men outside of the castes, many animals, the soil, even the utensils which one uses are so many impure things; whoever touches these is polluted and must at once purify himself. Life is consumed in purifications.

Penances.—For every defect in the rites, a penance is necessary, often a terrible one. He who involuntarily kills a cow must clothe himself in its skin, and for three months, day and night, follow and tend a herd of cows. Whoever has drunk of arrack[1] must swallow a boiling liquid which burns the internal organs until death results.

The Monks.—To escape so many dangers and maintain purity, it is better to leave the world. Often a Brahman when he has attained to a considerable age withdraws to the desert, fasts, watches, refrains from speech, exposes himself naked to the rain, holds himself erect between four fires under the burning sun. After some years, the solitary becomes "penitent"; then his only subsistence is from almsgiving; for whole days he lifts an arm in the air uttering not a word, holding his breath; or perchance, he gashes himself with razor-blades; or he may even keep his thumbs closed until the nails pierce the hands. By these mortifications he destroys passion, releases himself from this life, and by contemplation rises to Brahma. And yet, this way of

[1] A spirituous liquor made by the natives.—Ed.

salvation is open only to the Brahman; and even he has the right to withdraw to the desert only in old age, after having studied the Vedas all his life, practised all the rites, and established a family.

BUDDHISM

Buddha.—Millions of men who were not Brahmans, suffered by this life of minutiæ and anguish. A man then appeared who brought a doctrine of deliverance. He was not a Brahman, but of the caste of the Kchatrias, son of a king of the north. To the age of twenty-nine he had lived in the palace of his father. One day he met an old man with bald head, of wrinkled features, and trembling limbs; a second time he met an incurable invalid, covered with ulcers, without a home; again he fell in with a decaying corpse devoured by worms. And so, thought he, youth, health, and life are nothing for they offer no resistance to old age, to sickness, and to death. He had compassion on men and sought a remedy. Then he met a religious mendicant with grave and dignified air; following his example he decided to renounce the world. These four meetings had determined his calling.

Buddha fled to the desert, lived seven years in penitence, undergoing hunger, thirst, and rain. These mortifications gave him no repose. He ate, became strong, and found the truth. Then he reëntered the world to preach it; he made disciples in crowds who called him Buddha (the scholar); and when he died after forty-five years of preaching, Buddhism was established.

Nirvana.—To live is to be unhappy, taught Buddha. Every man suffers because he desires the goods of this world, youth, health, life, and cannot keep them. All life is a suffering; all suffering is born of desire. To suppress suffering, it is necessary to root out desire; to destroy it one must cease from wishing to live, "emancipate one's self from the thirst of being." The wise man is he who casts aside everything that attaches to this life and makes it unhappy. One must cease successively from feeling, wishing, thinking. Then, freed from passion, volition, even from reflection, he no longer suffers, and can, after his death, come to the supreme good, which consists in being delivered from all life and from all suffering. The aim of the wise man is the annihilation of personality: the Buddhists call it Nirvana.

Charity.—The Brahmans also considered life as a place of suffering and annihilation as felicity. Buddha came not with a new doctrine, but with new sentiments.

The religion of the Brahmans was egoistic. Buddha had compassion on men, he loved them, and preached love to his disciples. It was just this word of sympathy of which despairing souls were in need. He bade to love even those who do us ill. Purna, one of his disciples, went forth to preach to the barbarians. Buddha said to him to try him, "There are cruel, passionate, furious men; if they address angry words to you, what would you think?" "If they addressed angry words to me," said Purna, "I should think these are good men, these are gentle men, these men who attack me with wicked words but who strike me neither with the hand nor with stones." "But if they strike you, what would you think?" "I should think that those were good men who did not strike me with their staves or with their swords." "But if they did strike you with staff and sword, what would you think then?" "That those are good men who strike me with staff and sword, but do not take my life." "But if they should take your life?" "I should think them good men who delivered me with so little pain from this body filled as it is with pollution." "Well, well, Purna! You may dwell in the country of the barbarians. Go, proceed on the way to complete Nirvana and bring others to the same goal."

Fraternity.—The Brahmans, proud of their caste, assert that they are purer than the others. Buddha loves all men equally, he calls all to salvation even the pariahs, even the barbarians—all he declares are equal. "The Brahman," said he, "just like the pariah, is born of woman; why should he be noble and the other vile?" He receives as disciples street-sweepers, beggars, cripples, girls who sleep on dung-hills, even murderers and thieves; he fears no contamination in touching them. He preaches to them in the street in language simple with parables.

Tolerance.—The Brahmans passed their lives in the practice of minute rites, regarding as criminal whoever did not observe them. Buddha demanded neither rites nor exertions. To secure salvation it was enough to be charitable, chaste, and beneficent. "Benevolence," says he, "is the first of virtues. Doing a little good avails more than the fulfilment of the most arduous religious tasks. The perfect man is nothing unless he diffuses himself in benefits over creatures, unless he comforts the afflicted. My doctrine is a doctrine of mercy; this is why the fortunate in the world find it difficult."

Later History of Buddhism.—Thus was established about 500 years before Christ a religion of an entirely new sort. It is a religion without a god and without rites; it ordains only that one shall love his neighbor and become better; annihilation is offered as supreme recompense. But, for the first time in the history of the world, it preaches self-renunciation, the love of others, equality of mankind, charity and tolerance. The Brahmans made bitter war upon it and extirpated it in India. Missionaries carried it to the barbarians in Ceylon, in Indo-China, Thibet, China, and Japan. It is today the religion of about 500,000,000[1] people.

Changes in Buddhism.—During these twenty centuries Buddhism has undergone change. Buddha had himself formed communities of monks. Those who entered these renounced their family, took the vow of poverty and chastity; they had to wear filthy rags and beg their living. These religious rapidly multiplied; they founded convents in all Eastern Asia, gathered in councils to fix the doctrine, proclaimed dogmas and rules. As they became powerful they, like the Brahmans, came to esteem themselves as above the rest of the faithful. "The layman," they said, "ought to support the religious and consider himself much honored that the holy man accepts his offering. It is more commendable to feed one religious than many thousands of laymen." In Thibet the religious, men and women together, constitute a fifth of the entire population, and

[1] A high estimate.—ED.

their head, the Grand Lama, is venerated as an incarnation of God.

At the same time that they transformed themselves into masters, the Buddhist religious constructed a complicated theology, full of fantastic figures. They say there is an infinite number of worlds. If one surrounded with a wall a space capable of holding 100,000 times ten millions of those worlds, if this wall were raised to heaven, and if the whole space were filled with grains of mustard, the number of the grains would not even then equal one-half the number of worlds which occupy but one division of heaven. All these worlds are full of creatures, gods, men, beasts, demons, who are born and who die. The universe itself is annihilated and another takes its place. The duration of each universe is called *kalpa;* and this is the way we obtain an impression of a kalpa: if there were a rock twelve miles in height, breadth, and length, and if once in a century it were only touched with a piece of the finest linen, this rock would be worn and reduced to the size of a kernel of mango before a quarter of a kalpa had elapsed.

Buddha Transformed into a God.—It no longer satisfied the Buddhists to honor their founder as a perfect man; they made him a god, erecting idols to him, and offering him worship. They adored also the saints, his disciples; pyramids and shrines were built to preserve their bones, their. teeth, their cloaks. From every quarter the faithful came to venerate the impression of the foot of Buddha.

Mechanical Prayer.—Modern Buddhists regard prayer as a magical formula which acts of itself.

They spend the day reciting prayers as they walk or eat, often in a language which they do not understand. They have invented prayer-machines; these are revolving cylinders and around these are pasted papers on which the prayer is written; every turn of the cylinder counts for the utterance of the prayer as many times as it is written on the papers.

Amelioration of Manners.—And yet Buddhism remains a religion of peace and charity. Wherever it reigns, kings refrain from war, and even from the chase; they establish hospitals, caravansaries, even asylums for animals. Strangers, even Christian missionaries, are hospitably received; they permit the women to go out, and to walk without veiling themselves; they neither fight nor quarrel. At Bangkok, a city of 400,000 souls, hardly more than one murder a year is known.

Buddhism has enfeebled the intelligence and sweetened the character.[1]

[1] India is for us the country of the Vedas, the Brahmans, and Buddha. We know the religion of the Hindoos, but of their political history we are ignorant.

CHAPTER VI

THE PERSIANS

THE RELIGION OF ZOROASTER

Iran.—Between the Tigris and the Indus, the Caspian Sea and the Persian Gulf rises the land of Iran, five times as great as France,[1] but partly sterile. It is composed of deserts of burning sand and of icy plateaux cut by deep and wooded valleys. Mountains surround it preventing the escape of the rivers which must lose themselves in the sands or in the salt lakes. The climate is harsh, very uneven, torrid in summer, frigid in winter; in certain quarters one passes from 104° above zero to 40° below, from the cold of Siberia to the heat of Senegal. Violent winds blow which "cut like a sword." But in the valleys along the rivers the soil is fertile. Here the peach and cherry are indigenous; the country is a land of fruits and pastures.

The Iranians.—Aryan tribes inhabited Iran. Like all the Aryans, they were a race of shepherds, but well armed and warlike. The Iranians fought on horseback, drew the bow, and, to protect themselves from the biting wind of their country, wore garments of skin sewed on the body.

[1] That is, of about the same area as that part of the United States east of the Mississippi, with Minnesota and Iowa. Modern Persia is not two-thirds of this area.—Ed.

Zoroaster.—Like the ancient Aryans, they first adored the forces of nature, especially the sun (Mithra). Between the tenth and seventh[1] centuries before our era their religion was reformed by a sage, Zarathustra (Zoroaster). We know nothing certainly about him except his name.

The Zend-Avesta.—No writing from the hand of Zoroaster is preserved to us; but his doctrine, reduced to writing long after his death, is conserved in the Zend-Avesta (law and reform), the sacred books of the Persians. It was a compilation written in an ancient language (the Zend) which the faithful themselves no longer understood. It was divided into twenty-one books, inscribed on 12,000 cow skins, bound by golden cords. The Mohammedans destroyed it when they invaded Persia. But some Persian families, faithful to the teaching of Zoroaster, fled into India. Their posterity, whom we call Parsees, have there maintained the old religion. An entire book of the Zend-Avesta and fragments of two others have been found among them.

Ormuzd and Ahriman.—The Zend-Avesta is the sacred book of the religion of Zoroaster. According to these writings Ahura Mazda (Ormuzd), "the omniscient sovereign," created the world. He is addressed in prayer in the following language: "I invoke and celebrate the creator, Ahura Mazda, luminous, glorious, most intelligent and beautiful, eminent in purity, who possessest the good knowledge, source of joy, who hast created us, hast fashioned us, and hast nourished us." Since he is perfect in his goodness, he can create

[1] Most historians place Zoroaster before 1000 B.C.—Ed.

only that which is good. Everything bad in the world has been created by an evil deity, Angra Manyou, (Ahriman), the "spirit of anguish."

Angels and Demons.—Over against Ormuzd, the god and the creator, is Ahriman, wicked and destructive. Each has in his service a legion of spirits. The soldiers of Ormuzd are the good angels (yazatas), those of Ahriman the evil demons (devs). The angels dwell in the East in the light of the rising sun; the demons in the West in the shadows of the darkness. The two armies wage incessant warfare; the world is their battleground, for both troops are omnipresent. Ormuzd and his angels seek to benefit men, to make them good and happy; Ahriman and his demons gnaw around them to destroy them, to make them unhappy and wicked.

Creatures of Ormuzd and Ahriman.—Everything good on the earth is the work of Ormuzd and works for good; the sun and fire that dispel the night, the stars, fermented drinks that seem to be liquid fire, the water that satisfies the thirst of man, the cultivated fields that feed him, the trees that shade him, domestic animals—especially the dog,[1] the birds (because they live in the air), among all these the cock since he announces the day. On the other hand everything that is baneful comes from Ahriman and tends to evil: the night, drought, cold, the desert, poisonous plants, thorns, beasts of prey, serpents, parasites (mosquitoes, fleas, bugs) and animals that live in dark holes—

[1] "I created the dog," said Ormuzd, "with a delicate scent and strong teeth, attached to man, biting the enemy to protect the herds. Thieves and wolves come not near the sheep-fold when the dog is on guard, strong in voice and defending the flocks."

lizards, scorpions, toads, rats, ants. Likewise in the moral world life, purity, truth, work are good things and come from Ormuzd; death, filth, falsehood, idleness are bad, and issue from Ahriman.

Worship.—From these notions proceed worship and morality. Man ought to adore the good god[1] and fight for him. According to Herodotus, "The Persians are not accustomed to erect statues, temples, or altars to their gods; they esteem those who do this as lacking in sense for they do not believe, as the Greeks do, that the gods have human forms."[2] Ormuzd manifests himself only under the form of fire or the sun. This is why the Persians perform their worship in the open air on the mountains, before a lighted fire. To worship Ormuzd they sing hymns to his praise and sacrifice animals in his honor.

Morality.—Man fights for Ormuzd in aiding his efforts and in overcoming Ahriman's. He wars against darkness in supplying the fire with dry wood and perfumes; against the desert in tilling the soil and in building houses; against the animals of Ahriman in killing serpents, lizards, parasites, and beasts of prey. He battles against impurity in keeping himself clean, in banishing from himself everything that is dead, especially the nails and hair, for "where hairs and clipped nails are, demons and unclean animals assemble." He fights against falsehood by always being truthful. "The Persians," says Herodotus,[3] "consider nothing

[1] Certain Persian heretics of our day, on the contrary, adore only the evil god, for, they say, the principle of the good being in itself good and indulgent does not require appeasing. They are called Yezidis (worshippers of the devil).

[2] Herod., i., 131.

[3] i., 138.

so shameful as lying, and after falsehood nothing so shameful as contracting debts, for he who has debts necessarily lies." He wars against death by marrying and having many children. "Terrible," says the Zend-Avesta, "are the houses void of posterity."

Funerals.—As soon as a man is dead his body belongs to the evil spirit. It is necessary, then, to remove it from the house. But it ought not to be burned, for in this way the fire would be polluted; it should not be buried, for so is the soil defiled; nor is it to be drowned, and thus contaminate the water. These dispositions of the corpse would bring permanent pollution. The Persians resorted to a different method. The body with face toward the sun was exposed in an elevated place and left uncovered, securely fixed with stones; the bearers then withdrew to escape the demons, for they assemble "in the places of sepulture, where reside sickness, fever, filth, cold, and gray hairs." Dogs and birds, pure animals, then come to purify the body by devouring it.

Destiny of the Soul.—The soul of the dead separates itself from the body. In the third night after death it is conducted over the "Bridge of Assembling" (Schinvat) which leads to the paradise above the gulf of inferno. There Ormuzd questions it on its past life. If it has practised the good, the pure spirits and the spirits of dogs support it and aid it in crossing the bridge and give it entrance into the abode of the blest; the demons flee, for they cannot bear the odor of virtuous spirits. The soul of the wicked, on the other hand, comes to the dread bridge, and reeling, with no one to support it, is dragged by demons to hell, is seized by the evil spirit and chained in the abyss of darkness.

Character of Mazdeism.—This religion originated in a country of violent contrasts, luxuriant valleys side by side with barren steppes, cool oases with burning deserts, cultivated fields and stretches of sand, where the forces of nature seem engaged in an eternal warfare. This combat which the Iranian saw around him he assumed to be the law of the universe. Thus a religion of great purity was developed, which urged man to work and to virtue; but at the same time issued a belief in the devil and in demons which was to propagate itself in the west and torment all the peoples of Europe.

THE PERSIAN EMPIRE

The Medes.—Many were the tribes dwelling in Iran; two of these have become noted in history—the Medes and the Persians. The Medes at the west, nearer the Assyrians, destroyed Nineveh and its empire (625). But soon they softened their manners, taking the flowing robes, the indolent life, the superstitious religion of the degenerate Assyrians. They at last were confused with them.

The Persians.—The Persians to the east preserved their manners, their religion, and their vigor. "For twenty years," says Herodotus, "the Persians teach their children but three things—to mount a horse, to draw the bow, and to tell the truth."

Cyrus.—About 550 Cyrus, their chief, overthrew the king of the Medes, reunited all the peoples of Iran, and then conquered Lydia, Babylon, and all Asia Minor. Herodotus recounts in detail a legend which became attached to this prince. Cyrus himself in an inscription says of himself, "I am Cyrus, king of the legions, great king, mighty king, king of Babylon, king of Sumir and Akkad, king of the four regions, son of Cambyses, great king of Susiana, grand-son of Cyrus, king of Susiana."

The Inscription of Behistun.—The eldest son of Cyrus, Cambyses, put to death his brother Smerdis and conquered Egypt. What occurred afterward is known to us from an inscription. Today one may see on the frontier of Persia, in the midst of a plain, an enormous rock, cut perpendicularly, about 1,500 feet high, the rock of Behistun. A bas-relief carved on the rock represents a crowned king, with left hand on a bow; he tramples on one captive while nine other prisoners are presented before him in chains. An inscription in three languages relates the life of the king: "Darius the king declares, This is what I did before I became king. Cambyses, son of Cyrus, of our race, reigned here before me. This Cambyses had a brother Smerdis, of the same father and the same mother. One day Cambyses killed Smerdis. When Cambyses had killed Smerdis the people were ignorant that Smerdis was dead. After this Cambyses made an expedition to Egypt and while he was there the people became rebellious; falsehood was then rife in the country, in Persia, in Media and the other provinces. There was at that time a magus named Gaumata; he deceived the people by saying that he was Smerdis, the son of Cyrus. Then the whole people rose in revolt, forsook Cambyses and went over to the pretender. After this Cambyses died from a wound inflicted by himself.

"After Gaumata had drawn away Persia, Media, and the other countries from Cambyses, he followed out his purpose: he became king. The people feared him on account of his cruelty: he would have killed the people so that no one might learn that he was not Smerdis, the son of Cyrus. Darius the king declares there was not a man in all Persia or in Media who dared to snatch the crown from this Gaumata, the magus. Then I presented myself, I prayed Ormuzd. Ormuzd accorded me his protection. . . . Accompanied by faithful men I killed this Gaumata and his principal accomplices. By the will of Ormuzd I became king. The empire which had been stolen from our race I restored to it. The altars that Gaumata, the magus, had thrown down I rebuilt to the deliverance of the people; I received the chants and the sacred ceremonials." Having overturned the usurper, Darius had to make war on many of the revolting princes. "I have," said he, "won nineteen battles and overcome nine kings."

The Persian Empire.—Darius then subjected the peoples in revolt and reëstablished the empire of the Persians. He enlarged it also by conquering Thrace and a province of India. This empire reunited all the peoples of the Orient: Medes and Persians, Assyrians, Chaldeans, Jews, Phœnicians, Syrians, Lydians, Egyptians, Indians; it covered all the lands from the Danube on the west to the Indus on the east, from the Caspian Sea on the north to the cataracts of the

Nile on the south. It was the greatest empire up to this time. One tribe of mountaineers, the last to come, thus received the heritage of all the empires of Asia.

The Satrapies.—Oriental kings seldom concerned themselves with their subjects more than to draw money from them, levy soldiers, and collect presents; they never interfered in their local affairs. Darius, like the rest, left each of the peoples of his empire to administer itself according to its own taste, to keep its language, its religion, its laws, often its ancient princes. But he took care to regulate the taxes which his subjects paid him. He divided all the empire into twenty[1] districts called satrapies. There were in the same satrapy peoples who differed much in language, customs, and beliefs; but each satrapy was to pay a fixed annual tribute, partly in gold and silver, partly in natural products (wheat, horses, ivory). The satrap, or governor, had the tribute collected and sent it to the king.

Revenues of the Empire.—The total revenue of the king amounted to sixteen millions of dollars and this money was paid by weight. This sum was in addition to the tributes in kind. These sixteen millions of dollars, if we estimate them by the value of the metals at this time, would be equivalent to one hundred and twenty millions in our day. With this sum the king supported his satraps, his army, his domestic servants and an extravagant court; there still remained to him every year enormous ingots of metal which accumu-

[1] Herodotus mentions 20, but we find as many as 31 enumerated in the inscriptions.

lated in his treasuries. The king of Persia, like all the Orientals, exercised his vanity in possessing an immense treasure.

The Great King.—No king had ever been so powerful and rich. The Greeks called the Persian king The Great King. Like all the monarchs of the East, the king had absolute sway over all his subjects, over the Persians as well as over tributary peoples. From Herodotus one can see how Cambyses treated the great lords at his court. "What do the Persians think of me?" said he one day to Prexaspes, whose son was his cupbearer. "Master, they load you with praises, but they believe that you have a little too strong desire for wine." "Learn," said Cambyses in anger, "whether the Persians speak the truth. If I strike in the middle of the heart of your son who is standing in the vestibule, that will show that the Persians do not know what they say." He drew his bow and struck the son of Prexaspes. The youth fell; Cambyses had the body opened to see where the shot had taken effect. The arrow was found in the middle of the heart. The prince, full of joy said in derision to the father of the young man, "You see that it is the Persians who are out of their senses; tell me if you have seen anybody strike the mark with so great accuracy." "Master," replied Prexaspes, "I do not believe that even a god could shoot so surely."[1]

Services Rendered by the Persians.—The peoples of Asia have always paid tribute to conquerors and given allegiance to despots. The Persians, at least, ren-

[1] Herod., iii., 34, 35. Compare also iii., 78, 79; and the book of Esther.

dered them a great service: in subjecting all these peoples to one master they prevented them from fighting among themselves. Under their domination we do not see a ceaseless burning of cities, devastation of fields, massacre or wholesale enslavement of inhabitants. It was a period of peace.

Susa and Persepolis.—The kings of the Medes and Persians, following the example of the lords of Assyria, had palaces built for them. Those best known to us are the palaces at Susa and Persepolis. The ruins of Susa have been excavated by a French engineer,[1] who has discovered sculptures, capitals, and friezes in enameled bricks which give evidence of an advanced stage of art. The palace of Persepolis has left ruins of considerable mass. The rock of the hill had been fashioned into an enormous platform on which the palace was built. The approach to it was by a gently rising staircase so broad that ten horsemen could ascend riding side by side.

Persian Architecture.—Persian architects had copied the palaces of the Assyrians. At Persepolis and Susa, as in Assyria, are flat-roofed edifices with terraces, gates guarded by monsters carved in stone, bas-reliefs and enameled bricks, representing hunting-scenes and ceremonies. At three points, however, the Persians improved on their models:

(1) They used marble instead of brick; (2) they made in the halls painted floors of wood; (3) they erected eight columns in the form of trunks of trees, the slenderest that we know, twelve times as high as they were thick.

[1] M. Dieulafoi.

Thus their architecture is more elegant and lighter than that of Assyria.

The Persians had made little progress in the arts. But they seem to have been the most honest, the sanest, and the bravest people of the time. For two centuries they exercised in Asia a sovereignty the least cruel and the least unjust that it had ever known.

CHAPTER VII

THE PHŒNICIANS

THE PHŒNICIAN PEOPLE

The Land.—Phœnicia is the narrow strip of country one hundred and fifty miles long by twenty-four to thirty wide, shut in between the sea of Syria and the high range of Lebanon. It is a succession of narrow valleys and ravines confined by abrupt hills which descend towards the sea; little torrents formed by the snows or rain-storms course through these in the early spring; in summer no water remains except in wells and cisterns. The mountains in this quarter were always covered with trees; at the summit were the renowned cedars of Lebanon, on the ridges, pines and cypresses; while lower yet palms grew even to the sea-shore. In the valleys flourished the olive, the vine, the fig, and the pomegranate.

The Cities.—At intervals along the rocky coast promontories or islands formed natural harbors. On these the Phœnicians had founded their cities; Tyre and Arad were each built on a small island. The people housed themselves in dwellings six to eight stories in height. Fresh water was ferried over in ships. The other cities, Gebel, Beirut, and Sidon arose on the mainland. The soil was inadequate to support these swarms of men, and so the Phœnicians were before all else seamen and traders.

Phœnician Ruins.—Not a book of the Phœnicians has come down to us, not even their sacred book. The sites of their cities have been excavated. But, in the words of the scholar sent to do this work, "Ruins are not preserved, especially in countries where people are not occupied with them," and the Syrians are not much occupied with ruins. They have violated the tombs to remove the jewels of the dead, have demolished edifices to secure stone for building purposes, and Mussulman hatred of chiseled figures has shattered the sculptures.[1] Very little is found beyond broken marble, cisterns, wine-presses cut in the rock and some sarcophagi hewn in rock. All this débris gives us little information and we know very little more of the Phœnicians than Greek writers and Jewish prophets have taught us.

Political Organization of the Phœnicians.—The Phœnicians never built an empire. Each city had its little independent territory, its assemblies, its king, and its government. For general state business each city sent delegates to Tyre, which from the thirteenth century B.C. was the principal city of Phœnicia. The Phœnicians were not a military people, and so submitted themselves to all the conquerors—Egyptians, Assyrians, Babylonians, Persians. They fulfilled all their obligations to them in paying tribute.

Tyre.—From the thirteenth century Tyre was the most notable of the cities. Its island becoming too small to contain it, a new city was built on the coast

[1] Renan ("Mission de Phénicie," p. 818) says, "I noticed at Tripolis a sarcophagus serving as a public fountain and the sculptured face of it was turned to the wall. I was told that a governor had placed it thus so as not to provide distractions for the inhabitants."

opposite. Tyrian merchants had founded colonies in every part of the Mediterranean, receiving silver from the mines of Spain and commodities from the entire ancient world. The prophet Isaiah[1] calls these traders princes; Ezekiel[2] describes the caravans which came to them from all quarters. It is Hiram, a king of Tyre, from whom Solomon asked workmen to build his palace and temple at Jerusalem.

Carthage.—A colony of Tyre surpassed even her in power. In the ninth century some Tyrians, exiled by a revolution, founded on the shore of Africa near Tunis the city of Carthage. A woman led them, Elissar, whom we call Dido (the fugitive). The inhabitants of the country, says the legend, were willing to sell her only as much land as could be covered by a bull's hide; but she cut the hide in strips so narrow that it enclosed a wide territory; and there she constructed a citadel. Situated at the centre of the Mediterranean, provided with two harbors, Carthage flourished, sent out colonies in turn, made conquests, and at last came to reign over all the coasts of Africa, Spain, and Sardinia. Everywhere she had agencies for her commerce and subjects who paid her tribute.

The Carthaginian Army.—To protect her colonies from the natives, to hold her subjects in check who were always ready to revolt, a strong army was necessary. But the life of a Carthaginian was too valuable to risk it without necessity. Carthage preferred to pay mercenary soldiers, recruiting them among the barbarians of her empire and among the adventurers

[1] See ch. xxiii.
[2] See chs. xxvi., xxvii., xxviii.

of all countries. Her army was a bizarre aggregation in which all languages were spoken, all religions practised, and in which every soldier wore different arms and costume. There were seen Numidians clothed in lion skins which served them as couch, mounted bareback on small fleet horses, and drawing the bow with horse at full gallop; Libyans with black skins, armed with pikes; Iberians from Spain in white garments adorned with red, armed with a long pointed sword; Gauls, naked to the girdle, bearing enormous shields and a rounded sword which they held in both hands; natives of the Balearic Islands, trained from infancy to sling with stones or balls of lead. The generals were Carthaginians; the government distrusted them, watched them closely, and when they were defeated, had them crucified.

The Carthaginians.—Carthage had two kings, but the senate was the real power, being composed of the richest merchants of the city. And so every state question for this government became a matter of commerce. The Carthaginians were hated by all other peoples, who found them cruel, greedy, and faithless. And yet, since they had a good fleet, had money to purchase soldiers, and possessed an energetic government, they succeeded in the midst of barbarous and divided peoples in maintaining their empire over the western Mediterranean for 300 years (from the sixth to the third century B.C.).

The Phœnician Religion.—The Phœnicians and the Carthaginians had a religion similar to that of the Chaldeans. The male god, Baal, is a sun-god; for the sun and the moon are in the eyes of the Phœnicians the great forces which create and which destroy. Each of the cities of Phœnicia has therefore its divine pair: at Sidon it is Baal Sidon (the sun) and Astoreth (the moon); at Gebel, Baal Tammouz and Baaleth; at Carthage, Baal-Hamon, and Tanith. But the same god changes his name according as he is conceived as creator or destroyer; thus Baal as destroyer is worshipped at Carthage under the name of Moloch. These gods, represented by idols, have their temples, altars, and priests. As creators they are honored with orgies, with tumultuous feasts; as destroyers, by human victims. Astoreth, the great goddess of Sidon, whom they represented by the crescent of the moon and the dove, had her cult in the sacred woods. Baal Moloch is figured at Carthage as a bronze colossus with arms extended and lowered. When they wished to appease him they laid children in his hands who fell at once into a pit of fire. During the siege of Carthage by Agathocles the principal men of the city sacrificed to Moloch as many as two hundred of their children.

This sensual and sanguinary religion inspired other peoples with horror, but they imitated it. The Jews sacrificed to Baal on the mountains; the Greeks adored Astarte of Sidon under the name of Aphrodite, and Baal Melkhart of Tyre under the name of Herakles.

PHŒNICIAN COMMERCE

Phœnician Occupations.—Crowded into a small territory, the Phœnicians gained their livelihood mainly from commerce. None of the other peoples of the East—the Egyptians, the Chaldeans, the Assyrians, nor the barbarian tribes of the West (Spaniards, Gauls, Italians) had a navy. The Phœnicians alone in this time dared to navigate. They were the commission merchants of the old world; they went to every people to buy their merchandise and sold them in exchange the commodities of other countries. This traffic was by caravan with the East, by sea with the West.

Caravans.—On land the Phœnicians sent caravans in three directions:

1.—Towards Arabia, from which they brought gold, agate, and onyx, incense and myrrh, and the perfumes of Arabia; pearls, spices, ivory, ebony, ostrich plumes and apes from India.

2.—Towards Assyria, whence came cotton and linen cloths, asphalt, precious stones, perfumery, and silk from China.

3.—Towards the Black Sea, where they went to receive horses, slaves, and copper vases made by the mountaineers of the Caucasus.

Marine Commerce.—For their sea commerce they built ships from the cedars of Lebanon to be propelled by oars and sails. In their sailing it was not necessary to remain always in sight of the coast, for they knew how to direct their course by the polar star. Bold mariners, they pushed in their little boats to the mouth of the Mediterranean; they ventured even to pass through the strait of Gibraltar or, as the ancients called it, the Pillars of Hercules, and took the ocean course to the shores of England, and perhaps to Norway. Phœnicians in the service of a king of Egypt started in the seventh century B.C. to circumnavigate Africa, and returned, it is said, at the end of three years by the

Red Sea. An expedition issuing from Carthage skirted the coast of Africa to the Gulf of Guinea; the commander Hanno wrote an account of the voyage which is still preserved.

Commodities.—To civilized peoples the Phœnicians sold the products of their industry. In barbarous countries they went to search for what they could not find in the Orient. On the coast of Greece they gathered shell-fish from which they extracted a red tint, the purple; cloths colored with purple were used among all the peoples of ancient times for garments of kings and great lords.

From Spain and Sardinia they brought the silver which the inhabitants took from the mines. Tin was necessary to make bronze, an alloy of copper and tin, but the Orient did not furnish this, and so they sought it even on the coasts of England, in the Isles of Tin (the Cassiterides). In every country they procured slaves. Sometimes they bought them, as lately the slavers bought negroes on the coast of Africa, for all the peoples of this time made commerce in slaves; sometimes they swooped down on a coast, threw themselves on the women and children and carried them off to be retained in their own cities or to be sold abroad; for on occasion they were pirates and did not scruple to plunder strangers.

The Secrets Kept by the Phœnicians.—The Phœnicians did not care to have mariners of other peoples come into competition with them. On the return from these far countries they concealed the road which they had travelled. No one in antiquity knew where were the famous Isles of the Cassiterides from which they got their tin. It was by chance that a Greek ship discovered Spain, with which the Phœnicians had traded for centuries. Carthage drowned the foreign merchants whom they found in Sardinia or on the shore of Gibraltar. Once a Carthaginian merchantman, seeing a strange ship following it, was run aground by the pilot that the foreigner might not see where he was going.

Colonies.—In the countries where they traded, the Phœnicians founded factories, or branch-houses. They were fortified posts on a natural harbor. There they landed their merchandise, ordinarily cloths, pottery, ornaments, and idols.[1] The natives brought down their commodities and an exchange was made, just as now European merchants do with the negroes of Africa. There were Phœnician markets in Cyprus, in Egypt, and in all the then barbarous countries of the Mediterranean—in Crete, Greece, Sicily, Africa, Malta, Sardinia, on the coasts of Spain at Malaga and Cadiz, and perhaps in Gaul at Monaco. Often around these Phœnician buildings the natives set up their cabins and the mart became a city. The inhabitants adopted the Phœnician gods, and even after the city had become Greek, the cult of the dove-goddess was found there (as in Cythera), that of the god Melkhart (as at Corinth), or of the god with the bull-face that devours human victims (as in Crete).

Influence of the Phœnicians.—It is certain that the Phœnicians in founding their trading stations cared only for their own interest. But it came to pass that

[1] These idols, one of their principal exports, are found wherever the Phœnicians traded.

their colonies contributed to civilization. The barbarians of the West received the cloths, the jewels, the utensils of the peoples of the East who were more civilized, and, receiving them, learned to imitate them. For a long time the Greeks had only vases, jewels, and idols brought by the Phœnicians, and these served them as models. The Phœnicians brought simultaneously from Egypt and from Assyria industry and commodities.

The Alphabet.—At the same time they exported their alphabet. The Phœnicians did not invent writing. The Egyptians knew how to write many centuries before them, they even made use of letters each of which expressed its own sound, as in our alphabet. But their alphabet was still encumbered with ancient signs which represented, some a syllable, others an entire word. Doubtless the Phœnicians had need of a simpler system for their books of commerce. They rejected all the syllabic signs and ideographs, preserving only twenty-two letters, each of which marks a sound (or rather an articulation of the language). The other peoples imitated this alphabet of twenty-two letters. Some, like the Jews, wrote from right to left just as the Phœnicians themselves did; others, like the Greeks, from left to right. All have slightly changed the form of the letters, but the Phœnician alphabet is found at the basis of all the alphabets—Hebrew, Lycian, Greek, Italian, Etruscan, Iberian, perhaps even in the runes of the Norse. It is the Phœnicians that taught the world how to write.

CHAPTER VIII

THE HEBREWS

ORIGIN OF THE HEBREW PEOPLE

The Bible.—The Jews united all their sacred books into a single aggregation which we call by a Greek name the Bible, that is to say, the Book. It is the Book *par excellence*. The sacred book of the Jews became also the sacred book of the Christians. The Bible is at the same time the history of the Jewish nation, and all that we know of the sacred people we owe to the sacred books.

The Hebrews.—When the Semites had descended from the mountains of Armenia into the plains of the Euphrates, one of their tribes, at the time of the first Chaldean empire, withdrew to the west, crossed the Euphrates, the desert, and Syria and came to the country of the Jordan beyond Phœnicia. This tribe was called the Hebrews, that is to say, the people from beyond the river. Like the majority of the Semites they were a race of nomadic shepherds. They did not till the soil and had no houses; they moved from place to place with their herds of cattle, sheep, and camels, seeking pasturage and living in tents as the Arabs of the desert do to this day. In the book of Genesis one has a glimpse of this nomad life.

The Patriarchs.—The tribe was like a great family; it was composed of the chief, his wives, his children, and his servants. The chief had absolute authority over all; for the tribe he was father, priest, judge, and king. We call these tribal chiefs patriarchs. The principal ones were Abraham and Jacob; the former the father of the Hebrews, the latter of the Israelites. The Bible represents both of them as designed by God to be the scions of a sacred people. Abraham made a covenant with God that he and his descendants would obey him; God promised to Abraham a posterity more numerous than the stars of heaven. Jacob received from God the assurance that a great nation should issue from himself.

The Israelites.—Moved by a vision Jacob took the name of Israel (contender with God). His tribe was called Beni-Israel (sons of Israel) or Israelites. The Bible records that, driven by famine, Jacob abandoned the Jordan country to settle with all his house on the eastern frontier of Egypt, to which Joseph, one of his sons who had become minister of a Pharaoh, invited him. There the sons of Israel abode for several centuries. Coming hither but seventy in number, they multiplied, according to the Bible, until they became six hundred thousand men, without counting women and children.

The Call of Moses.—The king of Egypt began to oppress them, compelling them to make mortar and bricks for the construction of his strong cities. It was then that one of them, Moses, received from God the mission to deliver them. One day while he was keeping his herds on the mountain, an angel appeared to him in the midst of a burning bush, and he heard these words: "I am the God of Abraham, the God of Isaac, the God of Jacob. I have seen the affliction of my people which is in Egypt, I have heard their cry against their oppressors, I know their sorrows. And I am come down to deliver them out of the hands of the Egyptians and to bring them to a land flowing with milk and honey, to the place of the Canaanites. . . . Come now therefore and I will send thee unto Pharaoh that thou mayest bring forth my people, the children of Israel, out of Egypt."[1] The Israelites under the guidance of Moses fled from Egypt (the Exodus); they journeyed to the foot of Mount Sinai, where they received the law of God, and for an entire generation wandered in the deserts to the south of Syria.

Israel in the Desert.—Often the Israelites wished to turn back. "We remember," said they, "the fish which we ate in Egypt, the cucumbers, melons, leeks, and onions. Let us appoint a chief who will lead us back to Egypt." Moses, however, held them to obedience. At last they reached the land promised by God to their race.

The Promised Land.—It was called the land of Canaan or Palestine; the Jews named it the land of Israel, later Judea. Christians have termed it the Holy Land. It is an arid country, burning with heat in the summer, but a country of mountains. The Bible describes it thus: "Jehovah thy God bringeth thee into a good land, a land of brooks of water, of fountains and depths that spring out of valleys and hills, a land of wheat, and barley, and vines, and fig-

[1]Exodus iii., 1–10.

trees, and pomegranates; a land of oil olive and honey, wherein thou shalt eat bread without scarceness, thou shalt not lack anything in it." The Israelites according to their estimate were then 601,700 men capable of bearing arms, divided among twelve tribes, ten descended from Jacob, two from Joseph; this enumeration does not include the Levites or priests to the number of 23,000. The land was occupied by several small peoples who were called Canaanites. The Israelites exterminated them and at last occupied their territory.

THE RELIGION OF ISRAEL

One God.—The other ancient peoples adored many gods; the Israelites believed in but one God, immaterial, who made the world and governs it. "In the beginning," says the book of Genesis, "God created the heavens and the earth." He created plants and animals, he "created man in his own image." All men are the handiwork of God.

The People of God.—But among all mankind God has chosen the children of Israel to make of them "his people." He called Abraham and said to him, "I will establish my covenant between me and thee and thy seed after me . . . to be a God unto thee and to thy seed." He appeared to Jacob: "I am God," said he to him, "the God of thy father; fear not to go down into Egypt, for I will make of thee there a great nation." When Moses asks his name, he replies, "Thou shalt say to the children of Israel, The Lord, the God of thy fathers, the God of Abraham, the God of Isaac, the God of Jacob hath sent me unto you. This is my name forever."

The Covenant.—There is, then, a covenant between the Israelites and God. Jehovah (the Eternal) loves and protects the Israelites, they are "a holy nation," "his most precious jewel among all the nations." He promises to make them mighty and happy. In return, the Israelites swear to worship him, to serve him, to obey him in everything as a lawgiver, a judge, and a sovereign.

The Ten Commandments.—Jehovah, lawgiver of the Israelites, dictated his precepts to Moses on Mount Sinai amidst lightnings and thunderings. They were inscribed on two tables, the Tables of the Law, in these terms:

"Hear, O Israel, I am Jehovah, thy God, who brought you out of the land of Egypt, from the land of bondage." (Then follow the ten commandments to be found in the twentieth chapter of the book of Exodus.)

The Law.—Beside the ten commandments, the Israelites are required to obey many other divine ordinances. These are all delivered to them in the first five books of the Bible, the Pentateuch, and constitute the Law of Israel. The Law regulates the ceremonies of religion, establishes the feasts—including the Sabbath every seven days, the Passover in memory of the escape from Egypt, the week of harvest, the feast of Tabernacles during the vintage; it organizes marriage, the family, property, government, fixes the penalty of crimes, indicates even foods and remedies. It is a code at once religious, political, civil and penal. God the ruler of the Israelites has the right to regulate all the details of their lives.

Religion has made the Jewish People.—The Israelites did not receive with docility the government of God. Moses on his death-bed could say to the Levites in delivering to them the book of the law, "Take this book that it may be a witness against you, Israel, for I know thy rebellion and thy stiff neck" (Deut. xxxi. 27). "During my life you have been rebellious against the Lord, and how much more after my death." During these centuries some of the Israelites, often the majority of the nation, had been idolaters. They became similar to the other Semites of Syria. Only the Israelites who remained faithful to God formed the Jewish people. It is the religion of Jehovah which has transformed an obscure tribe into the holy nation, a small nation, but one of the most significant in the history of the world.

THE KINGDOM OF ISRAEL

The Judges.—Once established in Palestine the Hebrews remained divided for several centuries. "In those days," says the Bible, "there was no king in Israel; every man did that which was right in his own eyes." Often the Israelites forgot Jehovah and served the gods of neighboring tribes. Then "the anger of the Lord was kindled against the Israelites, and he delivered them into the hands of their enemies." When they had repented and had humbled themselves, "the Lord raised up judges who delivered them out of the hand of those that spoiled them." "But it came to pass that at the death of the judge they corrupted themselves anew . . . bowing themselves to other gods." These judges—Gideon, Jephthah, Samson—were warriors who came in the name of Jehovah to free the people. Then they fell at once into idolatry again and their servitude was repeated.

The Kings.—At last the Israelites were wearied and asked of Samuel, the high-priest, that he would give them a king. Samuel unwillingly placed Saul at their head. This king should have been the ready servant of the will of God; he dared to disobey him, upon which the high-priest said to him, "Thou hast rejected the word of the Lord and the Lord hath rejected thee from being king over Israel." A war-chief, David, was set in his place. He defeated all the enemies of Israel, captured from them Mount Zion, and transferred his capital thither. This was Jerusalem.

Jerusalem.—Compared with Babylon or Thebes, Jerusalem was a poor capital. The Hebrews were not builders; their religion prevented them from raising temples; the houses of individuals were shaped like cubes of rock which may be seen today on the sides of Lebanon in the midst of vines and fig-trees. But Jerusalem was the holy city of the Hebrews. The king had his palace there—the palace of Solomon, who astonished the Hebrews with his throne of ivory; Jehovah had his temple there, the first Hebrew temple.

The Tabernacle.—The emblem of the covenant between God and Israel was a great chest of cedar-wood furnished with rings of gold, which contained the tables of the Law. This was borne before the people on high feast-days; it was the Ark of the Covenant. To preserve this ark and necessary objects of worship, Moses is said to have made the Tabernacle—a pavilion of wood covered with skins and hangings. It was a portable temple which the Hebrews carried with them until they could erect a true temple in the promised land.

The Temple.—The Temple of Jerusalem, built at last under Solomon, was divided into three parts:

1.—To the rear, the Holy of Holies, in which rested the ark of the covenant; the high-priest only had the right to enter here, and that but once a year.

2.—In the middle, the Holy Place, in which were kept the altar of incense, the candle-stick with the seven arms, the table of shew-bread; the priests entered to burn incense and to present the offerings.

3.—At the front, the Court open to the people, where the victims were sacrificed on the great altar.

The Temple of Jerusalem was from the first the centre of the nation; from all Palestine the people came to be present at the ceremonies. The high-priest who directed the worship was a person sometimes of greater power than the king.

THE PROPHETS

Disasters of Israel.—Solomon was the last king who enjoyed great power. After him ten tribes separated themselves and constituted the kingdom of Israel, whose inhabitants worshipped the golden calves and the gods of the Phœnicians. Two tribes only remained faithful to Jehovah and to the king at Jerusalem; these formed the kingdom of Judah (977).[1]

[1] There is much uncertainty regarding the chronology of this period.—Ed.

The two kingdoms exhausted their energies in making war on each other. Then came the armies of the Eastern conquerors; Israel was destroyed by Sargon, king of Assyria (722); Judah, by Nabuchodonosor (Nebuchadrezzar), king of Chaldea (586).

Sentiments of the Israelites.—Faithful Israelites regarded these woes as a chastisement: God was punishing his people for their disobedience; as before, he delivered them from their conquerors. "The children of Israel had sinned against Jehovah, their God, they had built them high places in every city, they imitated the nations around them, although the Lord had forbidden them to do like them; they made them idols of brass; they bowed themselves before all the host of heaven [the stars], they worshipped Baal. It is for this that Jehovah rejected all the race of Israel, he afflicted them and delivered them into the hands of those that plundered them."

The Prophets.—Then appeared the prophets, or as they were called, the Seers: Elijah, Jeremiah, Isaiah, Ezekiel. Usually they came from the desert where they had fasted, prayed, and given themselves to meditation. They came in the name of Jehovah, not as warriors in judgment, but as preachers. They called the Israelites to repent, to overthrow their idols, to return to Jehovah; they foretold all the woes that would come upon them if they did not reconcile themselves to him. They preached and uttered prophecies at the same time.

The New Teaching.—These men on fire with the divine spirit found the official religion at Jerusalem mean and cold. Why should they, like the idolaters, slaughter cattle and burn incense to the honor of God? "Hear the word of Jehovah," says Isaiah: "To what purpose is the multitude of your sacrifices? I am full of the burnt offerings of rams and of the fat of fed beasts; and I delight not in the blood of bullocks, or of lambs, or of he-goats. . . . Bring no more vain oblations, your incense is an abomination to me. . . . When ye spread forth your hands, I will hide mine eyes from you . . . for your hands are full of blood. Wash you, make you clean . . . cease to do evil, learn to do well; seek judgment, relieve the oppressed, judge the fatherless, plead for the widow. . . . Though your sins be as scarlet, they shall be as white as snow." In place of sacrifices, the prophets would set justice and good works.

The Messiah.—Israel deserved its afflictions, but there would be a limit to the chastisement. "O my people," says Isaiah in the name of Jehovah, "be not afraid of the Assyrian: he shall smite thee with a rod . . . after the manner of Egypt . . . for yet a very little while and the indignation shall cease . . . and the burden shall be taken away from off thy shoulder." The prophets taught the people to look for the coming of Him who should deliver them; they prepared the way for the Messiah.

THE JEWISH PEOPLE

Return to Jerusalem.—The children of Judah, removed to the plain of the Euphrates, did not forget their country, but sang of it in their chants: "By the rivers of Babylon, there we sat down, yea, we wept when we remembered Zion. We hanged our harps upon the willows in the midst thereof, for there they that carried us away required a song . . . saying, 'Sing us one of the songs of Zion.' How shall we sing the Lord's song in a strange land?" After seventy years of captivity, Cyrus, victor over Babylon, allowed the Israelites to return to Palestine. They rebuilt Jerusalem, reconstructed the temple, restored the feasts, and recovered the sacred books. As a sign that they were again the people of Jehovah they renewed the covenant with him; it was a formal treaty, written and signed by the chiefs of the people.

The Jews.—The little kingdom of Jerusalem maintained itself for seven centuries, governed now by a king, now by the high-priest, but always paying tribute to the masters of Syria—to the Persians first, later to the Macedonians and the Syrians, and last of all to the Romans. Faithful to the end to Jehovah, the Jews (their proper name since the return) continued to live the law of Moses, to celebrate at Jerusalem the feasts and the sacrifices. The high-priest, assisted by a council of the elders, preserved the law; scribes copied it and doctors expounded it to the people. The faithful obliged themselves to observe it in the smallest details. The Pharisees were eminent among them for their zeal in fulfilling all its requirements.

The Synagogues.—Meanwhile the Jews for the sake of trade were pushing beyond the borders of Judæa into Egypt, Syria, Asia Minor, and even to Italy. Some of them were to be found in all the great cities

—Alexandria, Damascus, Antioch, Ephesus, Corinth and Rome. Dispersed among the Gentiles, the Jews were strenuous to preserve their religion. They raised no temples, for the law prevented this; there could be but one Jewish temple, that at Jerusalem, where they celebrated the solemn feasts. But they joined themselves together to read and comment on the word of God. These places of assembling were called Synagogues, from a Greek word signifying meetings.

Destruction of the Temple.—The Christ appeared at this moment. The Jews crucified him and persecuted his disciples not only in Judæa but in every city where they found them in any number. In the year 70 A.D. Jerusalem, in revolt against the Romans, was taken by assault, and all the inhabitants were massacred or sold into slavery. The Romans burnt the temple and carried away the sacred utensils. From that time there was no longer a centre of the Jewish religion.

Fortunes of the Jews after the Dispersion.—The Jewish nation survived the ruin of its capital. The Jews, scattered throughout the world, learned to dispense with the temple. They preserved their sacred books in the Hebrew tongue. Hebrew is the primitive language of Israel; the Jews since the return from Babylon no longer spoke it, but adopted the languages of the neighboring peoples—the Syriac, the Chaldean, and especially the Greek. The Rabbis, however, instructed in the religion, still learned the Hebrew, explained it, and commented on the Scripture.[1] Thus

[1] The Talmud is the accumulation of these commentaries.

the Jewish religion was preserved, and, thanks to it, the Jewish people. It made converts even among the Gentiles; there were in the empire proselytes, that is, people who practised the religion of Jehovah without being of the Jewish race.

The Christian Church, powerful since the fourth century, commenced to persecute the Jews. This persecution has endured to this day in all Christian countries. Usually the Jews were tolerated on account of their wealth and because they transacted all banking operations; but they were kept apart, not being permitted to hold any office. In the majority of cities they were compelled to wear a special costume, to live in a special quarter,[1] gloomy, filthy, unhealthy, and sometimes at Easter time to send one of their number to suffer insult. The people suspected them of poisoning fountains, of killing children, of profaning the consecrated host; often the people rose against them, massacred them, and pillaged their houses. Judges under the least pretext had them imprisoned, tortured, and burned. Sometimes the church tried to convert them by force; sometimes the government exiled them *en masse* from the country and confiscated their goods. The Jews at last disappeared from France,[2] from Spain, England, and Italy. In Portugal, Germany, and Poland, and in the Mohammedan lands they maintained themselves. From these countries after the cessation of persecution they returned to the rest of Europe.

[1] The Jewish Quarter at Rome was called the Ghetto. This name has since been applied to all Jewish quarters.

[2] Except at Avignon, on the domains of the Pope, and in Alsace-Lorraine.

CHAPTER IX

GREECE AND THE GREEKS

The Country.—Greece is a very little country (about 20,000 square miles), hardly larger than Switzerland; but it is a country of great variety, bristling with mountains, indented with gulfs—a country originally constituted to influence mightily the character of the men who inhabited it.

A central chain, the Pindus, traverses Greece through the centre and covers it with its rocky system. Toward the isthmus of Corinth it becomes lower; but the Peloponnesus, on the other side of the isthmus, is elevated about 2,000 feet above the sea level, like a citadel crowned with lofty chains, abrupt and snowy, which fall perpendicularly into the sea. The islands themselves scattered along the coast are only submerged mountains whose summits rise above the surface of the sea. In this diverse land there is little tillable ground, but almost everywhere bare rock. The streams, like brooks, leave between their half-dried channel and the sterile rock of the mountain only a narrow strip of fertile soil. In this beautiful country are found some forests, cypresses, laurels, palms, here and there vines scattered on the rocky hillsides; but there are no rich harvests and no green pasturages. Such a country produces wiry mountaineers, active and sober.

The Sea.—Greece is a land of shores: smaller than Portugal, it has as great a coast-line as Spain. The sea penetrates it to a great number of gulfs, coves, and indentations; it is ordinarily surrounded with projecting rocks, or with approaching islands that form a natural port. This sea is like a lake; it has not, like the ocean, a pale and sombre color; usually it is calm, lustrous, and, as Homer says, "of the color of violets."

No sea lends itself better to navigation with small ships. Every morning the north wind rises to conduct the barques of Athens to Asia; in the evening the south wind brings them back to port. From Greece to Asia Minor the islands are placed like stepping-stones; on a clear day the mariner always has land in view. Such a sea beckons people to cross it.

And so the Greeks have been sailors, traders, travellers, pirates, and adventurers; like the Phœnicians, they have spread over all the ancient world, carrying with them the merchandise and the inventions of Egypt, of Chaldea, and of Asia.

The Climate.—The climate of Greece is mild. In Athens it freezes hardly once in twenty years; in summer the heat is moderated by the breeze from the sea.[1] Today the people still lie in the streets from the month of May to September. The air is cool and transparent; for many leagues could once be seen the crest of the statue of Pallas. The contours of distant mountains are not, as with us, enveloped in haze, but show a clear line against the clear sky. It is a beautiful country which urges man to take life as a

[1] "Balmy and clement," says Euripides, "is our atmosphere. The cold of winter has no extremes for us, and the shafts of the sun do not wound."

feast, for everything is happy about him. "Walking at night in the gardens, listening to the grasshoppers, playing the lute in the clear of the moon, going to drink at the spring at the mountain, carrying with him some wine that he may drink while he sings, spending the days in dancing—these are Greek pleasures, the joys of a race poor, economical, and eternally young."

Simplicity of Greek Life.—In this country men are not melted with the heat nor stiffened with cold; they live in the open air gay and at slight expense. Food in great quantity is not required, nor warm clothing, nor a comfortable house. The Greek could live on a handful of olives and a sardine. His entire clothing consisted of sandals, a tunic, a large mantle; very often he went bare-footed and bare-headed. His house was a meagre and unsubstantial building; the air easily entered through the walls. A couch with some coverings, a coffer, some beautiful vases, a lamp, —this was his furniture. The walls were bare and whitened with lime. This house was only a sleeping place.

THE PEOPLE

Origin of the Greeks.—The people who inhabited this charming little land were an Aryan people, related to the Hindoos and the Persians, and like them come from the mountains of Asia or the steppes beyond the Caspian Sea. The Greeks had forgotten the long journey made by their ancestors; they said that they, like the grasshoppers, were the children of the soil.[1] But their language and the names of their

[1] Autochthones.

gods leave no doubt of their origin. . . . Like all the Aryans, the primitive Greeks nourished themselves with milk and with the flesh of their herds; they moved about under arms, always ready to fight, and grouped themselves in tribes governed by patriarchs.

The Legends.—The Greeks like all the other ancient peoples were ignorant of their origin. They neither knew whence their ancestors had come nor when they had established themselves in Greece, nor what they had done there. To preserve the exact memory of things as they occur, there is need of some means of fixing them; but the Greeks did not know how to write; they did not employ writing until about the eighth century B.C. They had no way of calculating the number of years. Later they adopted the usage of counting the years according to the great feast which was celebrated every four years at Olympia; a period of four years was called an olympiad. But the first olympiad was placed in 776 B.C., and the chronology of the Greeks does not rise beyond this date.

And yet they used to tell in Greece a great number of legends about this primitive period. These were especially the exploits of ancient kings and of heroes who were adored as demi-gods. These stories were so mingled with fable that it is impossible to know how much truth they may contain. They said at Athens that the first king, Cecrops, was half man and half serpent; at Thebes, that Cadmus, founder of the city, had come from Phœnicia to seek his sister Europa who had been stolen by a bull; that he had killed a dragon and had sowed his teeth, from which was sprung a race of warriors, and that the noble families of Thebes descended from these warriors. At Argos it was said that the royal family was the issue of Pelops to whom Zeus had given a shoulder of ivory to replace the one devoured by a goddess. Thus each country had its legends and the Greeks continued to the end to relate them and to offer worship to their ancient heroes—Perseus, Bellerophon, Herakles, Theseus, Minos, Castor and Pollux, Meleager, Œdipus. The majority of the Greeks, even among the better educated, admitted, at least in part, the truth of these traditions. They accepted as historical facts the war between the two sons of Œdipus, king of Thebes, and the expedition of the Argonauts, sailing forth in quest of the Golden Fleece, which was guarded by two brazen-footed bulls vomiting flames.

The Trojan War.—Of all these legends the most fully developed and the most celebrated was the legend of the Trojan War. It recounted that about the twelfth century, Troy, a rich and powerful city, held sway over the coast of Asia. Paris, a Trojan prince, having come to Greece, had abducted Helen, wife of Menelaus, king of Sparta. Agamemnon, king of Argos, made a league of the kings of Greece; a Greek army went in a fleet of two hundred galleys to besiege Troy. The siege endured ten years because the supreme god, Zeus, had taken the side of the Trojans. All the Greek chiefs participated in this adventure. Achilles, the bravest and the most beautiful of these, killed Hector, the principal defender of Troy, and dragged his corpse around the city; he fought clad in divine armor which had been presented him by his mother, a goddess of the sea; in turn he died, shot by an arrow in the heel. The Greeks, despairing of taking the city by force, employed a trick: they pretended to depart, and left an immense horse of wood in which were concealed the chiefs of the army. The Trojans drew this horse into the city; during the night the chiefs came forth and opened the city to the Greeks. Troy was burnt, the men slaughtered, the women led away as slaves. But the chiefs of the Greeks on their return were beset by tempest. Some perished in the sea, others were cast on foreign shores. Odysseus, the most crafty of the chiefs, was for ten years buffeted from one land to another, losing successively all his ships, himself the sole survivor of the disasters.

All antiquity had steadfast faith in the Trojan War. 1184 B.C. was set as the date of the ending of the siege, and men pointed out the site of the city. In 1874 Schliemann purposed to excavate this site; it was necessary to traverse the débris of many cities which lay over it; at last at a depth of about fifty feet he found in the deepest bed of débris the traces of a mighty city reduced to ashes, and in the ruins of the principal edifice a casket filled with gems of gold which he called the Treasury of Priam. There was no inscription, and the city, the whole wall of which we have been able to bring to light, was a very small one. A large number of small, very rude idols have been found, which represent an owl-headed goddess (the Greeks thus represented the goddess Pallas). Beyond this no proof has been found that this city was called Troy.

The Homeric Poems.—It is the two poems attributed to Homer which have made the taking of Troy renowned throughout the world—the Iliad, which related the combats of the Greeks and the exploits of Achilles before Troy; and the Odyssey, which recounts the adventures of Odysseus (Ulysses) after the capture of Troy.

These two poems were handed down for centuries without being committed to writing; the rhapsodists, wandering singers, knew long passages from them by heart and recited them at feasts. It is not till the sixth century that Pisistratus, a prince of Athens, had them collected and edited.[1] The two poems became from that time and always remained the most admired works of Greek literature.

The Greeks said that the author of these poems was Homer, a Greek of Ionia, who lived about the tenth or the ninth century B.C. They represented him as a blind old man, poor and a wanderer. Seven towns disputed the honor of being his birth-place. This tradition was received without hesitation. But at the end of the eighteenth century a German scholar, Wolf, noticed certain contradictions in these poems, and at last asserted that they were not the work of a single poet, but a collection of fragments from several different poets. This theory has been attacked and supported with great energy: for a half century men have flown into a passion for or against the existence of Homer. Today we begin to think the problem insoluble. What is certain is that these poems are very old, probably of the ninth century. The Iliad was composed in Asia Minor and is perhaps the result of

[1] The story of the collection of the Homeric poems by Pisistratus is without foundation—"eine blosse Fabel." Busolt, "Griechische Geschichte." Gotha, 1893, i., 127.—ED.

the union of two poems—one dedicated to the combats of the Trojans, and the other to the adventures of Achilles. The Odyssey appears to be the work of one author; but it cannot be affirmed that it is of the same author as the Iliad.

The Greeks at the Time of Homer.—We are not able to go back very far in the history of the Greeks; the Homeric poems are their oldest historical document. When these were composed, about the ninth century B.C., there was not yet any general name to designate all the inhabitants of Greece: Homer mentions them under the names of their principal tribes. From his description it appears that they have made some progress since their departure from Asia. They know how to till the ground, how to construct strong cities and to organize themselves into little peoples. They obey kings; they have a council of old men and an assembly of the people. They are proud of their institutions, they despise their less advanced neighbors, the Barbarians, as they call them. Odysseus, to show how rude the Cyclops were, says, "They have no rules of justice nor places where they deliberate; each one governs himself, his wife, and children, and has no association with others." But these Greeks themselves are half barbarians; they do not know how to write, to coin money, nor the art of working in iron. They hardly dare to trust themselves on the sea and they imagine that Sicily is peopled with monsters.

The Dorians.—Dorians was the name given to those sons of the mountaineers who had come from the north and had expelled or subjected those dwelling in the plains and on the shore of the Peloponnesus;

the latter, crowded into too narrow limits, sent colonies into Asia. Of these mountain bands the most renowned came from a little canton called Doris and preserved the name Dorians. These invaders told how certain kings of Sparta, the posterity of Herakles, having been thrust out by their subjects, had come to seek the Dorians in their mountains. These people of the mountains, moved by their love for Herakles, had followed his descendants and had replaced them on their throne. By the same stroke they dispossessed the inhabitants and took their place. They were a martial, robust, and healthy race, accustomed to cold, to meagre food, to a scant existence. Men and women wore a short tunic which did not reach to the knee. They spoke a rude and primitive dialect. The Dorians were a race of soldiers, always obliged to keep themselves under arms; they were the least cultivated in Greece, since, situated far from the sea, they preserved the customs of the barbarous age; they were the most Greek because, being isolated, they could neither mingle with strangers nor imitate their manners.

The Ionians.—The peoples of Attica, the isles, and the coast of Asia were called Ionians; no one knows the origin of the name. Unlike the Dorians, they were a race of sailors or traders, the most cultured of Greece, gaining instruction from contact with the most civilized peoples of the Orient; the least Greek, because they associated with Asiatics and had in part adopted their dress. They were peaceful and industrious, living luxuriously, speaking a smooth dialect, and wearing long flowing garments like the Orientals.

The Hellenes.—Dorians and Ionians—these are the two opposing races, the most remarkable of Greece, and the most powerful: Sparta is Dorian, Athens is Ionian. But the majority of the Greeks are neither Dorians nor Ionians: they are called Æolians, a vague name which covers very different peoples.

All the Greeks from early times take the name "Hellenes" which they have kept to this day. What is the origin of the term? They did not know any more than we: they said only that Dorus and Æolus were sons of Hellen, and Ion was his grandson.

Cities.—The Hellenes were still in little peoples as at the time of Homer. The land of Greece, cut by mountains and sea, breaks naturally into a large number of small cantons, each isolated from its neighbor by an arm of the sea or by a wall of rocks, so that it is easy to defend the land and difficult to communicate with other parts. Each canton constituted a separate state which was called a city. There were more than a hundred of these; counting the colonies, more than a thousand. To us a Greek state seems a miniature. The whole of Attica was but little larger than the state of Delaware, and Corinth or Megara was much smaller. Usually the state was only a city with a strip of shore and a harbor, or some villages scattered in the plain around a citadel. From one state one sees the citadel, mountains, or harbor of the next state. Many of them count their citizens only by thousands; the largest included hardly 200,000 or 300,000.

The Hellenes never formed one nation; they never ceased to fight and destroy one another. And yet all spoke the same language, worshipped the same gods, and lived the same sort of a life. In these respects they recognized the bonds of a common race and distinguished themselves from all other peoples whom they called barbarians and regarded with disdain.

THE HELLENES BEYOND SEA

Colonization.—The Hellenes did not inhabit Greece alone. Colonists from the Greek cities had gone forth to found new cities in all the neighboring countries. There were little states in all the islands of the Archipelago, over all the coast of Asia Minor, in Crete and Cyprus, on the whole circumference of the Black Sea as far as the Caucasus and the Crimea, along the shore of Turkey in Europe (then called Thrace), on the shore of Africa, in Sicily, in south Italy, and even on the coasts of France and Spain.

Character of These Colonies.—Greek colonies were being founded all the time from the twelfth century to the fifth; they issued from various cities and represented all the Greek races—Dorian, Ionian, and Æolian. They were established in the wilderness, in an inhabited land, by conquest, or by an agreement with the natives. Mariners, merchants, exiles, or adventurers were their founders. But with all this diversity of time, place, race, and origin, the colonies had common characteristics: they were established at one stroke and according to certain fixed rules. The colonists did not arrive one by one or in small bands; nor did they settle at random, building houses which little by little became a city, as is the case now with European colonists in America. All the colonists started at once under a leader, and the new city was founded in one day. The foundation was a religious ceremony; the "founder" traced a sacred enclosure, constructed a sacred hearth, and lighted there the holy fire.

Traditions Concerning the Colonists.—The old stories about the founding of some of these colonies enable us to see how they differed from modern colonies. The account of the settlement of Marseilles runs as follows: Euxenus, a citizen of Phocæa, coming to Gaul in a merchant galley, was invited by a Gallic chief to the marriage of his daughter; according to the custom of this people, the young girl about the time of the feast entered bearing a cup which she was to present to the one whom she would choose for a husband; she stopped before the Greek and offered him the cup. This unpremeditated act appeared to have been inspired from heaven; the Gallic chief gave his daughter to Euxenus and permitted him and his companions to found a city on the gulf of Marseilles. Later the Phocæans, seeing their city blockaded by the Persian army, loaded on their ships their families, their movables, the statues and treasures of their temple and went to sea, abandoning their city. As they started, they threw into the sea a mass of red-hot iron and swore never to return to Phocæa until the iron should rise to the surface of the water. Many violated this oath and returned; but the rest continued the voyage and after many adventures came to Marseilles.

At Miletus the Ionians who founded the city had brought no wives with them; they seized a city inhabited by the natives of Asia, slaughtered all the men, and forcibly married the women and girls of the families of their victims. It was said that the women, affronted in this manner, swore never to eat food with their captors and never to call them by the name of husband; this custom was for centuries preserved among the women of Miletus.[1]

The colony at Cyrene in Africa was founded according to the express command of the oracle of Apollo. The inhabitants of Thera, who had received this order, did not care to go to an unknown country. They yielded only at the end of seven years since their island was afflicted with dearth; they believed that Apollo had sent misfortune on them as a penalty. Nevertheless the citizens who were sent out attempted to abandon the enterprise, but their fellow-citizens attacked them and forced them to return. After having spent two years on an island where no success came to them, they at last came to settle at Cyrene, which soon became a prosperous city.[2]

Importance of the Colonies.—Wherever they settled, the colonists constituted a new state which in no respect obeyed the mother town from which they had come out. And so the whole Mediterranean found itself surrounded by Greek cities independent one of the others. Of these cities many became richer and more powerful than their mother towns; they had a territory which was larger and more fertile, and in consequence a greater population. Sybaris, it was said, had 300,000 men who were capable of bearing arms. Croton could place in the field an infantry

[1] Probably this custom has another origin the recollection of which was lost.—ED.

[2] Herodotus, iv., 150–158.

force of 120,000 men. Syracuse in Sicily, Miletus in Asia had greater armies than even Sparta and Athens. South Italy was termed Great Greece. In comparison with this great country fully peopled with Greek colonies the home country was, in fact, only a little Greece. And so it happened that the Greeks were much more numerous in the neighboring countries than in Greece proper; and among these people of the colonies figure a good share of the most celebrated names: Homer, Alcæus, Sappho, Thales, Pythagoras, Heraclitus, Democritus, Empedocles, Aristotle, Archimedes, Theocritus, and many others.

CHAPTER X

GREEK RELIGION

The Gods. Polytheism.—The Greeks, like the ancient Aryans, believed in many gods. They had neither the sentiment of infinity nor that of eternity; they did not conceive of God as one for whom the heavens are only a tent and the earth a foot-stool. To the Greeks every force of nature—the air, the sun, the sea—was divine, and as they did not conceive of all these phenomena as produced by one cause, they assigned each to a particular god. This is the reason that they believed in many gods. They were polytheists.

Anthropomorphism.—Each god was a force in nature and carried a distinct name. The Greeks, having a lively imagination, figured under this name a living being, of beautiful form and human characteristics. A god or goddess was represented as a beautiful man or woman. When Odysseus or Telemachus met a person peculiarly great and beautiful, they began by asking him if he were not a god. Homer in describing the army pictured on the shield of Achilles adds, "Ares and Athena led the army, both clad in gold, beautiful and great, as becomes the gods, for men were smaller." Greek gods are men; they have clothing, palaces, bodies similar to ours; if they cannot die, they can at least be wounded. Homer relates how

Ares, the god of war, struck by a warrior, fled howling with pain. This fashion of making gods like men is what is called *Anthropomorphism.*

Mythology.—The gods, being men, have parents, children, property. Their mothers were goddesses, their brothers were gods, and their children other gods or men who were half divine. This genealogy of the gods is what is called the *Theogony.* The gods have also a history; we are told the story of their birth, the adventures of their youth, their exploits. Apollo, for example, was born on the island of Delos to which his mother Latona had fled; he slew a monster which was desolating the country at the foot of Parnassus. Each canton of Greece had thus its tales of the gods. These are called myths; the sum of them is termed *Mythology,* or the history of the gods.

The Local Gods.—The Greek gods, even under their human form, remained what they were at first, phenomena of nature. They were thought of both as men and as forces of nature. The Naiad is a young woman, but at the same time a bubbling fountain. Homer represents the river Xanthus as a god, and yet he says, "The Xanthus threw itself on Achilles, boiling with fury, full of tumult, foam, and the bodies of the dead." The people itself continued to say "Zeus rains" or "Zeus thunders." To the Greek the god was first of all rain, storm, heaven, or sun, and not the heaven, sun, or earth in general, but that corner of the heaven under which he lived, the land of his canton, the river which traversed it. Each city, then, had its divinities, its sun-god, its earth-goddess, its sea-god, and these are not to be confounded with the sun, the earth, and the sea of the neighboring city. The Zeus of Sparta is not the same as the Zeus of Athens; in the same oath one sometimes invokes two Athenas or two Apollos. A traveller who would journey through Greece[1] would therefore meet thousands of local gods (they called them Poliades, or gods of the city). No torrent, no wood, no mountain was without its own deity,[2] although often a minor divinity, adored only by the people of the vicinity and whose sanctuary was only a grotto in the rock.

The Great Gods.—Above the innumerable legion of local gods of each canton the Greeks imagined certain great divinities—the heaven, the sun, the earth, and the sea—and these everywhere had the same name, and had their temple or sanctuary in every place. Each represented one of the principal forces of nature. These gods common to all the Greeks were never numerous; if all are included, we have hardly twenty.[3] We have the bad habit of calling them by the name of a Latin god. The following are their true names: Zeus (Jupiter), Hera (Juno), Athena (Minerva), Apollo, Artemis (Diana), Hermes (Mercury), Hephaistos (Vulcan), Hestia (Vesta), Ares (Mars), Aphrodite (Venus), Poseidon (Neptune), Amphitrite, Proteus, Kronos (Saturn), Rhea (Cybele), Demeter (Ceres), Persephone (Proserpina), Hades,

[1] See the account of the traveller Pausanias.

[2] "There are," says Hesiod, "30,000 gods on the fruitful earth."

[3] Greek scholars formed a select society of twelve gods and goddesses, but their choice was arbitrary, and all did not agree on the same series. The Greeks of different countries and of different epochs often represented the same god under different forms. Further, the majority of the gods seem to us to have vague and undetermined attributes; this is because they were not the same everywhere.

(Pluto), Dionysos (Bacchus). It is this little group of gods that men worshipped in all the temples, that men ordinarily invoked in their prayers.

Attributes of the Gods.—Each of these great gods had his form, his costume, his instruments (which we call his attributes); it is thus that the faithful imagined him and that the sculptors represented him. Each has his character which is well known to his worshippers. Each has his rôle in the world, performing his determined functions, ordinarily with the aid of secondary divinities who obey him.

Athena, virgin of clear eye, is represented standing, armed with a lance, a helmet on the head, and gleaming armor on the breast. She is the goddess of the clear air, of wisdom, and of invention, a goddess of dignity and majesty.

Hephaistos, the god of fire, is figured with a hammer and in the form of a lame and ugly blacksmith. It is he who forges the thunderbolt.

Artemis, shy maiden, armed with bow and quiver, courses the forests hunting with a troop of nymphs. She is the goddess of the woods, of the chase, and of death.

Hermes, represented with winged sandals, is the god of the fertile showers. But he has other offices; he is the god of streets and squares, the god of commerce, of theft, and of eloquence. He it is who guides the souls of the dead, the messenger of the gods, the deity presiding over the breeding of cattle.

Almost always a Greek god has several functions, quite dissimilar to our eyes, but to the Greeks bearing some relation to one another.

Olympus and Zeus.—Each one of these gods is like a king in his own domain. Still the Greeks had remarked that all the forces of nature do not operate by chance and that they act in harmony; the same word served them for the idea of order and of universe. They supposed, then, that the gods were in accord for the administration of the world, and that they, like men, had laws and government among them.

In the north of Greece there was a mountain to whose snowy summit no man had ever climbed. This was Olympus. On this summit, which was hidden by clouds from the eyes of men, it was imagined the gods assembled. Meeting under the light of heaven, they conferred on the affairs of the world. Zeus, the mightiest of them, presided over the gathering: he was god of the heavens and of the light, the god "who masses the clouds," who launches the thunderbolt—an old man of majestic mien, with long beard, sitting on a throne of gold. It is he who commands and the other gods bow before him. Should they essay to resist, Zeus menaces them; Homer makes him say,[1] "Bind to heaven a chain of gold, and all of you, gods or goddesses, throw your weight upon it; all your united efforts cannot draw Zeus, the sovereign ordainer, to the earth. On the contrary, if I wished to draw the chain to myself, I should bring with it the earth and the very sea. Then I would attach it to the summit of Olympus and all the universe would be suspended. By so much am I superior to gods and men."

Morality of the Greek Mythology.—The greater part

[1] Iliad, viii., 18.

of their gods were conceived by the Greeks as violent, sanguinary, deceitful, dissolute. They ascribed to them scandalous adventures or dishonest acts. Hermes was notorious for his thieving, Aphrodite for her coquetry, Ares for his ferocity. All were so vain as to persecute those who neglected to offer sacrifices to them. Niobe had seen all her children pierced with arrows by Apollo because she herself had boasted of her numerous family. The gods were so jealous that they could not endure seeing a man thoroughly happy; prosperity for the Greeks was the greatest of dangers, for it never failed to draw the anger of the gods, and this anger became a goddess (Nemesis) about whom were told such anecdotes as the following: Once Polycrates of Samos, become very powerful, feared the jealousy of the gods; and so a ring of gold which he still retained was cast into the sea that his good fortune might not be unmixed with evil. Some time after, a fisherman brought to Polycrates an enormous fish and in its belly was found the ring. This was a certain presage of evil. Polycrates was besieged in his city, taken, and crucified. The gods punished him for his good fortune.

Greek mythology was immoral in that the gods gave bad examples to men. The Greek philosophers were already saying this and were inveighing against the poets who had published these stories. A disciple of Pythagoras affirmed that his master, descending to hell, had seen the soul of Homer hanging to a tree and that of Hesiod bound to a column to punish them for calumniating the gods. "Homer and Hesiod," said Xenophanes, "attribute to the gods all the acts which among men are culpable and shameful; there is but one god who neither in body nor in soul resembles men." And he added this profound remark: "If oxen and lions had hands and could manipulate like men, they would have made gods with bodies similar to their own, horses would have framed gods with horses' bodies, and cattle with cattle's. . . . Men think that the gods have their feelings, their voice, and their body." Xenophanes was right; the primitive Greeks had created their gods in their own image. As they were then sanguinary, dissolute, jealous, and vain, their gods were the same. Later, as the people became better, their descendants were shocked with all these vices; but the history and the character of the gods were fixed by the ancient traditions, and later generations, without daring to change them, had received the gross and dishonest gods of their ancestors.

THE HEROES

The Hero.—The hero in Greece is a man who has become illustrious, and after death a mighty spirit—not a god, but a demi-god. The heroes do not live on Olympus in the heaven of the gods, they do not direct the life of the world. And yet they, too, possess a power higher than that of any human, and this permits them to aid their friends and destroy their enemies. For this reason the Greeks rendered them worship as to the gods and implored their protection. There was not a city, not a tribe, not a family but had its hero, a protecting spirit which it adored.

Different Kinds of Heroes.—Of these heroes many are legendary persons (Achilles, Odysseus, Agamemnon); some without doubt never existed (Herakles, Œdipus); others like Hellen, Dorus, Æolus are only names. But their worshippers regarded them as men of the olden time; and, in fact, the most of the heroes lived at one time. Many are historical personages: generals like Leonidas, Lysander; philosophers like Democritus and Aristotle; legislators like Lycurgus and Solon. The people of Croton adored even one of their fellow-citizens, Philip by name, because he had been in his time the most beautiful man in Greece. The leader who had guided a band of colonists and founded a city became for the inhabitants the Founder; a temple was raised to him and every year sacrifices were offered to him. The Athenian Miltiades was thus worshipped in a city of Thrace. The Spartiate Brasidas, killed in the defence of Amphipolis, had divine honors paid to him in that city, for the inhabitants had come to regard him as their Founder.

Presence of the Heroes.—The hero continued to reside in the place where his body was interred, either in his tomb or in the neighborhood. A story told by Herodotus (v. 67) depicts this belief in a lively way. The city of Sicyon adored the hero Adrastus and in a public place was a chapel dedicated to his honor. Cleisthenes, the tyrant of Sicyon, took a fancy to rid himself of this hero. He went to the oracle at Delphi to ask if it would aid him in expelling Adrastus. The oracle replied to his question that Adrastus was king of the Sicyonians and Cleisthenes was a brigand. The tyrant, not daring to evict the hero, adopted a ruse; he sent to Thebes to seek the bones of Melanippas, another hero, and installed them with great pomp in the sanctuary of the city. "He did this," says Herodotus, "because Melanippus during his life had been the greatest enemy of Adrastus and had killed his brother and his son-in-law." Then he transferred to Melanippus the festivals and the sacrifices formerly paid to the honor of Adrastus. He was persuaded, and all the Greeks with him, that the hero would be irritated and would flee.

Intervention of the Heroes.—The heroes have divine power; like the gods, they can according to their whim send good or evil. The poet Stesichorus had spoken ill of the famous Helen (that Helen who the legend states was carried away to Troy); he suddenly became blind; when he retracted what he had said, the heroine restored his sight.

The protecting heroes of a city kept it from plagues and famine and even fought against its enemies. At the battle of the Marathon the Athenian soldiers saw in the midst of them Theseus, the mythical founder of Athens, clad in shining armor. During the battle of Salamis the heroes Ajax and Telamon, once kings of Salamis, appeared on the highest point of the island extending their hands to the Greek fleet. "It is not we," said Themistocles, "that have vanquished the Persians; it is the gods and heroes." In "Œdipus at Colonus," a tragedy of Sophocles, Œdipus at the point of death receives the visit of the king of Athens and of the king of Thebes, both of whom as gods request him to have his body interred in their territory, and to become a protecting hero. Œdipus at last consents to be buried in the soil of the Athenians, and says to the king, "Dead, I shall not be a useless inhabitant of this country, I shall be a rampart for you, stronger than millions of warriors." In himself alone a hero was as efficient as a whole army; his spirit was mightier than all living men.

WORSHIP

Principles of Worship of the Gods.—Gods and heroes, potent as they were, bestowed on men all good or evil fortune according to their will. It was dangerous to have them against you, wise to have them on your side. They were conceived as like men, irritated if they were neglected, contented if they were venerated. On this principle worship was based. It consisted in doing things agreeable to the gods to obtain their favor. Plato expresses as follows[1] the thought of the common man, "To know how to say and do those things that are pleasing to the gods, either in prayers or in offerings, this is piety which brings prosperity to individuals and to states. The reverse is impiety which ruins everything." "It is natural," says Xenophon at the end of his treatise on Cavalry, "that the gods should favor those especially who not only consult them in need, but honor them in the day of prosperity." Religion was first of all a contract; the Greek sought to delight the gods and in return required their services. "For a long time," says a priest of Apollo to his god, "I have burned fat bullocks

[1] In the dialogue "Eutyphron."

for you; now grant my petitions and discharge your arrows against my enemies."

The Great Festivals.—Since the gods had the feelings of men they were to be pleased in the same way as men. Wine, cakes, fruits, food were brought to them. Palaces were built for them. Festivals were given in their honor, for they were "joyous gods" who loved pleasure and beautiful spectacles. A festival was not, as with us, purely an occasion of rejoicing, but a religious ceremony. On those days free from the daily toil men were required to rejoice in public before the god. The Greek, without doubt, delighted in these fêtes; but it is for the god and not for himself that he celebrates them. "The Ionians," says an ancient hymn to Apollo, "delight thee with trial of strength, the hymn, and the dance."

The Sacred Games.—From these diversions offered to the gods originated the solemn games. Each city had them to the honor of its gods; ordinarily only its citizens were admitted to them; but in four districts of Greece were celebrated games at which all Greeks could be present and participate. These are called the Four Great Games.

The principal of these four festivals was that at Olympia. This was given every four years in honor of Zeus and continued five or six days. The multitude coming from all parts of Greece filled the amphitheatre. They commenced by sacrificing victims and addressing prayers to Zeus and the other gods. Then came the contests; they were:

The foot-race around the stadion.

The Pentathlon, so called because it comprised five

exercises. The competitors were to leap, run from one end of the stadion to the other, make a long throw of the metal discus, hurl the javelin, and wrestle.

Boxing, in which one fought with arms bound with thongs of hide.

The chariot races, which were held in the hippodrome; the cars were light and were drawn by four horses.

The judges of the games were clothed in purple, crowned with laurel. After the combat a herald proclaimed before the whole assembly the name of the victor and of his city. A crown of olive was the only reward given him; but his fellow-citizens on his return received him as a conquering hero; sometimes they threw down a section of the city wall to give him entrance. He arrived in a chariot drawn by four horses, clothed in purple, escorted by all the people. "These victories which we leave today to the athletes of the public shows appeared then the greatest of all. Poets of greatest renown celebrated them; Pindar, the most illustrious lyric poet of antiquity, has hardly done more than sing of chariot races. It is related that a certain Diagoras, who had seen his two sons crowned on the same day, was borne in triumph by them in the sight of the spectators. The people, holding such an honor too great for a mortal, cried out, 'Perish, Diagoras, for after all you cannot become a god.' Diagoras, suffocated with emotion, died in the arms of his sons. In his eyes and the eyes of the Greeks the fact that his sons possessed the stoutest fists and the nimblest limbs in Greece was the acme of earthly happiness."[1] The

[1] Taine, "Philosophy of Art."

Greeks had their reasons for thus admiring physical prowess: in their wars in which they fought hand to hand the most vigorous athletes were the best soldiers.

Omens.—In return for so much homage, so many festivals and offerings, the Greeks expected no small amount of service from their gods. The gods protected their worshippers, gave them health, riches, victory. They preserved them from the evils that menaced them, sending signs which men interpreted. These are called Omens. "When a city," says Herodotus,[1] "is about to suffer some great misfortune, this is usually anticipated by signs. The people of Chios had omens of their defeat: of a band of one hundred youths sent to Delphi but two returned; the others had died of the plague. About the same time the roof of a school of the city fell on the children who were learning to read; but one escaped of the one hundred and twenty. Such were the anticipating signs sent them by the deity."

The Greeks regarded as supernatural signs, dreams, the flight of birds in the heavens, the entrails of animals sacrificed—in a word, everything that they saw, from the tremblings of the earth and eclipses to a simple sneeze. In the expedition to Sicily, Nicias, the general of the Athenians, at the moment of embarking his army for the retreat, was arrested by an eclipse of the moon; the gods, thought he, had sent this prodigy to warn the Athenians not to continue their enterprise. And so Nicias waited; he waited twenty-seven days offering sacrifices to appease the gods. During this inactivity the enemy closed the port, destroyed the

[1] Herodotus, vi., 27.

fleet, and exterminated his army. The Athenians on learning this news found but one thing with which to reproach Nicias: he should have known that for an army in retreat the eclipse of the moon was a favorable sign. During the retreat of the Ten Thousand, Xenophon, the general, making an address to his soldiers, uttered this sentiment: "With the help of the gods we have the surest hope that we shall save ourselves with glory." At this point a soldier sneezed. At once all adored the god who had sent this omen. "Since at the very instant when we are deliberating concerning our safety," exclaimed Xenophon, "Zeus the savior has sent us an omen, let us with one consent offer sacrifices to him."[1]

The Oracles.—Often the god replies to the faithful who consult him not by a mute sign, but by the mouth of an inspired person. The faithful enter the sanctuary of the god seeking responses and counsel. These are Oracles.

There were oracles in many places in Greece and Asia. The most noted were at Dodona in Epirus, and at Delphi, at the foot of Mount Parnassus. At Dodona it was Zeus who spoke by the rustling of the sacred oaks. At Delphi it was Apollo who was consulted. Below his temple, in a grotto, a current of cool air issued from a rift in the ground. This air the Greeks thought[2] was sent by the god, for he threw into a frenzy those who inhaled it. A tripod was placed over the orifice, a woman (the Pythia), prepared by a bath in the sacred spring, took her seat on

[1] Xenophon, "Anabasis," iii., 2.

[2] This idea gained currency only in the later periods of Grecian history.—Ed.

the tripod, and received the inspiration. At once, seized with a nervous frenzy, she uttered cries and broken sentences. Priests sitting about her caught these expressions, set them to verse, and brought them to him who sought advice of the god.

The oracles of the Pythia were often obscure and ambiguous. When Crœsus asked if he should make war on the Persians, the reply was, "Crœsus will destroy a great empire." In fact, a great empire was destroyed, but it was that of Crœsus.

The Spartans had great confidence in the Pythia, and never initiated an expedition without consulting her. The other Greeks imitated them, and Delphi thus became a sort of national oracle.

Amphictyonies.—To protect the sanctuary of Delphi twelve of the principal peoples of Greece had formed an association called an Amphictyony.[1] Every year deputies from these peoples assembled at Delphi to celebrate the festival of Apollo and see that the temple was not threatened; for this temple contained immense wealth, a temptation to pillage it. In the sixth century the people of Cirrha, a neighboring city of Delphi, appropriated these treasures.[2] The Amphictyons declared war against them for sacrilege. Cirrha was taken and destroyed, the inhabitants sold as slaves, the territory left fallow. In the fourth century the Amphictyons made war on the Phocidians also who had seized the treasury of Delphi, and on the people of Amphissa who had tilled a field dedicated to Apollo.

[1] There were similar amphictyonies at Delos, Calauria, and Onchestus.

[2] The special charge against Cirrha was the levying of toll on pilgrims coming to Delphi.—Ed.

Still it is not necessary to believe that the assembly of the Amphictyons ever resembled a Greek senate. It was concerned only with the temple of Apollo, not at all with political affairs. It did not even prevent members of the Amphictyony fighting one another. The oracle and the Amphictyony of Delphi were more potent than the other oracles and the other amphictyonies; but they never united the Greeks into a single nation.

CHAPTER XI

SPARTA

THE PEOPLE

Laconia.—When the Dorian mountaineers invaded the Peloponnesus, the main body of them settled at Sparta in Laconia. Laconia is a narrow valley traversed by a considerable stream (the Eurotas) flowing between two massive mountain ranges with snowy summits. A poet describes the country as follows: "A land rich in tillable soil, but hard to cultivate, deep set among perpendicular mountains, rough in aspect, inaccessible to invasion." In this enclosed country lived the Dorians of Sparta in the midst of the ancient inhabitants who had become, some their subjects, others their serfs. There were, then, in Laconia three classes: Helots, Periœci, Spartiates.

The Helots.—The Helots dwelt in the cottages scattered in the plain and cultivated the soil. But the land did not belong to them—indeed, they were not even free to leave it. They were, like the serfs of the Middle Ages, peasants attached to the soil, from father to son. They labored for a Spartiate proprietor who took from them the greater part of the harvest. The Spartiates instructed them, feared them, and ill treated them. They compelled them to wear rude garments, beat them unreasonably to remind them of their servile condition, and sometimes made them intoxicated to disgust their children with the sight of drunkenness. A Spartiate poet compares the Helots to "loaded asses stumbling under their burdens and the blows inflicted."

The Periœci.—The Periœci (those who live around) inhabited a hundred villages in the mountains or on the coast. They were sailors, they engaged in commerce, and manufactured the objects necessary to life. They were free and administered the business of their village, but they paid tribute to the magistrates of Sparta and obeyed them.

Condition of the Spartiates.—Helots and Periœci despised the Spartiates, their masters. "Whenever one speaks to them of the Spartiates," says Xenophon,[1] "there isn't one of them who can conceal the pleasure he would feel in eating them alive." Once an earthquake nearly destroyed Sparta: the Helots at once rushed from all sides of the plain to massacre those of the Spartiates who had escaped the catastrophe. At the same time the Periœci rose and refused obedience. The Spartiates' bearing toward the Periœci was certain to exasperate them. At the end of a war in which many of the Helots had fought in their army, they bade them choose those who had especially distinguished themselves for bravery, with the promise of freeing them. It was a ruse to discover the most energetic and those most capable of revolting. Two thousand were chosen; they were conducted about the temples with heads crowned as an evidence of their

[1] "Hellenica," iii., 3, 6.

manumission; then the Spartiates put them out of the way, but how it was done no one ever knew.[1]

And yet the oppressed classes were ten times more numerous than their masters. While there were more than 200,000 Helots and 120,000 Periœci, there were never more than 9,000 Spartiate heads of families. In a matter of life and death, then, it was necessary that a Spartiate be as good as ten Helots. As the form of battle was hand-to-hand, they needed agile and robust men. Sparta was like a camp without walls; its people was an army always in readiness.

EDUCATION

The Children.—They began to make soldiers of them at birth. The newly-born infant was brought before a council; if it was found deformed, it was exposed on the mountain to die; for an army has use only for strong men. The children who were permitted to grow up were taken from their parents at the age of seven years and were trained together as members of a group. Both summer and winter they went bare-foot and had but a single mantle. They lay on a heap of reeds and bathed in the cold waters of the Eurotas. They ate little and that quickly and had a rude diet. This was to teach them not to satiate the stomach. They were grouped by hundreds, each under a chief. Often they had to contend together with blows of feet and fists. At the feast of Artemis they were beaten before the statue of the goddess till

[1] See Thucydides, iv., 80.

the blood flowed; some died under this ordeal, but their honor required them not to weep. They were taught to fight and suffer.

Often they were given nothing to eat; provision must be found by foraging. If they were captured on these predatory expeditions, they were roughly beaten. A Spartiate boy who had stolen a little fox and had hidden it under his mantle, rather than betray himself let the animal gnaw out his vitals. They were to learn how to escape from perplexing situations when they were in the field.

They walked with lowered glance, silent, hands under the mantle, without turning the head and "making no more noise than statues." They were not to speak at table and were to obey all men that they encountered. This was to accustom them to discipline.

The Girls.—The other Greeks kept their daughters secluded in the house, spinning flax. The Spartiates would have robust women capable of bearing vigorous children. The girls, therefore, were trained in much the same manner as the boys. In their gymnasia they practised running, leaping, throwing the disc and javelin. A poet describes a play in which Spartiate girls "like colts with flowing manes make the dust fly about them." They were reputed the healthiest and bravest women in Greece.

The Discipline.—The men, too, have their regular life and this a soldier's life. The presence of many enemies requires that no one shall weaken. At seventeen years the Spartiate becomes a soldier and this he remains until he is sixty. The costume, hour of rising and retiring, meals, exercise—everything is fixed by regulations as in barracks.

Since the Spartiate engages only in war, he is to prepare himself for that; he exercises himself in running, leaping, and wielding his arms; he disciplines all the members of the body—the neck, the arms, the shoulders, the legs, and that too, every day. He has no right to engage in trade, to pursue an industry, nor to cultivate the earth; he is a soldier and is not to allow himself to be diverted to any other occupation. He cannot live at his pleasure with his own family; the men eat together in squads; they cannot leave the country without permission. It is the discipline of a regiment in the enemy's territory.

Laconism.—These warriors had a rude life, with clean-cut aims and proud disposition. They spoke in short phrases—or as we say, laconically—the word has still persisted. The Greeks cited many examples of these expressions. To a garrison in danger of being surprised the government sent this message, "Attention!" A Spartan army was summoned by the king of Persia to lay down his arms; the general replied, "Come and take them." When Lysander captured Athens, he wrote simply, "Athens is fallen."

Music. The Dance.—The arts of Sparta were those that pertained to an army. The Dorian conquerors brought with them a peculiar sort of music—the Dorian style, serious, strong, even harsh. It was military music; the Spartiates went into battle to the sound of the flute so that the step might be regular.

Their dance was a military movement. In the "Pyrrhic" the dancers were armed and imitated all the movements of a battle; they made the gestures of striking, of parrying, of retreating, and of throwing the javelin.

Heroism of the Women.—The women stimulated the men to combat; their exhibitions of courage were celebrated in Greece, so much so that collections of stories of them were made.[1] A Spartan mother, seeing her son fleeing from battle, killed him with her own hand, saying, "The Eurotas does not flow for deer." Another, learning that her five sons had perished, said, "This is not what I wish to know; does victory belong to Sparta?" "Yes." "Then let us render thanks to the gods."

THE INSTITUTIONS OF SPARTA

The Kings and the Council.—The Spartiates had at first, like the other Greeks, an assembly of the people. All these institutions were preserved, but only in form. The kings, descendants of the god Herakles, were loaded with honors; they were given the first place at the feasts and were served with a double portion; when they died all the inhabitants made lamentation for them. But no power was left to them and they were closely watched.

The Senate was composed of twenty-eight old men taken from the rich and ancient families, appointed for life; but it did not govern.

The Ephors.—The real masters of Sparta were the Ephors (the name signifies overseers), five magistrates who were renewed every year. They decided peace

[1] A collection by Plutarch is still preserved.

and war, and had judicial functions; when the king commanded the army, they accompanied him, directed the operations, and sometimes made him return. Usually they consulted the senators and took action in harmony with them. Then they assembled the Spartiates in one place, announced to them what had been decided and asked their approbation. The people without discussing the matter approved the action by acclamation. No one knew whether he had the right to refuse assent; accustomed to obey, the Spartiate never refused. It was, therefore, an aristocracy of governing families. Sparta was not a country of equality. There were some men who were called Equals, but only because they were equal among themselves. The others were termed Inferiors and had no part in the government.

The Army.—Thanks to this régime, the Spartiates preserved the rude customs of mountaineers; they had no sculptors, no architects, no orators, no philosophers. They had sacrificed everything to war; they became "adepts in the military art,"[1] and instructors of the other Greeks. They introduced two innovations especially: a better method of combat, a better method of athletic exercise.

The Hoplites.—Before them the Greeks marched into battle in disorder; the chiefs, on horseback or in a light chair, rushed ahead, the men following on foot, armed each in his own fashion, helter-skelter, incapable of acting together or of resisting. A battle reduced itself to a series of duels and to a massacre. At Sparta all the soldiers had the same arms; for de-

[1] A phrase of Xenophon.

fence, the breastplate covering the chest, the casque which protected the head, the greaves over the legs, the buckler held before the body. For offence the soldier had a short sword and a long lance. The man thus armed was called a hoplite. The Spartan hoplites were drawn up in regiments, battalions, companies, squads, almost like our armies. An officer commanded each of these groups and transmitted to his men the orders of his superior officer, so that the general in chief might have the same movement executed throughout the whole army. This organization which appears so simple to us was to the Greeks an astonishing novelty.

The Phalanx.—Come into the presence of the enemy, the soldiers arrange themselves in line, ordinarily eight ranks deep, each man close to his neighbor, forming a compact mass which we call a Phalanx. The king, who directs the army, sacrifices a goat to the gods; if the entrails of the victim are propitious, he raises a chant which all the army takes up in unison. Then they advance. With rapid and measured step, to the sound of the flute, with lance couched and buckler before the body, they meet the enemy in dense array, overwhelm him by their mass and momentum, throw him into rout, and only check themselves to avoid breaking the phalanx. So long as they remain together each is protected by his neighbor and all form an impenetrable mass on which the enemy could secure no hold. These were rude tactics, but sufficient to overcome a disorderly troop. Isolated men could not resist such a body. The other Greeks understood this, and all, as far as they were able, imitated the

Spartans; everywhere men were armed as hoplites and fought in phalanx.

Gymnastics.—To rush in orderly array on the enemy and stand the shock of battle there was need of agile and robust men; every man had to be an athlete. The Spartans therefore organized athletic exercises, and in this the other Greeks imitated them; gymnastics became for all a national art, the highest esteemed of all the arts, the crowning feature of the great festivals.

In the most remote countries, in the midst of the barbarians of Gaul or of the Black Sea, a Greek city was recognized by its gymnasium. There was a great square surrounded by porticoes or walks, usually near a spring, with baths and halls for exercise. The citizens came hither to walk and chat: it was a place of association. All the young men entered the gymnasium; for two years or less they came here every day; they learned to leap, to run, to throw the disc and the javelin, to wrestle by seizing about the waist. To harden the muscles and strengthen the skin they plunged into cold water, dispensed with oil for the body, and rubbed the flesh with a scraper (the strigil).

Athletes.—Many continued these exercises all their lives as a point of honor and became Athletes. Some became marvels of skill. Milo of Croton in Italy, it was said, would carry a bull on his shoulders; he stopped a chariot in its course by seizing it from behind. These athletes served sometimes in combats as soldiers, or as generals. Gymnastics were the school of war.

Rôle of the Spartiates.—The Spartans taught the

other Greeks to exercise and to fight. They always remained the most vigorous wrestlers and the best soldiers, and were recognized as such by the rest of Greece. Everywhere they were respected. When the rest of the Greeks had to fight together against the Persians, they unhesitatingly took the Spartans as chiefs—and with justice, said an Athenian orator.

CHAPTER XII

ATHENS

THE ATHENIAN PEOPLE

Attica.—The Athenians boasted of having always lived in the same country; their ancestors, according to their story, originated from the soil itself. The mountaineers who conquered the south land passed by the country without invading it; Attica was hardly a temptation to them.

Attica is composed of a mass of rocks which in the form of a triangle advances into the sea. These rocks, renowned for their blocks of marble and for the honey of their bees,[1] are bare and sterile. Between them and the sea are left three small plains with meagre soil, meanly watered (the streams are dry in summer), and incapable of supporting a numerous population.

Athens.—In the largest of these plains, a league from the sea, rises a massive isolated rock: Athens was built at its foot. The old city, called the Acropolis, occupied the summit of the rock.

The inhabitants of Attica commenced, not by forming a single state, but by founding scattered villages, each of which had its own king and its own government. Later all these villages united under one king,[2]

[1] The marble of Pentelicus and the honey of Hymettus.
[2] This legendary king was called Theseus.

the king of Athens, and established a single city. This does not mean that all the people came to dwell in one town. They continued to have their own villages and to cultivate their lands; but all adored one and the same protecting goddess, Athena, divinity of Athens, and all obeyed the same king.

Athenian Revolutions.—Later still the kings were suppressed. In their place Athens had nine chiefs (the archons) who changed every year. This whole history is little known to us for no writing of the time is preserved. They used to say that for centuries the Athenians had lived in discord; the nobles (Eupatrids) who were proprietors of the soil oppressed the peasants on their estates; creditors held their debtors as slaves. To reëstablish order the Athenians commissioned Solon, a sage, to draft a code of laws for them (594).

Solon made three reforms:

1. He lessened the value of the money, which allowed the debtors to release themselves more easily.

2. He made the peasants proprietors of the land that they cultivated. From this time there were in Attica more small proprietors than in any other part of Greece.

3. He grouped all the citizens into four classes according to their incomes. Each had to pay taxes and to render military service according to his wealth, the poor being exempt from taxation and military service.

After Solon the Athenians were subject to Pisistratus, one of their powerful and clever citizens; but in 510 the dissensions revived.

Reforms of Cleisthenes.—Cleisthenes, leader of one of the parties, used the occasion to make a thoroughgoing revolution.

There were many strangers in Athens, especially seamen and traders who lived in Piræus near the harbor. Cleisthenes gave them the rights of citizenship and made them equal[1] to the older inhabitants. From this time there were two populations side by side—the people of Attica and those of Piræus. A difference of physical features was apparent for three centuries afterward: the people of Attica resembled the rest of the Greeks; those in Piræus resembled Asiatics. The Athenian people thus augmented was a new people, the most active in Greece.

THE ATHENIAN PEOPLE

In the fifth century the society of Athens was definitely formed: three classes inhabited the district of Attica—slaves, foreigners, and citizens.

The Slaves.—The slaves constituted the great majority of the population; there was no man so poor that he did not have at least one slave; the rich owned a multitude of them, some as many as five hundred. The larger part of the slaves lived in the house occupied with grinding grain, kneading bread, spinning and weaving cloth, performing the service of the kitchens, and in attendance on their masters. Others labored in the shops as blacksmiths, as dyers, or in stone quarries or silver mines. Their master fed them,

[1] Certain limitations, however, are referred to below, under "Metics."—ED.

but sold at a profit everything which they produced, giving them in return nothing but their living. All the domestic servants, all the miners, and the greater part of the artisans were slaves. These men lived in society but without any part in it; they had not even the disposition of their own bodies, being wholly the property of other men. They were thought of only as objects of property; they were often referred to as "a body" (σῶμα). There was no other law for them than the will of their master, and he had all power over them—to make them work, to imprison them, to deprive them of their sustenance, to beat them. When a citizen went to law, his adversary had the right to require that the former's slaves should be put to the torture to tell what they knew. Many Athenian orators commend this usage as an ingenious means for obtaining true testimony. "Torture," says the orator Isæus, "is the surest means of proof; and so when you wish to clear up a contested question, you do not address yourselves to freemen, but, placing the slaves to the torture, you seek to discover the truth."

Foreigners.—The name Metics was applied to people of foreign origin who were established in Athens. To become a citizen of Athens it was not enough, as with us, to be born in the country; one must be the son of a citizen. It might be that some aliens had resided in Attica for several generations and yet their family not become Athenian. The metics could take no part in the government, could not marry a citizen, nor acquire land. But they were personally free, they had the right of commerce by sea, of banking and of trade on condition that they take a patron to represent them in the courts. There were in Athens more than ten thousand families of metics, the majority of them bankers or merchants.

The Citizens.—To be a citizen of Athens it was necessary that both parents should be citizens. The young Athenian, come to maturity at about eighteen years of age, appeared before the popular assembly, received the arms which he was to bear and took the following oath: "I swear never to dishonor these sacred arms, not to quit my post, to obey the magistrates and the laws, to honor the religion of my country." He became simultaneously citizen and soldier. Thereafter he owed military service until he was sixty years of age. With this he had the right to sit in the assembly and to fulfil the functions of the state.

Once in a while the Athenians consented to receive into the citizenship a man who was not the son of a citizen, but this was rare and a sign of great favor. The assembly had to vote the stranger into its membership, and then nine days after six thousand citizens had to vote for him on a secret ballot. The Athenian people was like a closed circle; no new members were admitted except those pleasing to the old members, and they admitted few beside their sons.

THE GOVERNMENT OF ATHENS

The Assembly.—The Athenians called their government a democracy (a government by the people). But this people was not, as with us, the mass of inhabitants, but the body of citizens, a true aristocracy of 15,000 to 20,000 men who governed the whole nation as masters. This body had absolute power, and was the true sovereign of Athens. It assembled at least three times a month to deliberate and to vote. The assembly was held in the open air on the Pnyx; the citizens sat on stone benches arranged in an amphitheatre; the magistrates before them on a platform opened the session with a religious ceremony and a prayer, then a herald proclaimed in a loud voice the business which was to occupy the assembly, and said, "Who wishes to speak?" Every citizen had the right to this privilege; the orators mounted the tribune according to age. When all had spoken, the president put the question; the assembly voted by a show of hands, and then dissolved.

The Courts.—The people itself, being sovereign, passed judgment in the courts. Every citizen of thirty years of age could participate in the judicial assembly (the Heliæa). The heliasts sat in the great halls in sections of five hundred; the tribunal was, then, composed of one thousand to fifteen hundred judges. The Athenians had no prosecuting officer as we have; a citizen took upon himself to make the accusation. The accused and the accuser appeared before the court; each delivered a plea which was not to exceed the time marked off by a water-clock. Then the judges voted by depositing a black or white stone. If the accuser did not obtain a certain number of votes, he himself was condemned.

The Magistrates.—The sovereign people needed a council to prepare the business for discussion and magistrates to execute their decisions. The council was composed of five hundred citizens drawn by lot for one year. The magistrates were very numerous: ten generals to command the army, thirty officials for financial administration, sixty police officials to superintend the streets, the markets, weights and measures, etc.[1]

Character of This Government.—The power in Athens did not pertain to the rich and the noble, as in Sparta. In the assembly everything was decided by a majority of votes and all the votes were equal. All the jurors, all the members of the council, all the magistrates except the generals were chosen by lot. The citizens were equal not only in theory, but also in practice. Socrates said[2] to a well-informed Athenian who did not dare to speak before the people: "Of what are you afraid? Is it of the fullers, the shoemakers, the masons, the artisans, or the merchants? for the assembly is composed of all these people."

Many of these people had to ply their trade in order to make a living, and could not serve the state gratuitously; and so a salary was instituted: every citizen who sat in the assembly or in the courts received for every day of session three obols (about eight cents of our money), a sum just sufficient to maintain life at that time. From this day the poor administered the government.

The Demagogues.—Since all important affairs whether in the assembly or in the courts were decided by discussion and discourse, the influential men were those who knew how to speak best. The people accustomed themselves to listen to the orators, to follow

[1] Not to mention the Archons, whom they had not ventured to suppress.

[2] Xenophon, "Memorabilia," iii., 7, 6.

their counsels, to charge them with embassies, and even to appoint them generals. These men were called Demagogues (leaders of the people). The party of the rich scoffed at them: in a comedy Aristophanes represents the people (Demos) under the form of an old man who has lost his wits: "You are foolishly credulous, you let flatterers and intriguers pull you around by the nose and you are enraptured when they harangue you." And the chorus, addressing a charlatan, says to him, "You are rude, vicious; you have a strong voice, an impudent eloquence, and violent gestures; believe me, you have all that is necessary to govern Athens."

PRIVATE LIFE

The Athenians created so many political functions that a part of the citizens was engaged in fulfilling them. The citizen of Athens, like the functionary or soldier of our days, was absorbed in public affairs. Warring and governing were the whole of his life. He spent his days in the assembly, in the courts, in the army, at the gymnasium, or at the market. Almost always he had a wife and children, for his religion commanded this, but he did not live at home.

The Children.—When a child came into the world, the father had the right to reject it. In this case it was laid outside the house where it died from neglect, unless a passer-by took it and brought it up as a slave. In this custom Athens followed all the Greeks. It was especially the girls that were exposed to death. "A son," says a writer of comedy, "is always raised even if the parents are in the last stage of misery; a daughter is exposed even though the parents are rich."

If the father accepted the child, the latter entered the family. He was left at first in the women's apartments with the mother. The girls remained there until the day of their marriage; the boys came out when they were seven years old. The boy was then entrusted to a preceptor (pedagogue), whose business it was to teach him to conduct himself well and to obey. The pedagogue was often a slave, but the father gave him the right to beat his son. This was the general usage in antiquity.

Later the boy went to school, where he learned to read, write, cipher, recite poetry, and to sing in the chorus or to the sound of the flute. At last came gymnastics. This was the whole of the instruction; it made men sound in body and calm in spirit—what the Greeks called "good and beautiful."

To the young girl, secluded with her mother, nothing of the liberal arts was taught; it was thought sufficient if she learned to obey. Xenophon represents a rich and well-educated Athenian speaking thus of his wife with Socrates: "She was hardly twenty years old when I married her, and up to that time she had been subjected to an exacting surveillance; they had no desire that she should live, and she learned almost nothing. Was it not enough that one should find in her a woman who could spin the flax to make garments, and who had learned how to distribute duties to the slaves?" When her husband proposed that she become his assistant, she replied with great surprise, "In what can I aid you? Of what am I capable?

My mother has always taught me that my business was to be prudent." Prudence or obedience was the virtue which was required of the Greek woman.

Marriage.—At the age of fifteen the girl married. The parents had chosen the husband; it might be a man from a neighboring family, or a man who had been a long-time friend of the father, but always a citizen of Athens. It was rare that the young girl knew him; she was never consulted in the case. Herodotus, speaking of a Greek, adds: "This Callias deserves mention for his conduct toward his daughters; for when they were of marriageable age he gave them a rich dowry, permitted them to choose husbands from all the people, and he then married them to the men of their choice."

Athenian Women.—In the inner recess of the Athenian house there was a retired apartment reserved for the women—the Gynecæum. Husband and relatives were the only visitors; the mistress of the household remained here all day with her slaves; she directed them, superintended the house-keeping, and distributed to them the flax for them to spin. She herself was engaged with weaving garments. She left the house seldom save for the religious festivals. She never appeared in the society of men: "No one certainly would venture," says the orator Isæus, "to dine with a married woman; married women do not go out to dine with men or permit themselves to eat with strangers." An Athenian woman who frequented society could not maintain a good reputation.

The wife, thus secluded and ignorant, was not an agreeable companion. The husband had taken her not for his life-long companion, but to keep his house in order, to be the mother of his children, and because Greek custom and religion required that he should marry. Plato says that one does not marry because he wants to, but "because the law constrains him." And the comic poet Menander had found this saying: "Marriage, to tell the truth, is an evil, but a necessary evil." And so the women in Athens, as in most of the other states of Greece, always held but little place in society.

CHAPTER XIII

WARS OF THE GREEKS

THE PERSIAN WARS

Origin of the Persian Wars.—While the Greeks were completing the organization of their cities, the Persian king was uniting all the nations of the East in a single empire. Greeks and Orientals at length found themselves face to face. It is in Asia Minor that they first meet.

On the coast of Asia Minor there were rich and populous colonies of the Greeks;[1] Cyrus, the king of Persia, desired to subject them. These cities sent for help to the Spartans, who were reputed the bravest of the Greeks, and this action was reported to Cyrus; he replied,[2] "I have never feared this sort of people that has in the midst of the city a place where the people assemble to deceive one another with false oaths." (He was thinking of the market-place.) The Greeks of Asia were subdued and made subject to the Great King.

Thirty years later King Darius found himself in the presence of the Greeks of Europe. But this time it was the Greeks that attacked the Great King. The Athenians sent twenty galleys to aid the revolting Ionians; their soldiers entered Lydia, took Sardis by

[1] Twelve Ionian colonies, twelve Æolian, four Dorian.
[2] Herod., i., 153.

surprise and burned it. Darius revenged himself by destroying the Greek cities of Asia, but he did not forget the Greeks of Europe. He had decreed, they say, that at every meal an officer should repeat to him: "Master, remember the Athenians." He sent to the Greek cities to demand earth and water, a symbol in use among the Persians to indicate submission to the Great King. Most of the Greeks were afraid and yielded. But the Spartans cast the envoys into a pit, bidding them take thence earth and water to carry to the king. This was the beginning of the Median wars.

Comparison of the Two Adversaries.—The contrast between the two worlds which now entered into conflict is well marked by Herodotus[1] in the form of a conversation of King Xerxes with Demaratus, a Spartan exile: " 'I venture to assure you,' said Demaratus, 'that the Spartans will offer you battle even if all the rest of the Greeks fight on your side, and if their army should not amount to more than one thousand men.' 'What!' said Xerxes, 'one thousand men attack so immense an army as mine! I fear your words are only boasting; for although they be five thousand, we are more than one thousand to one. If they had a master like us, fear would inspire them with courage; they would march under the lash against a larger army; but being free and independent, they will have no more courage than that with which nature has endowed them.' 'The Spartans,' replied Demaratus, 'are not inferior to anybody in a hand-to-hand contest, and united in a phalanx they are the bravest of all men. Yet,

[1] Herod., vii., 103, 104.

though free, they have an absolute master, the Law, which they dread more than all your subjects do you; they obey it, and this law requires them to stand fast to their post and conquer or die.'" This is the difference between the two parties to the conflict: on the one side, a multitude of subjects united by force under a capricious master; on the other, little martial republics whose citizens govern themselves according to laws which they respect.

First Persian War.—There were two Persian wars. The first was simply an expedition against Athens; six hundred galleys sent by Darius disembarked a Persian army on the little plain of Marathon, seven hours distant from Athens.

Religious sentiment prevented the Spartans from taking the field before the full moon, and it was still only the first quarter; the Athenians had to fight alone.[1] Ten thousand citizens armed as hoplites camped before the Persians. The Athenians had ten generals, having the command on successive days; of these Miltiades, when his turn came, drew up the army for battle. The Athenians charged the enemy in serried ranks, but the Persians seeing them advancing without cavalry and without archers, thought them fools. It was the first time that the Greeks had dared to face the Persians in battle array. The Athenians began by turning both flanks, and then engaged the centre, driving the Persians in disorder to the sea and forcing them to reëmbark on their ships.

The victory of Marathon delivered the Athenians and made them famous in all Greece (490).

[1] 1,000 Platæans came to the assistance of the Athenians.—Ed.

Second Persian War.—The second war began ten years later with an invasion. Xerxes united all the peoples of the empire, so that the land force amounted, as some say, to 1,700,000 men.[1] There were Medes and Persians clad in sleeved tunics, armed with cuirasses of iron, bucklers, bows and arrows; Assyrians with cuirass of linen, armed with clubs pointed with iron; Indians clad in cotton with bows and arrows of bamboo; savages of Ethiopia with leopard skins for clothing; nomads armed only with lassos; Phrygians armed with short pikes; Lydians equipped like Greeks; Thracians carrying javelins and daggers. The enumeration of these fills twenty chapters in Herodotus.[2] These warriors brought with them a crowd equally numerous of non-combatants, of servants, slaves, women, together with a mass of mules, horses, camels, and baggage wagons.

This horde crossed the Hellespont by a bridge of boats in the spring of 480. For seven days and nights it defiled under the lash. Then traversing Thrace, it marched on Greece, conquering the peoples whom it met.

The Persian fleet, 1,200 galleys strong, coasted the shores of Thrace, passing through the canal at Mount Athos which Xerxes had had built for this very purpose.

The Greeks, terrified, submitted for the most part to the Great King and joined their armies to the Persian force. The Athenians sent to consult the oracle of Delphi, but received only the reply: "Athens will

[1] Herodotus's statements of the numbers in Xerxes' army are incredible.—ED.

[2] Herod., vii., 61–80.

be destroyed from base to summit." The god being asked to give a more favorable response, replied, "Zeus accords to Pallas [protectress of Athens] a wall of wood which alone shall not be taken; in that shall you and your children find safety." The priests of whom they asked the interpretation of this oracle bade the Athenians quit Attica and go to establish themselves elsewhere. But Themistocles explained the "wall of wood" as meaning the ships; they should retire to the fleet and fight the Persians on sea.

Athens and Sparta, having decided on resistance, endeavored to form a league of the Greeks against the Persians. Few cities had the courage to enter it, and these placed themselves under the command of the Spartans. Four battles in one year settled the war. At Thermopylæ, Leonidas, king of Sparta, who tried to bar the entrance to a defile was outflanked and overwhelmed. At Salamis, the Persian fleet, crowded into a narrow space where the ships embarrassed one another, was defeated by the Greek navy (480). At Platæa the rest of the Persian army left in Greece was annihilated by the Greek hoplites; of 300,000 men but 40,000 escaped. The same day at Mycale, on the coast of Asia, an army of the Greeks landed and routed the Persians (479). The Greeks had conquered the Great King.

Reasons for the Greek Victory.—The Median war was not a national war between Greeks and barbarians. All the Greeks of Asia and half the Greeks of Europe fought on the Persian side. Many of the other Greeks gave no assistance. In reality it was a fight of the

Great King and his subjects against Sparta, Athens, and their allies.

The conquest of this great horde by two small peoples appeared at that time as a prodigy. The gods, said the Greeks, had fought for them. But there is less wonder when we examine the two antagonists more closely: the Persian army was innumerable, and Xerxes had thought that victory was a matter of numbers. But this multitude was an embarrassment to itself. It did not know where to secure food for itself, it advanced but slowly, and it choked itself on the day of combat. Likewise the ships arranged in too close order drove their prows into neighboring ships and shattered their oars. Then in this immense crowd there were, according to Herodotus, many men but few soldiers. Only the Persians and Medes, the flower of the army, fought with energy; the rest advanced only under the lash, they had come under pressure to a war which had no interest for them, ill-armed and without discipline, ready to desert as soon as no one was watching them. At Platæa the Medes and Persians were the only ones to do any fighting; the subjects kept aloof.

The Persian soldiers were ill-equipped; they were embarrassed by their long robes, the head was poorly protected by a felt hat, the body ill-defended by a shield of wicker-work. For arms they had a bow, a dagger, and a very short pike; they could fight only at a great distance or hand-to-hand. The Spartans and their allies, on the contrary, secure in the protection of great buckler, helmet and greaves, marched in solid line and were irresistible; they broke the enemy with their long pikes and at once the battle became a massacre.

Results of the Persian Wars.—Sparta had commanded the troops, but as Herodotus says,[1] it was Athens who had delivered Greece by setting an example of resistance and constituting the fleet of Salamis. It was Athens who profited by the victory. All the Ionian cities of the Archipelago and of the coast of Asia revolted and formed a league against the Persians. The Spartans, men of the mountains, could not conduct a maritime war, and so withdrew; the Athenians immediately became chiefs of the league. In 476[2] Aristides, commanding the fleet, assembled the delegates of the confederate cities. They decided to continue the war against the Great King, and engaged to provide ships and warriors and to pay each year a contribution of 460 talents ($350,000). The treasure was deposited at Delos in the temple of Apollo, god of the Ionians. Athens was charged with the leadership of the military force and with collecting the tax. To make the agreement irrevocable Aristides had a mass of hot iron cast into the sea, and all swore to maintain the oaths until the day that the iron should mount to the surface.

A day came, however, when the war ceased, and the Greeks, always the victors, concluded a peace, or at least a truce,[3] with the Great King. He surrendered his claim on the Asiatic Greeks (about 449).

[1] vii., 139.
[2] The chronology of these events is uncertain.—ED.
[3] Called the Peace of Cimon, but it is very doubtful whether Cimon really concluded a treaty. [With more right may it be called the Peace of Callias, who was probably principal ambassador.—ED.]

What was to become of the treaty of Aristides? Were the confederate cities still to pay their contribution now that there was no more fighting? Some refused it even before the war was done. Athens asserted that the cities had made their engagements in perpetuity and forced them to pay them.

The war finished, the treasury at Delos had no further use; the Athenians transferred the money to Athens and used it in building their monuments. They maintained that the allies paid for deliverance from the Persians; they, therefore, had no claim against Athens so long as she defended them from the Great King. The allies had now become the tributaries of Athens: they were now her subjects. Athens increased the tax on them, and required their citizens to bring their cases before the Athenian courts; she even sent colonists to seize a part of their lands. Athens, mistress of the league, was sovereign over more than three hundred cities spread over the islands and the coasts of the Archipelago, and the tribute paid her amounted to six hundred talents a year.

STRIFE AMONG THE GREEK STATES

The Peloponnesian War.—After the foundation of the Athenian empire in the Archipelago the Greeks found themselves divided between two leagues—the maritime cities were subject to Athens; the cities of the interior remained under the domination of Sparta. After much preliminary friction war arose between Sparta and her continental allies on the one side and Athens and her maritime subjects on the other. This was the *Peloponnesian War.* It continued twenty-seven years (431-404), and when it ceased, it was revived under other names down to 360.

These wars were complicated affairs. They were fought simultaneously on land and sea, in Greece, Asia, Thrace, and Sicily, ordinarily at several points at once. The Spartans had a better army and ravaged Attica; the Athenians had a superior fleet and made descents on the coasts of the Peloponnesus. Then Athens sent its army to Sicily where it perished to the last man (413); Lysander, a Spartan general, secured a fleet from the Persians and destroyed the Athenian fleet in Asia (405). The Athenian allies who fought only under compulsion abandoned her. Lysander took Athens, demolished its walls, and burnt its ships.

Wars against Sparta.—Sparta was for a time mistress on both land and sea. "In those days," says Xenophon, "all cities obeyed when a Spartan issued his orders." But soon the allies of Sparta, wearied of her domination, formed a league against her. The Spartans, driven at first from Asia, still maintained their power in Greece for some years by virtue of their alliance with the king of the Persians (387). But the Thebans, having developed a strong army under the command of Epaminondas, fought them at Leuctra (371) and at Mantinea (362). The allies of Sparta detached themselves from her, but the Thebans could not secure from the rest of the Greeks the recognition of their supremacy. From this time no Greek city was sovereign over the others.

Savage Character of These Wars.—These wars between the Greek cities were ferocious. A few incidents suffice to show their character. At the opening of the war the allies of Sparta threw into the sea all the merchants from cities hostile to them. The Athenians in return put to death the ambassadors of Sparta without allowing them to speak a word. The town of Platæa was taken by capitulation, and the Spartans had promised that no one should be punished without a trial; but the Spartan judges demanded of every prisoner if during the war he had rendered any service to the Peloponnesians; when the prisoner replied in the negative, he was condemned to death. The women were sold as slaves. The city of Mitylene having revolted from Athens was retaken by her. The Athenians in an assembly deliberated and decreed that all the people of Mitylene should be put to death. It is true that the next day the Athenians revised the decree and sent a second ship to carry a more favorable commission, but still more than one thousand Mityleneans were executed.

After the Syracusan disaster all the Athenian army was taken captive. The conquerors began by slaughtering all the generals and many of the soldiers. The remainder were consigned to the quarries which served as prison. They were left there crowded together for seventy days, exposed without protection to the burning sun of summer, and then to the chilly nights of autumn. Many died from sickness, from cold and hunger—for they were hardly fed at all; their corpses remained on the ground and infected the air. At last the Syracusans drew out the survivors and sold them into slavery.

Ordinarily when an army invaded a hostile state

it levelled the houses, felled the trees, burned the crops and killed the laborers. After battle it made short shrift of the wounded and killed prisoners in cold blood. In a captured city everything belonged to the captor: men, women, children were sold as slaves. Such was at this time the right of war. Thucydides sums up the case as follows:[1] "Business is regulated between men by the laws of justice when there is obligation on both sides; but the stronger does whatever is in his power, and the weaker yields. The gods rule by a necessity of their nature because they are strongest; men do likewise."

Results of These Wars.—These wars did not result in uniting the Greeks into one body. No city, Sparta more than Athens, was able to force the others to obey her. They only exhausted themselves by fighting one another. It was the king of Persia who profited by the strife. Not only did the Greek cities not unite against him, but all in succession allied themselves with him against the other Greeks. In the notorious Peace of Antalcidas (387) the Great King declared that all the Greek cities of Asia belonged to him, and Sparta recognized this claim. Athens and Thebes did as much some years later. An Athenian orator said, "It is the king of Persia who governs Greece; he needs only to establish governors in our cities. Is it not he who directs everything among us? Do we not summon the Great King as if we were his slaves?" The Greeks by their strife had lost the vantage that the Median war had gained for them.

[1] In his chapters on the Mityleneans.

CHAPTER XIV

THE ARTS IN GREECE

ATHENS AT THE TIME OF PERICLES

Pericles.—In the middle of the fifth century Athens found herself the most powerful city in Greece. Pericles, descended from one of the noble families, was then the director of the affairs of the state. He wasted neither speech nor personality, and never sought to flatter the vanity of the people. But the Athenians respected him and acted only in accordance with his counsels; they had faith in his knowledge of all the details of administration, of the resources of the state, and so they permitted him to govern. For forty years Pericles was the soul of the politics of Athens; as Thucydides his contemporary said, "The democracy existed in name; in reality it was the government of the first citizen."

Athens and Her Monuments.—In Athens, as in the majority of Greek cities, the houses of individuals were small, low, packed closely together, forming narrow streets, tortuous and ill paved. The Athenians reserved their display for their public monuments. Ever after they levied heavy war taxes on their allies they had large sums of money to expend, and these were employed in erecting beautiful edifices. In the market-place they built a portico adorned with paintings (the Poikile), in the city a theatre, a temple in honor of Theseus, and the Odeon for the contests in music. But the most beautiful monuments rose on the rock of the Acropolis as on a gigantic pedestal. There were two temples of which the principal, the Parthenon, was dedicated to Athena, protecting goddess of the city; a colossal statue of bronze which represented Athena; and a staircase of ornamental character leading up to the Propylæa. Athens was from this time the most beautiful of the Greek cities.[1]

Importance of Athens.—Athens became at the same time the city of artists. Poets, orators, architects, painters, sculptors—some Athenians by birth, others come from all corners of the Greek world—met here and produced their masterpieces. There were without doubt many Greek artists elsewhere than at Athens; there had been before the fifth century, and there were a long time afterward; but never were so many assembled at one time in the same city. Most of the Greeks had fine sensibilities in matters of art; but the Athenians more than all others had a refined taste, a cultivated spirit and love of the beautiful. If the Greeks have gained renown in the history of civilization, it is that they have been a people of artists; neither their little states nor their small armies have played a great rôle in the world. This is why the fifth century is the most beautiful moment in the history of Greece; this is why Athens has remained renowned above all the rest of the Greek cities.

[1] The moderns have called this time the Age of Pericles, because Pericles was then governing and was the friend of many of these artists; but the ancients never employed the phrase.

LETTERS

The Orators.—Athens is above all the city of eloquence. Speeches in the assembly determine war, peace, taxes, all state business of importance; speeches before the courts condemn or acquit citizens and subjects. Power is in the hands of the orators; the people follow their counsels and often commit to them important public functions: Cleon is appointed general; Demosthenes directs the war against Philip.

The orators have influence; they employ their talents in eloquence to accuse their political enemies. Often they possess riches, for they are paid for supporting one party or the other: Æschines is retained by the king of Macedon; Demosthenes accepts fees from the king of Persia.

Some of the orators, instead of delivering their own orations, wrote speeches for others. When an Athenian citizen had a case at court, he did not desire, as we do, that an advocate plead his case for him; the law required that each speak in person. He therefore sought an orator and had him compose a speech which he learned by heart and recited before the tribunal.

Other orators travelled through the cities of Greece speaking on subjects which pleased their fancy. Sometimes they gave lectures, as we should say.

The oldest orators spoke simply, limiting themselves to an account of the facts without oratorical flourishes; on the platform they were almost rigid without loud speaking or gesticulation. Pericles delivered his orations with a calm air, so quietly, indeed, that no fold of his mantle was disturbed. When he appeared at the tribune, his head, according to custom, crowned with leaves, he might have been taken, said the people, "for a god of Olympus." But the orators who followed wished to move the public. They assumed an animated style, pacing the tribune in a declamatory and agitated manner. The people became accustomed to this form of eloquence. The first time that Demosthenes came to the tribune the assembly shouted with laughter; the orator could not enunciate, he carried himself ill. He disciplined himself in declamation and gesture and became the favorite of the people. Later when he was asked what was the first quality of the orator, he replied, "Action, and the second, action, and the third, action." Action, that is delivery, was more to the Greeks than the sense of the discourse.

The Sages.—For some centuries there had been, especially among the Greeks of Asia, men who observed and reflected on things. They were called by a name which signifies at once wise men and scholars. They busied themselves with physics, astronomy, natural history, for as yet science was not separated from philosophy. Such were in the seventh century the celebrated Seven Sages of Greece.

The Sophists.—About the time of Pericles there came to Athens men who professed to teach wisdom. They gathered many pupils and charged fees for their lessons. Ordinarily they attacked the religion, customs, and institutions of Greek cities, showing that they were not founded on reason. They concluded that men could not know anything with certainty (which was quite true for their time), that men can know nothing at all, and that nothing is true or false: "Nothing exists," said one of them, "and if it did exist, we could not know it." These professors of scepticism were called sophists. Some of them were at the same time orators.

Socrates and the Philosophers.—Socrates, an old man of Athens, undertook to combat the sophists. He was a poor man, ugly, and without eloquence. He opened no school like the sophists but contented himself with going about the city, conversing with those he met, and leading them by the force of his questions to discover what he himself had in mind. He sought especially the young men and gave them instruction and counsel. Socrates made no pretensions as a scholar: "All my knowledge," said he, "is to know that I know nothing." He would call himself no longer a sage, like the others, but a philosopher, that is to say, a lover of wisdom. He did not meditate on the nature of the world nor on the sciences; man was his only interest. His motto was, "Know thyself." He was before all a preacher of virtue.

As he always spoke of morals and religion, the Athenians took him for a sophist.[1] In 399 he was brought before the court, accused "of not worshipping the gods of the city, of introducing new gods, and of corrupting the youth." He made no attempt to defend himself, and was condemned to death. He was then seventy years old.

Xenophon, one of his disciples, wrote out his conversations and an apology for him.[2] Another disciple,

[1] See Aristophanes' "Clouds."
[2] The "Memorabilia" and "Apologia."

Plato, composed dialogues in which Socrates is always the principal personage. Since this time Socrates has been regarded as the "father of philosophy." Plato himself was the head of a school (429-348); Aristotle (384-322), a disciple of Plato, summarized in his books all the science of his time. The philosophers that followed attached themselves to one or the other of these two masters: the disciples of Plato called themselves Academicians,[1] those of Aristotle, Peripatetics.[2]

The Chorus.—It was an ancient custom of the Greeks to dance in their religious ceremonies. Around the altar dedicated to the god a group of young men passed and repassed, assuming noble and expressive attitudes, for the ancients danced with the whole body. Their dance, very different from ours, was a sort of animated procession, something like a solemn pantomime. Almost always this religious dance was accompanied by chants in honor of the god. The group singing and dancing at the same time was called the Chorus. All the cities had their festival choruses in which the children of the noblest families participated after long time of preparation. The god required the service of a troop worthy of him.

Tragedy and Comedy.—In the level country about Athens the young men celebrated in this manner each year religious dances in honor of Dionysos, the god of the vintage. One of these dances was grave; it represented the actions of the god. The leader of the

[1] Because Plato had lectured in the gardens of a certain Academus.

[2] Because Aristotle had given instruction while moving about. [Or rather from a favorite walk (Peripatus) in the Lyceum.—Ed.]

chorus played Dionysos, the chorus itself the satyrs, his companions. Little by little they came to represent also the life of the other gods and the ancient heroes. Then some one (the Greeks call him Thespis) conceived the idea of setting up a stage on which the actor could play while the chorus rested. The spectacle thus perfected was transferred to the city near the black poplar tree in the market. Thus originated Tragedy.

The other dance was comic. The masked dancers chanted the praises of Dionysos mingled with jeers addressed to the spectators or with humorous reflections on the events of the day. The same was done for the comic chorus as for the tragic chorus: actors were introduced, a dialogue, all of a piece, and the spectacle was transferred to Athens. This was the origin of Comedy. This is the reason that from this time tragedy has been engaged with heroes, and comedy with every-day life.

Tragedy and comedy preserved some traces of their origin. Even when they were represented in the theatre, they continued to be played before the altar of the god. Even after the actors mounted on the platform had become the most important personages of the spectacle, the choir continued to dance and to chant around the altar. In the comedies, like the masques in other days, sarcastic remarks on the government came to be made; this was the Parabasis.

The Theatre.—That all the Athenians might be present at these spectacles there was built on the side of the Acropolis the theatre of Dionysos which could hold 30,000 spectators. Like all the Greek theatres, it was open to heaven and was composed of tiers of rock ranged in a half-circle about the orchestra where the chorus performed and before the stage where the play was given.

Plays were produced only at the time of the festivals of the god, but then they continued for several days in succession. They began in the morning at sunrise and occupied all the time till torch-light with the production of a series of three tragedies (a trilogy) followed by a satirical drama. Each trilogy was the work of one author. Other trilogies were presented on succeeding days, so that the spectacle was a competition between poets, the public determining the victor. The most celebrated of these competitors were Æschylus, Sophocles, and Euripides. There were also contests in comedy, but there remain to us only the works of one comic poet, Aristophanes.

THE ARTS

Greek Temples.—In Greece the most beautiful edifices were constructed to the honor of the gods, and when we speak of Greek architecture it is their temples that we have in mind.

A Greek temple is not, like a Christian church, designed to receive the faithful who come thither to pray. It is the palace[1] where the god lives, represented by his idol, a palace which men feel under compulsion to make splendid. The mass of the faithful do not enter the interior of the temple; they remain without, surrounding the altar in the open air.

[1] The Greek word for temple signifies "dwelling."

At the centre of the temple is the "chamber" of the god, a mysterious sanctuary without windows, dimly lighted from above.[1] On the pavement rises the idol of wood, of marble, or of ivory, clad in gold and adorned with garments and jewels. The statue is often of colossal size; in the temple of Olympia Zeus is represented sitting and his head almost touches the summit of the temple. "If the god should rise," they said, "his head would shatter the roof." This sanctuary, a sort of reliquary for the idol, is concealed on every side from the eyes. To enter, it is necessary to pass through a porch formed by a row of columns.

Behind the "chamber" is the "rear-chamber" in which are kept the valuable property of the god—his riches,[2] and often the gold and silver of the city. The temple is therefore storehouse, treasury, and museum.

Rows of columns surround the building on four sides, like a second wall protecting the god and his treasures. There are three orders of columns which differ in base and capital, each bearing the name of the people that invented it or most frequently used it. They are, in the order of age, the Doric, the Ionic, and the Corinthian. The temple is named from the style of the columns supporting it.

Above the columns, around the edifice are sculptured surfaces of marble (the metopes) which alternate with plain blocks of marble (the triglyphs). Metopes and triglyphs constitute the frieze.

[1] But not by a square opening in the roof as formerly supposed. —Ed. See Gardner, "Ancient Athens," N. Y., 1902, p. 268.

[2] The Parthenon contained vases of gold and silver, a crown of gold, shields, helmets, swords, serpents of gold, an ivory table, eighteen couches, and quivers of ivory.

The temple is surmounted with a triangular pediment adorned with statues.

Greek temples were polychrome, that is to say, were painted in several colors, yellow, blue, and red. For a long time the moderns refused to believe this; it was thought that the Greeks possessed too sober taste to add color to an edifice. But traces of painting have been discovered on several temples, which cannot leave the matter in doubt. It has at last been concluded, on reflection, that these bright colors were to give a clearer setting to the lines.

Characteristics of Greek Architecture.—A Greek temple appears at first a simple, bare edifice; it is only a long box of stone set upon a rock; the façade is a square surmounted by a triangle. At first glance one sees only straight lines and cylinders. But on nearer inspection "it is discovered[1] that not a single one of these lines is truly straight." The columns swell at the middle, vertical lines are slightly inclined to the centre, and horizontal lines bulge a little at the middle. And all this is so fine that exact measurements are necessary to detect the artifice. Greek architects discovered that, to produce a harmonious whole, it is necessary to avoid geometrical lines which would appear stiff, and take account of illusions in perspective. "The aim of the architect," says a Greek writer, "is to invent processes for deluding the sight."

Greek artists wrought conscientiously for they worked for the gods. And so their monuments are elaborated in all their parts, even in those that are least in view, and are constructed so solidly that they

[1] Boutmy, "Philosophie de l'Architecture en Grèce."

exist to this day if they have not been violently destroyed. The Parthenon was still intact in the seventeenth century. An explosion of gunpowder wrecked it.

The architecture of the Greeks was at once solid and elegant, simple and scientific. Their temples have almost all disappeared; here and there are a very few,[1] wholly useless, in ruins, with roofs fallen in, often nothing left but rows of columns. And yet, even in this state, they enrapture those who behold them.

Sculpture.—Among the Egyptians and the Assyrians sculpture was hardly more than an accessory ornament of their edifices; the Greeks made it the principal art. Their most renowned artists, Phidias, Praxiteles, and Lysippus, were sculptors.

They executed bas-reliefs to adorn the walls of a temple, its façade or its pediment. Of this style of work is the famous frieze of the Panathenaic procession which was carved around the Parthenon, representing young Athenian women on the day of the great festival of the goddess.[2]

They sculptured statues for the most part, of which some represented gods and served as idols; others represented athletes victorious in the great games, and these were the recompense of his victory.

The most ancient statues of the Greeks are stiff and rude, quite similar to the Assyrian sculptures. They are often colored. Little by little they become graceful and elegant. The greatest works are those of Phidias in the fifth century and of Praxiteles in the

[1] The most noted are the Parthenon at Athens and the temple of Poseidon at Pæstum, in south Italy.

[2] Knights and other subjects were also shown.—ED.

fourth. The statues of the following centuries are more graceful, but less noble and less powerful.

There were thousands of statues in Greece,[1] for every city had its own, and the sculptors produced without cessation for five centuries. Of all this multitude there remain to us hardly fifteen complete statues. Not a single example of the masterpieces celebrated among the Greeks has come down to us. Our most famous Greek statues are either copies, like the Venus of Milo, or works of the period of the decadence, like the Apollo of the Belvidere.[2] Still there remains enough, uniting the fragments of statues and of bas-reliefs which are continually being discovered,[3] to give us a general conception of Greek sculpture.

Greek sculptors sought above everything else to represent the most beautiful bodies in a calm and noble attitude. They had a thousand occasions for viewing beautiful bodies of men in beautiful poses, at the gymnasium, in the army, in the sacred dances and choruses. They studied them and learned to reproduce them; no one has ever better executed the human body.

Usually in a Greek statue the head is small, the face without emotion and dull. The Greeks did not seek, as we do, the expression of the face; they strove for beauty of line and did not sacrifice the limbs for the head. In a Greek statue it is the whole body that is beautiful.

[1] Even in the second century after the Romans had pillaged Greece to adorn their palaces, there were many thousands of statues in the Greek cities.

[2] It is not certain that the Apollo Belvidere was not a Roman copy.

[3] In the ruins of Olympia has been found a statue of Hermes, the work of Praxiteles.

Pottery.—The Greeks came to make pottery a real art. They called it Ceramics (the potter's art), and this name is still preserved. Pottery had not the same esteem in Greece as the other arts, but for us it has the great advantage of being better known than the others. While temples and statues fell into ruin, the achievements of Greek potters are preserved in the tombs. This is where they are found today. Already more than 20,000 specimens have been collected in all the museums of Europe. They are of two sorts:

1. Painted vases, with black or red figures, of all sizes and every form;

2. Statuettes of baked earth; hardly known twenty years ago, they have now attained almost to celebrity since the discovery of the charming figurines of Tanagra in Bœotia. The most of them are little idols, but some represent children or women.

Painting.—There were illustrious painters in Greece—Zeuxis, Parrhasius, and Apelles. We know little of them beyond some anecdotes, often doubtful, and some descriptions of pictures. To obtain an impression of Greek painting we are limited to the frescoes found in the houses of Pompeii, an Italian city of the first century of our era. This amounts to the same as saying we know nothing of it.

CHAPTER XV

THE GREEKS IN THE ORIENT

ASIA BEFORE ALEXANDER

Decadence of the Persian Empire.—The Greeks, engaged in strife, ceased to attack the Great King; they even received their orders from him. But the Persian empire still continued to become enfeebled. The satraps no longer obeyed the government; each had his court, his treasure, his army, made war according to his fancy, and in short, became a little king in his province. When the Great King desired to remove a satrap, he had scarcely any way of doing it except by assassinating him. The Persians themselves were no longer that nation before which all the Asiatic peoples were wont to tremble. Xenophon, a Greek captain, who had been in their pay, describes them as follows: "They recline on tapestries wearing gloves and furs. The nobles, for the sake of the pay, transform their porters, their bakers, and cooks into knights—even the valets who served them at table, dressed them or perfumed them. And so, although their armies were large, they were of no service, as is apparent from the fact that their enemies traversed the empire more freely than their friends. They no longer dared to fight. The infantry as formerly was equipped with buckler, sword, and axe, but they had no courage to use them. The drivers of chariots before facing the enemy basely allowed themselves to be overthrown at once or leaped down from the cars, so that these being no longer under control injured the Persians more than the enemy. For the rest, the Persians do not disguise their military weakness, they concede their inferiority and do not dare to take the field except there are Greeks in their army. They have for their maxim 'never to fight Greeks without Greek auxiliaries on their side.' "

Expedition of the Ten Thousand.—This weakness was very apparent when in 400 Cyrus, brother of the Great King Artaxerxes, marched against him to secure his throne. There were then some thousands of adventurers or Greek exiles who hired themselves as mercenaries. Cyrus retained ten thousand of them. Xenophon, one of their number, has written the story of their expedition.

This army crossed the whole of Asia even to the Euphrates without resistance from any one.[1] They at last came to battle near Babylon. The Greeks according to their habit broke into a run, raising the war-cry. The barbarians took flight before the Greeks had come even within bow-shot. The Greeks followed in pursuit urging one another to keep ranks.

[1] An episode told by Xenophon shows what fear the Greeks inspired. One day, to make a display before the queen of Cilicia, Cyrus had his Greeks drawn up in battle array. "They all had their brazen helmets, their tunics of purple, their gleaming shields and greaves. The trumpet sounded, and the soldiers, with arms in action, began the charge; hastening their steps and raising the war-cry, they broke into a run. The barbarians were terrified; the Cilician queen fled from her chariot, the merchants of the market abandoning their goods took to flight, and the Greeks returned with laughter to their tents."

When the war-chariots attacked them, they opened their ranks and let them through. Not a Greek received the least stroke with the exception of one only who was wounded with an arrow. Cyrus was killed; his army disbanded without fighting, and the Greeks remained alone in the heart of a hostile country threatened by a large army. And yet the Persians did not dare to attack them, but treacherously killed their five generals, twenty captains, and two hundred soldiers who had come to conclude a truce.

The friendless mercenaries elected new chiefs, burned their tents and their chariots, and began their retreat. They broke into the rugged mountains of Armenia, and notwithstanding famine, snow, and the arrows of the natives who did not wish to let them pass, they came to the Black Sea and returned to Greece after traversing the whole Persian empire. At their return (399) their number amounted still to 8,000.

Agesilaus.—Three years after, Agesilaus, king of Sparta, with a small army invaded the rich country of Asia Minor, Lydia, and Phrygia. He fought the satraps and was about to invade Asia when the Spartans ordered his return to fight the armies of Thebes and Athens. Agesilaus was the first of the Greeks to dream of conquering Persia. He was distressed to see the Greeks fighting among themselves. When they announced to him the victory at Corinth where but eight Spartans had perished and 10,000 of the enemy, instead of rejoicing he sighed and said, "Alas, unhappy Greece, to have lost enough men to have subjugated all the barbarians!" He refused one day to destroy a Greek city. "If we exterminate all the Greeks who fail of their duty," said he, "where shall we find the men to vanquish the barbarians?" This feeling was rare at that time. In relating these words of Agesilaus Xenophon, his biographer, exclaims, "Who else regarded it as a misfortune to conquer when he was making war on peoples of his own race?"

CONQUEST OF ASIA BY ALEXANDER

Macedon.—Sparta and Athens, exhausted by a century of wars, had abandoned the contest against the king of Persia. A new people resumed it and brought it to an end; these were the Macedonians. They were a very rude people, crude, similar to the ancient Dorians, a people of shepherds and soldiers. They lived far to the north of Greece in two great valleys that opened to the sea. The Greeks had little regard for them, rating them as half barbarians; but since the kings of Macedon called themselves sons of Herakles they had been permitted to run their horses in the races of the Olympian games. This gave them standing as Greeks.

Philip of Macedon.—These kings ruling in the interior, remote from the sea, had had but little part in the wars of the Greeks. But in 359 B.C. Philip ascended the throne of Macedon, a man young, active, bold, and ambitious. Philip had three aims:

1. To develop a strong army;
2. To conquer all the ports on the coast of Macedon;

3. To force all the other Greeks to unite under his command against the Persians.

He consumed twenty-four years in fulfilling these purposes and succeeded in all. The Greeks let him alone, often even aided him; in every city he bribed partisans who spoke in his favor. "No fortress is impregnable," said he, "if only one can introduce within it a mule laden with gold." And by these means he took one after another all the cities of northern Greece.

Demosthenes.—The most illustrious opponent of Philip was the orator Demosthenes. The son of an armorer, he was left an orphan at the age of seven, and his guardians had embezzled a part of his fortune. As soon as he gained his majority he entered a case against them and compelled them to restore the property. He studied the orations of Isæus and the history of Thucydides which he knew by heart. But when he spoke at the public tribune he was received with shouts of laughter; his voice was too feeble and his breath too short. For several years he labored to discipline his voice. It is said that he shut himself up for months with head half shaved that he might not be tempted to go out, that he declaimed with pebbles in his mouth, and on the sea-shore, in order that his voice might rise above the uproar of the crowd. When he reappeared on the tribune, he was master of his voice, and, as he preserved the habit of carefully preparing all his orations, he became the most finished and most potent orator of Greece.

The party that then governed Athens, whose chief was Phocion, wished to maintain the peace: Athens had neither soldiers nor money enough to withstand the king of Macedon. "I should counsel you to make war," said Phocion, "when you are ready for it." Demosthenes, however, misunderstood Philip, whom he regarded as a barbarian; he placed himself at the service of the party that wished to make war on him and employed all his eloquence to move the Athenians from their policy of peace. For fifteen years he seized every occasion to incite them to war; many of his speeches have no other object than an attack on Philip. He himself called these Philippics, and there are three of them. (The name Olynthiacs has been applied to the orations delivered with the purpose of enlisting the Athenians in the aid of Olynthus when it was besieged by Philip.) The first Philippic is in 352. "When, then, O Athenians, will you be about your duty? Will you always roam about the public places asking one of another: What is the news? Ah! How can there be anything newer than the sight of a Macedonian conquering Athens and dominating Greece? I say, then, that you ought to equip fifty galleys and resolve, if necessary, to man them yourselves. Do not talk to me of an army of 10,000 or of 20,000 aliens that exists only on paper. I would have only citizen soldiers."

In the third Philippic (341) Demosthenes calls to the minds of the Athenians the progress made by Philip, thanks to their inaction. "When the Greeks once abused their power to oppress others, all Greece rose to prevent this injustice; and yet today we suffer an unworthy Macedonian, a barbarian of a hated race, to destroy Greek cities, celebrate the Pythian games, or have them celebrated by his slaves. And the Greeks look on without doing anything, just as one sees hail falling while he prays that it may not touch him. You let him increase his power without taking a step to stop it, each regarding it as so much time gained when he is destroying another, instead of planning and working for the safety of Greece, when everybody knows that the disaster will end with the inclusion of the most remote."

At last, when Philip had taken Elatea on the borders of Bœotia, the Athenians, on the advice of Demosthenes, determined to make war and to send envoys to Thebes. Demosthenes was at the head of the embassy; he met at Thebes an envoy come from Philip; the Thebans hesitated. Demosthenes besought them to bury the old enmities and to think only of the safety of Greece, to defend its honor and its liberty. He persuaded them to an alliance with Athens and to undertake the war. A battle was fought at Chæronea in Bœotia, Demosthenes, then at the age of forty-eight, serving as a private hoplite. But the army of the Athenians and Thebans, levied in haste, was not equal to the veterans of Philip and was thrown into rout.

The Macedonian Supremacy.—Philip, victorious at Chæronea, placed a garrison in Thebes and offered peace to Athens. He then entered the Peloponnesus and was received as a liberator among the peoples whom Sparta had oppressed. From this time he met with no resistance. He came to Corinth and assembled delegates from all the Greek states (337)[1] except Sparta.

[1] There were two assemblies in Corinth—the first in 338, the second in 337.—ED.

Here Philip published his project of leading a Greek army to the invasion of Persia. The delegates approved the proposition and made a general confederation of all the Greek states. Each city was to govern itself and to live at peace with its neighbors. A general council was initiated to prevent wars, civil dissensions, proscriptions, and confiscations.

This confederacy made an alliance with the king of Macedon and conferred on him the command of all the Greek troops and navies. Every Greek was prohibited making war on Philip on pain of banishment.

Alexander.—Philip of Macedon was assassinated in 336. His son Alexander was then twenty years old. Like all the Greeks of good family he was accustomed to athletic exercises, a vigorous fighter, an excellent horseman (he alone had been able to master Bucephalus, his war-horse). But at the same time he was informed in politics, in eloquence, and in natural history, having had as teacher from his thirteenth to his seventeenth year Aristotle, the greatest scholar of Greece. He read the Iliad with avidity, called this the guide to the military art, and desired to imitate its heroes. He was truly born to conquer, for he loved to fight and was ambitious to distinguish himself. His father said to him, "Macedon is too small to contain you."

The Phalanx.—Philip left a powerful instrument of conquest, the Macedonian army, the best that Greece had seen. It comprised the phalanx of infantry and a corps of cavalry.

The phalanx of Macedonians was formed of 16,000 men ranged with 1,000 in front and 16 men deep. Each had a sarissa, a spear about twenty feet in length.

On the field of battle the Macedonians, instead of marching on the enemy facing all in the same direction, held themselves in position and presented their pikes to the enemy on all sides, those in the rear couching their spears above the heads of the men of the forward ranks. The phalanx resembled "a monstrous beast bristling with iron," against which the enemy was to throw itself. While the phalanx guarded the field of battle, Alexander charged the enemy at the head of his cavalry. This Macedonian cavalry was a distinguished body formed of young nobles.

Departure of Alexander.—Alexander started in the spring of 334 with 30,000 infantry (the greater part of these Macedonians) and 4,500 knights; he carried only seventy talents (less than eighty thousand dollars) and supplies for forty days. He had to combat not only the crowd of ill-armed peoples such as Xerxes had brought together, but an army of 50,000 Greeks enrolled in the service of the Great King under a competent general, Memnon of Rhodes. These Greeks might have withstood the invasion of Alexander, but Memnon died and his army dispersed. Alexander, delivered from his only dangerous opponent, conquered the Persian empire in two years.

Victories of Granicus, Issus, and Arbela.—Three victories gave the empire to Alexander. In Asia Minor he overthrew the Persian troops stationed behind the river Granicus (May, 333). At Issus, in the ravines of Cilicia, he routed King Darius and his army of 600,000 men (November, 333). At Arbela, near the Tigris, he scattered and massacred a still more numerous army (331).

This was a repetition of the Median wars. The Persian army was ill equipped and knew nothing of manœuvring; it was embarrassed with its mass of soldiers, valets, and baggage. The picked troops alone gave battle, the rest were scattered and massacred. Between the battles the conquest was only a triumphal progress. Nobody resisted (except the city of Tyre, commercial rival of the Greeks); what cared the peoples of the empire whether they were subject to Darius or Alexander? Each victory gave Alexander the whole of the country: the Granicus opened Asia Minor, Issus Syria and Egypt, Arbela the rest of the empire.

Death of Alexander.—Master now of the Persian empire Alexander regarded himself as the heir of the Great King. He assumed Persian dress, adopted the ceremonies of the Persian court and compelled his Greek generals to prostrate themselves before him according to Persian usage. He married a woman of the land and united eighty of his officers to daughters of the Persian nobles. He aimed to extend his empire to the farthest limits of the ancient kings and advanced even to India, warring with the combative natives. After his return with his army to Babylon (324), he died at the age of thirty-three, succumbing to a fever of brief duration (323).

Projects of Alexander.—It is very difficult to know exactly what Alexander's purposes were. Did he conquer for the mere pleasure of it? Or did he have a plan? Did he wish to fuse into one all the peoples of his empire? Was he following the example already set him by Persia? Or did he, perhaps, imitate the

Great King simply for vain-glory? And so of his intentions we know nothing. But his acts had great results. He founded seventy cities—many Alexandrias in Egypt, in Tartary, and even in India. He distributed to his subjects the treasures that had been uselessly hoarded in the chests of the Great King. He stimulated Greek scholars to study the plants, the animals, and the geography of Asia. But what is of special importance, he prepared the peoples of the Orient to receive the language and customs of the Greeks. This is why the title "Great" has been assigned to Alexander.

THE HELLENES IN THE ORIENT

Dissolution of the Empire of Alexander.—Alexander had united under one master all the ancient world from the Adriatic to the Indus, from Egypt to the Caucasus. This vast empire endured only while he lived. Soon after his death his generals disputed as to who should succeed him; they made war on one another for twenty years, at first under the pretext of supporting some one of the house of Alexander—his brother, his son, his mother, his sisters or one of his wives, later openly in their own names.

Each had on his side a part of the Macedonian army or some of the Greek mercenary soldiers. The Greeks were thus contending among themselves who should possess Asia. The inhabitants were indifferent in these wars as they had been in the strife between the Greeks and the Persians. When the war ceased, there remained but three generals; from the empire of Alexander each of them had carved for himself a great kingdom: Ptolemy had Egypt, Seleucus Syria, Lysimachus Macedonia. Other smaller kingdoms were already separated or detached themselves later: in Europe Epirus; in Asia Minor, Pontus, Bithynia, Galatia, Cappadocia, Pergamos; in Persia, Bactriana and Parthia. Thus the empire of Alexander was dismembered.

The Hellenistic Kingdoms.—In these new kingdoms the king was a Greek; accustomed to speak Greek, to adore the Greek gods, and to live in Greek fashion, he preserved his language, his religion, and his customs. His subjects were Asiatics, that is to say, barbarians; but he sought to maintain a Greek court about him; he recruited his army with Greek mercenaries, his administrative officers were Greeks, he invited to his court Greek poets, scholars, and artists.

Already in the time of the Persian kings there were many Greeks in the empire as colonists, merchants, and especially soldiers. The Greek kings attracted still more of these. They came in such numbers that at last the natives adopted the costume, the religion, the manners, and even the language of the Greeks. The Orient ceased to be Asiatic, and became Hellenic. The Romans found here in the first century B.C. only peoples like the Greeks and who spoke Greek.[1]

Alexandria.—The Greek kings of Egypt, descendants of Ptolemy,[2] accepted the title of Pharaoh held by the ancient kings, wore the diadem, and, like the earlier sovereigns, had themselves worshipped as

[1] The Gospels and the Acts of the Apostles composed in Asia Minor were written in Greek.

[2] They were called Lagidæ from the father of Ptolemy I.

children of the Sun. But they surrounded themselves with Greeks and founded their capital on the edge of the sea in a Greek city, Alexandria, a new city established by the order of Alexander.

Built on a simple plan, Alexandria was more regular than other Greek cities. The streets intersected at right angles; a great highway 100 feet broad and three and one-half miles in length traversed the whole length of the city. It was bordered with great monuments—the Stadium where the public games were presented, the Gymnasium, the Museum, and the Arsineum. The harbor was enclosed with a dike nearly a mile long which united the mainland to the island of Pharos. At the very extremity of this island a tower of marble was erected, on the summit of which was maintained a fire always burning to guide the mariners who wished to enter the port. Alexandria superseded the Phœnician cities and became the great port of the entire world.

The Museum.—The Museum was an immense edifice of marble connected with the royal palace. The kings of Egypt purposed to make of it a great scientific institution.

The Museum contained a great library.[1] The chief librarian had a commission to buy all the books that he could find. Every book that entered Egypt was brought to the library; copyists transcribed the manuscript and a copy was rendered the owner to indemnify him. Thus they collected 400,000 volumes, an

[1] The library of the Museum was burnt during the siege of Alexandria by Cæsar. But it had a successor in the Serapeum which contained 300,000 volumes. This is said to have been burnt in the seventh century by the Arabs. [The tale of the destruction of the library under orders of Omar is doubtful.—Ed.]

unheard-of number before the invention of printing. Until then the manuscripts of celebrated books were scarce, always in danger of being lost; now it was known where to find them. In the Museum were also a botanical and zoölogical garden, an astronomical observatory, a dissecting room established notwithstanding the prejudices of the Egyptians, and even a chemical laboratory.[1]

The Museum provided lodgings for scholars, mathematicians, astronomers, physicians, and grammarians. They were supported at the expense of the state; often to show his esteem for them the king dined with them. These scholars held conferences and gave lectures. Auditors came from all parts of the Greek world; it was to Alexandria that the youth were sent for instruction. In the city were nearly 14,000 students.

The Museum was at once a library, an academy, and a school—something like a university. This sort of institution, common enough among us, was before that time completely unheard of. Alexandria, thanks to its Museum, became the rendezvous for all the Orientals—Greeks, Egyptians, Jews, and Syrians; each brought there his religion, his philosophy, his science, and all were mingled together. Alexandria became and remained for several centuries the scientific and philosophical capital of the world.

Pergamum.—The kingdom of Pergamum in Asia Minor was small and weak. But Pergamum, its capital, was, like Alexandria, a city of artists and of letters. The sculptors of Pergamum constituted a cele-

[1] King Ptolemy Philadelphus who had great fear of death passed many years searching for an elixir of life.

brated school in the third century before our era.[1] Pergamum, like Alexandria, possessed a great library where King Attalus had assembled all the manuscripts of the ancient authors.

It was at Pergamum that, to replace the papyrus on which down to that time they used to write, they invented the art of preparing skins. This new paper of Pergamum was the parchment on which the manuscripts of antiquity have been preserved.

[1] There still remain to us some of the statues executed by the orders of King Attalus to commemorate his victory over the Gauls of Asia.

CHAPTER XVI

THE LAST YEARS OF GREECE

DECADENCE OF THE GREEK CITIES

Rich and Poor.—In almost all the Greek cities the domains, the shops of trade, the merchant ships, in short, all the sources of financial profit were in the hands of certain rich families. The other families, that is to say, the majority of the citizens,[1] had neither lands nor money. What, then, could a poor citizen do to gain a livelihood? Hire himself as a farmer, an artisan, or a sailor? But the proprietors already had their estates, their workshops, their merchantmen manned by slaves who served them much more cheaply than free laborers, for they fed them ill and did not pay them. Could he work on his own account? But money was very scarce; he could not borrow, since interest was at the rate of ten per cent. Then, too, custom did not permit a citizen to become an artisan. "Trade," said the philosophers, "injures the body, enfeebles the soul and leaves no leisure to engage in public affairs." "And so," says Aristotle, "a well-constituted city ought not to receive the artisan into citizenship." The citizens in Greece constituted a noble

[1] In almost all the Greek cities there was no middle class. In this regard Athens with its thirteen thousand small proprietors is a remarkable exception.

class whose only honorable functions, like the nobles of ancient France, were to govern and go to war; working with the hands was degrading. Thus by the competition of slaves and their exalted situation the greater part of the citizens were reduced to extreme misery.

Social Strife.—The poor governed the cities and had no means of living. The idea occurred to them to despoil the rich, and the latter, to resist them, organized associations. Then every Greek city was divided into two parties: the rich, called the minority, and the poor, called the majority or the people. Rich and poor hated one another and fought one another. When the poor got the upper hand, they exiled the rich and confiscated their goods; often they even adopted these two radical measures:

1. The abolition of debts;
2. A new partition of lands.

The rich, when they returned to power, exiled the poor. In many cities they took this oath among themselves: "I swear always to be an enemy to the people and to do them all the injury I can."

No means were found of reconciling the two parties: the rich could not persuade themselves to surrender their property; the poor were unwilling to die of hunger. According to Aristotle all revolutions have their origin in the distribution of wealth. "Every civil war," says Polybius, "is initiated to subvert wealth."

They fought savagely, as is always the case between neighbors. "At Miletus the poor were at first predominant and forced the rich to flee the city. But afterwards, regretting that they had not killed them all, they took the children of the exiles, assembled them in barns and had them trodden under the feet of cattle. The rich reëntered the city and became masters of it. In their turn they seized the children of the poor, coated them with pitch, and burned them alive."

Democracy and Oligarchy.—Each of the two parties —rich and poor—had its favorite form of government and set it in operation when the party held the city. The party of the rich was the Oligarchy which gave the government into the hands of a few people. That of the poor was the Democracy which gave the power to an assembly of the people. Each of the two parties maintained an understanding with the similar party in the other cities. Thus were formed two leagues which divided all the Greek cities: the league of the rich, or Oligarchy, the league of the poor, or Democracy. This régime began during the Peloponnesian War. Athens supported the democratic party, Sparta the oligarchic. The cities in which the poor had the sovereignty allied themselves with Athens; the cities where the rich governed, with Sparta. Thus at Samos when the poor gained supremacy they slew two hundred of the rich, exiled four hundred of them, and confiscated their lands and houses. Samos then adopted a democratic government and allied itself with Athens. The Spartan army came to besiege Samos, bringing with it the rich exiles of Samos who wished to return to the city by force. The city was captured, set up an oligarchy, and joined the league of Sparta.

The Tyrants.—At length, the poor perceived that the democratic form of government did not give them strength enough to maintain the contest. In most of the cities they consented to receive a chief. This chief was called Tyrant. He governed as master without obeying any law, condemning to death, and confiscating property at will. Mercenames defended him against his enemies. The following anecdote represents the policy of the tyrants: "Periander, tyrant of Corinth, sent one day to Thrasybulus, tyrant of Miletus, to ask what conduct he ought to follow in order to govern with safety. Thrasybulus led the envoy into the field and walked with him through the wheat, striking off with his staff all heads that were higher than the others. He sent off the envoy without further advice. The messenger took him for a fool, but Periander understood: Thrasybulus was counselling him to slay the principal citizens.

Everywhere the rich were killed by the tyrant and their goods confiscated; often the wealth was distributed among the poor. This is why the populace always sustained the tyrant.

There were tyrants in Greece from the sixth century; some, like Pisistratus, Polycrates, and Pittacus, were respected for their wisdom. At that time every man was called tyrant who exercised absolute power outside the limits of the constitution; it was not a title of reproach.

But when the tyrants made incessant warfare on the rich they became sanguinary and so were detested. Their situation is depicted in the famous story of Damocles. This Damocles said to Dionysius, tyrant of Syracuse, "You are the happiest of men." "I will show you the delight of being a tyrant," replied Dionysius. He had Damocles served with a sumptuous feast and ordered his servants to show the guest the same honors as to himself. During the feast Damocles raised his eyes and perceived a sword suspended to the ceiling held only by a horse hair, and hanging directly over his head. The comparison was a striking one—the tyrant's life hung only by a thread. The rich, his enemies, watched for an opportunity to cut it, for it was regarded as praiseworthy to assassinate a tyrant. This danger irritated him and made him suspicious and cruel. He dared not trust anybody, believed himself secure only after the massacre of all his enemies, and condemned the citizens to death on the slightest suspicion. Thus the name tyrant became a synonym of injustice.

Exhaustion of Greece.—The civil wars between rich and poor continued for nearly three centuries (430-150 B.C.). Many citizens were massacred, a greater number exiled. These exiles wandered about in poverty. Knowing no trade but that of a soldier, they entered as mercenaries into the armies of Sparta, Athens, the Great King, the Persian satraps—in short, of anybody who would hire them. There were 50,000 Greeks in the service of Darius against Alexander. It was seldom that such men returned to their own country.

Thus the cities lost their people. At the same time families became smaller, many men preferring not to marry or raise children, others having but one or two. "Is not this," says Polybius, "the root of the evil, that of these two children war or sickness removes one, then the home becomes deserted and the city enfeebled?" A time came when there were no longer enough citizens in the towns to resist a conqueror.

THE ROMAN CONQUEST

The Greek Leagues.—The most discerning of the Greeks commenced to see the danger during the second war of Rome with Carthage. In an assembly held at Naupactus in 207 B.C. a Greek orator said, "Turn your eyes to the Occident; the Romans and Carthaginians are disputing something else than the possession of Italy. A cloud is forming on that coast, it increases, and impends over Greece."[1]

The Greek cities at this time grouped themselves in two leagues hostile to each other. Two little peoples, the Ætolians and Achæans, had the direction of them; they commanded the armies and determined on peace and war, just as Athens and Sparta once did. Each league supported in the Greek states one of the two political parties—the Ætolian League the democratic, the Achæan League[2] the oligarchical.

The Roman Allies.—Neither of the two leagues was strong enough to unite all the Greek states. The Romans then appeared. Philip, the king of Macedon (197), and later Antiochus,[3] the king of Syria (193-169), made war on them. Both were beaten. Rome destroyed their armies and made them surrender their fleets.

[1] Polybius, v., 104.

[2] The Achæan league had illustrious leaders. In the third century, Aratus, who for twenty-seven years (251–224) traversed Greece, expelling tyrants, recalling the rich and returning to them their property and the government; in the second century Philopœmen, who fought the tyrants of Sparta and died by poison.

[3] There were two kings of Syria by the name of Antiochus, between 193 and 169.—ED.

Perseus, the new king of Macedon, was conquered, made prisoner, and his kingdom overthrown (167).[1] The Greeks made no effort to unite for the common defence; rich and poor persisted in their strife, and each hated the other more than the foreigner. The democratic party allied itself with Macedon, the oligarchical party called in the Romans.[2] While the Theban democrats were fighting in the army of Philip, the Theban oligarchs opened the town to the Roman general. At Rhodes all were condemned to death who had acted or spoken against Rome. Even among the Achæans, Callicrates, a partisan of the Romans, prepared a list of a thousand citizens whom he accused of having been favorable to Perseus; these suspects were sent to Rome where they were held twenty years without trial.

The Last Fight.—The Romans were not at first introduced as enemies. In 197 the consul Flamininus, after conquering the king of Macedon, betook himself to the Isthmus of Corinth and before the Greeks assembled to celebrate the games, proclaimed that "all the Greek peoples were free." The crowd in transports of joy approached Flamininus to thank him; they wished to salute their liberator, see his form, touch his hand; crowns and garlands were cast upon him. The pressure upon him was so great that he was nearly suffocated.

[1] The decisive battle (Pydna) was fought in 168. Perseus walked in the triumph of Paullus the next year.—ED.

[2] The party policies of the Greeks of this period were hardly so clearly drawn as the above would seem to indicate. Thus the Achæan League allied itself with Macedon against the Ætolians and against Sparta. The Ætolians leagued with the Romans against Macedon.—ED.

The Romans seeing themselves in control soon wished to command. The rich freely recognized their sovereignty; Rome served them by shattering the party of the poor. This endured for forty years. At last in 147, Rome being engaged with Carthage, the democratic party gained the mastery in Greece and declared war on the Romans. A part of the Greeks were panic-stricken; many came before the Roman soldiers denouncing their compatriots and themselves; others betook themselves to a safe distance from the cities; some hurled themselves into wells or over precipices. The leaders of the opposition confiscated the property of the rich, abolished debts, and gave arms to the slaves. It was a desperate contest. Once overcome, the Achæans reassembled an army and marched to the combat with their wives and children. The general Diœus shut himself in his house with his whole family and set fire to the building. Corinth had been the centre of the resistance; the Romans entered it, massacred the men, and sold the women and children as slaves. The city full of masterpieces of art was pillaged and burnt; pictures of the great painters were thrown into the dust, Roman soldiers lying on them and playing at dice.

THE HELLENES IN THE OCCIDENT

Influence of Greece on Rome.—The Romans at the time of their conquest of the Greeks were still only soldiers, peasants, and merchants; they had no statues, monuments, literature, science, or philosophy. All this was found among the Greeks. Rome sought to imitate these, as the Assyrian conquerors imitated the Chaldeans, as the Persians did the Assyrians. The Romans kept their costume, tongue, and religion, and never confused these with those of the Greeks. But thousands of Greek scholars and artists came to establish themselves in Rome and to open schools of literature and of eloquence. Later it was the fashion for the youth of the great Roman families to go as students to the schools of Athens and Alexandria. Thus the arts and science of the Greeks were gradually introduced into Rome. "Vanquished Greece overcame her savage conqueror," says Horace, the Roman poet; "she brought the arts to uncultured Latium."

Architecture.—The Romans had a national architecture. But they borrowed the column from the Greeks and often imitated their buildings. Many Roman temples resemble a Greek temple.

A wealthy Roman's house is composed ordinarily of two parts: the first, the ancient Roman house; the other is only a Greek house added to the first.

Sculpture.—The Greeks had thousands of statues, in temples, squares of the city, gymnasia, and in their dwellings. The Romans regarded themselves as the owners of everything that had belonged to the vanquished people. Their generals, therefore, removed a great number of statues, transporting them to the temples and the porticos of Rome. In the triumph of Æmilius Paullus, victor over the king of Macedon (Perseus), a notable spectacle was two hundred and fifty cars full of statues and paintings.

Soon the Romans became accustomed to adorn with

statues their theatres, council-halls, and private villas; every great noble wished to have some of them and gave commissions for them to Greek artists. Thus a Roman school of sculpture was developed which continued to imitate ancient Greek models. And so it was Greek sculpture, a little blunted and disfigured, which was spread over all the world subject to the Romans.

Literature.—The oldest Latin writer was a Greek, Livius Andronicus, a freedman, a schoolmaster, and later an actor. The first works in Latin were translations from the Greek. Livius Andronicus had translated the Odyssey and several tragedies. The Roman people took pleasure in Greek pieces and would have no others. Even the Roman authors who wrote for the theatre did nothing but translate or arrange Greek tragedies and comedies. Thus the celebrated works of Plautus and of Terence are imitations of the comedies of Menander and of Diphilus, now lost to us.

The Romans imitated also the Greek historians. For a long time it was the fashion to write history, even Roman history, in Greek.

The only great Roman poets declare themselves pupils of the Greeks. Lucretius writes only to expound the philosophy of Epicurus; Catullus imitates the poets of Alexander; Vergil, Theocritus and Homer; Horace translates the odes of the Greek lyrics.

Epicureans and Stoics.—The Romans had a practical and literal spirit, very indifferent to pure science and metaphysics. They took interest in Greek philosophy only so far as they believed it had a bearing on morals.

Epicureans and Stoics were two sects of Greek philosophers. The Epicureans maintained that pleasure is the supreme good, not sensual pleasure, but the calm and reasonable pleasure of the temperate man; happiness consists in the quiet enjoyment of a peaceful life, surrounded with friends and without concern for imaginary goods. For the Stoics the supreme good is virtue, which consists in conducting one's self according to reason, with a view to the good of the whole universe. Riches, honor, health, beauty, all the goods of earth are nothing for the wise man; even if one torture him, he remains happy in the possession of the true good.

The Romans took sides for one or the other philosophy, usually without thoroughly comprehending either. Those who passed for Epicureans spent their lives in eating and drinking and even compared themselves to swine. Those calling themselves Stoics, like Cato and Brutus, affected a rude language, a solemn demeanor and emphasized the evils of life. Nevertheless these doctrines, spreading gradually, aided in destroying certain prejudices of the Romans. Epicureans and Stoics were in harmony on two points: they disdained the ancient religion and taught that all men are equal, slaves or citizens, Greeks or barbarians. Their Roman disciples renounced in their school certain old superstitions, and learned to show themselves less cruel to their slaves, less insolent toward other peoples.

The conquest of Greece by the Romans gave the arts, letters, and morals of the Greeks currency in the west, just as the conquest of the Persian empire by the Greeks had carried their language, customs, and religion into the Orient.

CHAPTER XVII

ROME

ANCIENT PEOPLES OF ITALY

THE ETRUSCANS

Etruria.—The word Italy never signified for the ancients the same as for us: the Po Valley (Piedmont and Lombardy) was a part of Gaul. The frontier country at the north was Tuscany. The Etruscans who dwelt there have left it their name (Tusci).

Etruria was a country at once warm and humid; the atmosphere hung heavily over the inhabitants. The region on the shore of the sea where the Etruscans had most of their cities is the famous Maremma, a wonderfully fertile area, covered with beautiful forests, but where the water having no outlet forms marshes that poison the air. "In the Maremma," says an Italian proverb, "one gets rich in a year, but dies in six months."

The Etruscan People.—The Etruscans were for the ancients, and are still for us, a mysterious people. They had no resemblance to their neighbors, and doubtless they came from a distance—from Germany, Asia, or from Egypt; all these opinions have been maintained, but no one of them is demonstrated.

We are ignorant even of the language that they spoke. Their alphabet resembles that of the Greeks, but the Etruscan inscriptions present only proper names, and these are too short to furnish a key to the language.

The Etruscans established twelve cities in Tuscany, united in a confederation, each with its own fortress, its king, and its government. They had colonies on both coasts, twelve in Campania in the vicinity of Naples, and twelve more in the valley of the Po.

Etruscan Tombs.—There remain to us from the Etruscans only city walls and tombs.

When an Etruscan tomb is opened, one perceives a porch supported by columns and behind this chambers with couches, and bodies laid on these. Round about are ornaments of gold, ivory, and amber; purple cloths, utensils, and especially large painted vases. On the walls are paintings of combats, games, banquets, and fantastic scenes.

Industry and Commerce.—The Etruscans knew how to turn their fertile soil to some account, but they were for the most part mariners and traders. Like the Phœnicians they made long journeys to seek the ivory of India, amber from the Baltic, tin, the Phœnician purple, Egyptian jewels adorned with hieroglyphics, and even ostrich eggs. All these objects are found in their tombs. Their navies sailed to the south as far as Sicily. The Greeks hated them and called them "savage Tyrrhenians" or "Etruscan pirates." At this time every mariner on occasion was a pirate, and the Etruscans were especially interested to exclude the Greeks so that they might keep for themselves the trade of the west coast of Italy.

The famous Etruscan vases, which have been taken

from the tombs by the thousand to enrich our museums, were imitations of Greek vases, but manufactured by the Etruscans. They represent scenes from Greek mythology, especially the combats about Troy; the human figures are in red on a black ground.

Religion.—The Etruscans were a sombre people. Their gods were stern, often malevolent. The two most exalted gods were "the veiled deities," of whom we know nothing. Below these were the gods who hurled the lightning and these form a council of twelve gods. Under the earth, in the abode of the dead, were gods of evil omen. These are represented on the Etruscan vases. The king of the lower world, Mantus, a winged genius, sits with crown on his head and torch in his hand. Other demons armed with sword or club with serpents in their hands receive the souls of the dead; the principal of these under the name Charun (the Charon of the Greeks), an old man of hideous form, bears a heavy mallet to strike his victims. The souls of the dead (the Manes) issue from the lower world three days in the year, wandering about the earth, terrifying the living and doing them evil. Human victims are offered to appease their lust for blood. The famous gladiatorial combats which the Romans adopted had their origin in bloody sacrifices in honor of the dead.

The Augurs.—The Etruscans used to say that a little evil spirit named Tages issued one day from a furrow and revealed to the people assembled the secrets of divination. The Etruscan priests who called themselves haruspices or augurs had rules for predicting the future. They observed the entrails of victims, the thunderbolt, but especially the flight of birds (whence their name "augurs"). The augur at first with face turned to the north, holding a crooked staff in his hand, describes a line which cuts the heavens in two sections; the part to the right is favorable, to the left unfavorable. A second line cutting the first at right angles, and others parallel to these form in the heavens a square which was called the Temple. The augur regarded the birds that flew in this square: some like the eagle have a lucky significance; others like the owl presage evil.

The Etruscans predicted the future destiny of their own people. They are the only people of antiquity who did not expect that they were to persist forever. Etruria, they said, was to endure ten centuries. These centuries were not of exactly one hundred years each, but certain signs marked the end of each period. In the year 44, the year of the death of Cæsar, a comet appeared; an Etruscan haruspex stated to the Romans in an assembly of the people that this comet announced the end of the ninth century and the beginning of the tenth, the last of the Etruscan people.

Influence of the Etruscans.—The Romans, a semi-barbarous people, always imitated their more civilized neighbors, the Etruscans. They drew from them especially the forms of their religion: the costume of the priests and of the magistrates, the religious rites, and the art of divining the future from birds (the auspices). When the Romans found a city, they observe the Etruscan rites: the founder traces a square enclosure with a plough with share of bronze, drawn by a white bull and a white heifer. Men follow the founder and carefully cast the clods of earth from the side of the furrow. The whole ditch left by the plough is sacred and is not to be crossed. To allow entrance to the enclosure, it is necessary that the founder break the ditch at certain points, and he does this by lifting the plough and carrying it an instant; the interval made in this manner remains profane and it becomes the gate by which one enters. Rome itself was founded according to these rites. It was called Roma Quadrata, and it was said that the founder had killed his brother to punish him for crossing the sacred furrow. Later the limits of Roman colonies and of camps, and even the bounds of domains were always traced in conformity with religious rules and with geometrical lines.

The Roman religion was half Etruscan. The Fathers of the church were right, therefore, in calling Etruria the "Mother of Superstitions."

THE ITALIAN PEOPLE

Umbrians and Oscans.—In the rugged mountains of the Apennines, to the east and south of the Roman plain, resided numerous tribes. These peoples did not bear the same name and did not constitute a single nation. They were Umbrians, Sabines, Volscians, Æquians, Hernicans, Marsians, and Samnites. But all spoke almost the same language, worshipped the same gods, and had similar customs. Like the Persians, Hindoos, and Greeks, they were of Aryan race; secluded in their mountains, remote from strangers, they remained like the Aryans of the ancient period; they lived in groups with their herds scattered in the plains;

they had no villages nor cities. Fortresses erected on the mountains defended them in time of war. They were brave martial people, of simple and substantial manners. They later constituted the strength of the Roman armies. A proverb ran: "Who could vanquish the Marsians without the Marsians?"

The Sacred Spring.—In the midst of a pressing danger, the Sabines, according to a legend, believing their gods to be angry, decided to appease their displeasure by sacrificing to the god of war and of death everything that was born during a certain spring. This sacrifice was called a "Sacred Spring." All the children born in this year belonged to the god. Arrived at the age of manhood, they left the country and journeyed abroad. These exiles formed several groups, each taking for guide one of the sacred animals of Italy, a woodpecker, a wolf, or a bull, and followed it as a messenger of the god. Where the animal halted the band settled itself. Many peoples of Italy, it was said, had originated in these colonies of emigrants and still preserved the name of the animal which had led their ancestors. Such were, the Hirpines (people of the wolf), the Picentines (people of the woodpecker), and the Samnites whose capital was named Bovianum (city of the ox).

The Samnites.—The Samnites were the most powerful of all. Settled in the Abruzzi, a paradise for brigands, they descended into the fertile plains of Naples and of Apulia and put Etruscan and Greek towns to ransom.

The Samnites fought against the Romans for two centuries; although always beaten because they had no central administration and no discipline they yet re-opened the war. Their last fight was heroic. An old man brought to the chiefs of the army a sacred book written on linen. They formed in the interior of the camp a wall of linen, raised an altar in the midst of it, and around this stood soldiers with unsheathed swords. One by one the bravest of the warriors entered the precinct. They swore not to flee before the enemy and to kill the fugitives. Those who took the oath, to the number of 16,000, donned linen garments. This was the "linen legion"; it engaged in battle, and was slaughtered to the last man.

The Greeks of Italy.—All south Italy was covered with Greek colonies, some, like Sybaris, Croton, and Tarentum, very populous and powerful. But the Greeks did not venture on the Roman coast for fear of the Etruscans. Except the city of Cumæ the Greek colonies down to the third century had almost no relations with the Romans.

The Latins.—The Latins dwelt in the country of hills and ravines to the south of the Tiber, called today the Roman Campagna. They were a small people, their territory comprising no more than one hundred square miles. They were of the same race as the other Italians, similar to them in language, religion, and manners, but slightly more advanced in civilization. They cultivated the soil and built strong cities. They separated themselves into little independent peoples. Each people had its little territory, its city, and its government. This miniature state was called a city. Thirty Latin cities had formed among themselves a religious association analogous to the Greek amphictyonies.

Every year they celebrated a common festival, when their delegates, assembled at Alba, sacrificed a bull in honor of their common god, the Latin Jupiter.

Rome.—On the frontier of Latium, on the borders of Etruria, in the marshy plain studded with hills that followed the Tiber, rose the city of Rome, the centre of the Roman people scattered in the plain. The land was malarial and dreary; but the situation was good. The Tiber served as a barrier against the enemy from Etruria, the hills were fortresses. The sea was but six leagues away, far enough to escape fear of pirates, and near enough to permit the transportation of merchandise. The port of Ostia at the mouth of the Tiber was a suburb of Rome, as Piræus was of Athens. The locality was therefore agreeable to a people of soldiers and merchants.

Roma Quadrata and the Capitol.—Of the first centuries of Rome we know only some legends, and the Romans knew no more than we. Rome, they said, was a little square town, limited to the Palatine Hill. The founder whom they called Romulus had according to the Etruscan forms traced the circuit with the plough. Every year, on the 21st of April, the Romans celebrated the anniversary of these ceremonies: a procession marched about the primitive enclosure and a priest fixed a nail in a temple in commemoration of it. It was calculated that the founding had occurred in the year 754[1] B.C.

On the other hills facing the Palatine other small cities rose. A band of Sabine mountaineers established themselves on the Capitoline, a group of Etrus-

[1] Rather 753 B.C.—ED.

can adventurers[1] on Mount Cœlius; perhaps there were still other peoples. All these small settlements ended with uniting with Rome on the Palatine. A new wall was built to include the seven hills. The Capitol was then for Rome what the Acropolis was for Athens: here rose the temples of the three protecting deities of the city—Jupiter, Juno, and Minerva, and the citadel that contained the treasure and the archives of the people. In laying the foundations, it was said there was found a human head recently cleft from the body; this head was a presage that Rome should become the head of the world.

[1] There were three tribes in old Rome, the Ramnes on the Palatine, the Tities or Sabines on the Capitoline, and the Luceres; but whether the last were Etruscans or Ramnians or neither is uncertain.—Ed.

CHAPTER XVIII

ROMAN RELIGION

The Roman Gods.—The Romans, like the Greeks, believed that everything that occurs in the world was the work of a deity. But in place of a God who directs the whole universe, they had a deity for every phenomenon which they saw. There was a divinity to make the seed sprout, another to protect the bounds of the fields, another to guard the fruits. Each had its name, its sex, and its functions.

The principal gods were Jupiter, god of the heaven; Janus, the two-faced god (the deity who opens); Mars, god of war; Mercury, god of trade; Vulcan, god of fire; Neptune, god of the sea; Ceres, goddess of grains, the Earth, the Moon, Juno, and Minerva.

Below these were secondary deities. Some personified a quality—for example, Youth, Concord, Health, Peace. Others presided over a certain act in life: when the infant came into the world there were a god to teach him to speak, a goddess to teach him to drink, another charged with knitting his bones, two to accompany him to school, two to take him home again. In short, there was a veritable legion of minor special deities.

Other gods protected a city, a certain section of the city, a mountain, a forest; every river, every fountain, every tree had its little local divinity. It is this that makes an old woman in a Latin romance exclaim, "Our country is so full of gods that it is much easier to find a god than a man."

Form of the Gods.—The Romans, unlike the Greeks, did not give their gods a precise form. For a long time there was no idol in Rome; they worshipped Jupiter under the form of a rock, Mars under that of a sword. It was later that they imitated the wooden statues of the Etruscans and the marbles of the Greeks. Perhaps they did not at first conceive of the gods as having human forms.

Unlike the Greeks they did not imagine marriage and kinship among their gods; they had no legends to tell of these relationships; they knew of no Olympus where the gods met together. The Latin language had a very significant word for designating the gods: they were called Manifestations. They were the manifestations of a mysterious divine power. This is why they were formless, without family relationship, without legends. Everything that was known of the gods was that each controlled a natural force and could benefit or injure men.

Principles of the Roman Religion.—The Roman was no lover of these pale and frigid abstractions; he even seemed to fear them. When he invoked them, he covered his face, perhaps that he might not see them. But he thought that they were potent and that they would render him service, if he knew how to please them. "The man whom the gods favor," says Plautus, "they cause to gain wealth."

The Roman conceives of religion as an exchange

of good offices; the worshipper brings offerings and homage; the god in return confers some advantage.[1] If after having made a present to the god the man receives nothing, he considers himself cheated. During the illness of Germanicus the people offered sacrifices for his restoration. When it was announced that Germanicus was dead, the people in their anger overturned the altars and cast the statues of the gods into the streets, because they had not done what was expected of them. And so in our day the Italian peasant abuses the saint who does not give him what he asks.

Worship.—Worship, therefore, consists in doing those things that please the gods. They are presented with fruits, milk, wine, or animal sacrifices. Sometimes the statues of the gods are brought from their temples, laid on couches, and served with a feast. As in Greece, magnificent homes (temples[2]) were built for them, and diversions were arranged for them.

Formalism.—But it is not enough that one make a costly offering to the gods. The Roman gods are punctilious as to form; they require that all the acts of worship, the sacrifices, games, dedications, shall proceed according to the ancient rules (the rites). When one desires to offer a victim to Jupiter, one must select a white beast, sprinkle salted meal on its head, and strike it with an axe; one must stand erect

[1] A legend represents King Numa debating with Jupiter the terms of a contract: "You will sacrifice a head to me?" says Jupiter. "Very well," says Numa, "the head of an onion that I shall take in my garden." "No," replies Jupiter, "but I want something that pertains to a man." "We will give you then the tip of the hair." "But it must be alive." "Then we will add to this a little fish." Jupiter laughed and consented to this.

[2] In Rome, as in Greece, the temple was called a house.

with hands raised to heaven, the abode of Jupiter, and pronounce a sacred formula. If any part of the ceremonial fails, the sacrifice is of no avail; the god, it is thought, will have no pleasure in it. A magistrate may be celebrating games in honor of the protecting deities of Rome; "if he alters a word in his formula, if a flute-player rests, if the actor stops short, the games do not conform to the rites; they must be recommenced."[1]

And so the prudent man secures the assistance of two priests, one to pronounce the formula, the other to follow the ritual accurately.

Every year the Arval Brothers, a college of priests, assemble in a temple in the environs of Rome where they perform a sacred dance and recite a prayer; this is written in an archaic language which no one any longer comprehends, so much so that at the beginning of the ceremony a written formulary must be given to each of the priests. And yet, ever since the time that they ceased to comprehend it, they continued to chant it without change. This is because the Romans hold before all to the letter of the law in dealing with their gods. This exactness in performing the prescribed ritual is for them their religion. And so they regarded themselves as "the most religious of men." "On all other points we are the inferiors or only the equals of other peoples, but we excel all in religion, that is, the worship we pay the gods."

Prayer.—When the Roman prays, it is not to lift his soul and feel himself in communion with a god, but to ask of him a service. He is concerned, then, first

[1] The remark is Cicero's.

to find the god who can render it. "It is as important," says Varro, "to know what god can aid us in a special case as to know where the carpenter and baker live." Thus one must address Ceres if one wants rich harvests, Mercury to make a fortune, Neptune to have a happy voyage. Then the suppliant dons the proper garments, for the gods love neatness; he brings an offering, for the gods love not that one should come with empty hands. Then, erect, the head veiled, the worshipper invokes the god. But he does not know the exact name of the god, for, say the Romans, "no one knows the true names of the gods." He says, then, for example, "Jupiter, greatest and best, or whatever is the name that thou preferrest . . . ." Then he proposes his request, taking care to use always the clearest expressions so that the god may make no mistake. If a libation is offered, one says, "Receive the homage of this wine that I am pouring"; for the god might think that one would present other wine and keep this back. The prayers, too, are long, verbose, and full of repetitions.

Omens.—The Romans, like the Greeks, believe in omens. The gods, they think, know the future, and they send signs that permit men to divine them. Before undertaking any act, the Roman consults the gods. The general about to engage in battle examines the entrails of victims; the magistrates before holding an assembly regards the passing birds (called "taking the auspices"). If the signs are favorable, the gods are thought to approve the enterprise; if not, they are against it. The gods often send a sign that had not been requested. Every unexpected phenomenon is the presage of an event. A comet appeared before the death of Cæsar and was thought to have announced it.

When the assembly of the people deliberates and it thunders, it is because Jupiter does not wish that anything shall be decided on that day and the assembly must dissolve. The most insignificant fact may be interpreted as a sign—a flash of lightning, a word overheard, a rat crossing the road, a diviner met on the way. And so when Marcellus had determined on an enterprise, he had himself carried in a closed litter that he might be sure of not seeing anything which could impose itself on him as a portent.

These were not the superstitions of the populace; the republic supported six augurs charged with predicting the future. It carefully preserved a collection of prophecies, the Sibylline Books. It had sacred chickens guarded by priests. No public act—assembly, election, deliberation—could be done without the taking of the auspices, that is to say, observation of the flight of birds. In the year 195 it was learned that lightning had struck a temple of Jupiter and that it had hit a hair on the head of the statue of Hercules; a governor wrote that a chicken with three feet had been hatched; the senate assembled to discuss these portents.

The Priests.—The priest in Rome, as in Greece, is not charged with the care of souls, he exists only for the service of the god. He guards his temple, administers his property, and performs the ceremonies in his honor. Thus the guild of the Salii (the leapers) watches over a shield which fell from heaven, they said, and which was adored as an idol; every year they perform a dance in arms, and this is their sole function.

The augurs predict the future. The pontiffs superintend the ceremonies of worship; they regulate the calendar and fix the festivals to be celebrated on the various days of the year.

Neither the priests, the augurs, nor the pontiffs form a separate class. They are chosen from among the great families and continue to exercise all the functions of state—judging, presiding over assemblies, and commanding armies. This is the reason that the Roman priests, potent as they were, did not constitute, as in Egypt, a sacerdotal caste. At Rome it was a state religion, but not a government by the priests.

The Dead.—The Romans, like the Hindoos and the Greeks, believed that the soul survived the body. If care were taken to bury the body according to the proper rites, the soul went to the lower world and became a god; otherwise the soul could not enter the abode of the dead, but returned to the earth terrifying the living and tormenting them until suitable burial was performed. Pliny the Younger[1] relates the story of a ghost which haunted a house and terrified to death all the inhabitants of the dwelling; a philosopher who was brave enough to follow it discovered at the place where the spectre stopped some bones which had not been buried in the proper manner. The shade of the Emperor Caligula wandered in the gardens of the palace; it was necessary to disinter the body and bury it anew in regular form.

[1] Pliny, Epistles, vii., 27. See another story in Plautus's Mostellaria.

Cult of the Dead.—It was of importance, therefore, to both the living and the dead that the rites should be observed. The family of the deceased erected a funeral pile, burned the body on it, and placed the ashes in an urn which was deposited in the tomb, a little chapel dedicated to the Manes,[1] *i.e.*, the souls that had become gods. On fixed days of the year the relatives came to the tomb to bring food; doubtless they believed that the soul was in need of nourishment, for wine and milk were poured on the earth, flesh of victims was burned, and vessels of milk and cakes were left behind. These funeral ceremonies were perpetuated for an indefinite period; a family could not abandon the souls of its ancestors, but continued to maintain their tomb and the funeral feasts. In return, these souls which had become gods loved and protected their posterity. Each family, therefore, had its guardian deities which they called Lares.

Cult of the Hearth.—Each family had a hearth, also, that it adored. For the Romans, as for the Hindoos, fire was a god and the hearth an altar. The flame was to be maintained day and night, and offerings made on the hearth of oil, fat, wine, and incense; the fire then became brilliant and rose higher as if nourished by the offering.

Before beginning his meal the Roman thanked the god of the hearth, gave him a part of the food, and poured out for him a little wine (this was the libation). Even the sceptical Horace supped with his slaves before the hearth and offered libation and prayer.

[1] The letters D.M. found on Roman tombs are the initials of Dei Manes.

Every Roman family had in its house a sanctuary where were to be found the Lares, the souls of the ancestors, and the altar of the hearth. Rome also had its sacred hearth, called Vesta, an ancient word signifying the hearth itself. Four virgins of the noblest families, the Vestals, were charged with keeping the hearth, for it was necessary that the flame should never be extinguished, and the care of it could be confided only to pure beings. If a Vestal broke her vow, she was buried alive in a cave, for she had committed sacrilege and had endangered the whole Roman people.

THE FAMILY

Religion of the Family.—All the members of a family render worship to the same ancestors and unite about the same hearth. They have therefore the same gods, and these are their peculiar possession. The sanctuary where the Lares[1] were kept was concealed in the house and no stranger was to approach it. Thus the Roman family was a little church; it had its religion and its worship to which no others than its members had access. The ancient family was very different from the modern, having its basis in the principles of religion.

Marriage.—The first rule of this religion is that one should be the issue of a regular marriage if one is to have the right of adoring the ancestors of the family. Roman marriage, therefore, is at the start a religious ceremony. The father of the bride gives her away outside the house when a procession conducts her to

[1] They were called the Penates, that is to say, the gods of the interior.

the house of the groom chanting an ancient sacred refrain, "Hymen, O Hymen!" The bride is then led before the altar of the husband where water and fire are presented, and there in the presence of the gods of the family the bride and groom divide between them a cake of meal. Marriage at this period was called confarreatio (communion through the cake). Later another form of marriage was invented. A relative of the bride in the presence of witnesses sells her to the husband who declares that he buys her for his wife. This is marriage by sale (coemptio).

For the Romans as for the Greeks marriage is a religious duty; religion ordains that the family should not become extinct. The Roman, therefore, declares when he marries that he takes his wife to perpetuate the family through their children. A noble Roman who sincerely loved his wife repudiated her because she brought him no children.

The Roman Woman.—The Roman woman is never free. As a young girl, she belongs to her father who chooses her husband for her; married, she comes under the power of her husband—the jurisconsults say she is under his "manus," *i.e.,* she is in the same position as his daughter. The woman always has a master who has the right of life and death over her. And yet, she is never treated like a slave. She is the equal in dignity of her husband; she is called the mother of the family (materfamilias) just as her husband is called the father of the family (paterfamilias). She is the mistress in the house, as he is the master. She gives orders to the slaves whom she charges with all the heavy tasks—the grinding of the grain, the making of bread, and the cooking. She sits in the seat of honor (the atrium), spins and weaves, apportions work to the slaves, watches the children, and directs the house. She is not excluded from association with the men, like the Greek woman; she eats at the table with her husband, receives visitors, goes into town to dinner, appears at the public ceremonies, at the theatre, and even at the courts. And still she is ordinarily uncultured; the Romans do not care to instruct their daughters; the quality which they most admire in woman is gravity, and on her tomb they write by way of eulogy, "She kept the house and spun linen."

The Children.—The Roman child belongs to the father like a piece of property. The father has the right of exposing him in the street. If he accepts the child, the latter is brought up at first in the house. Girls remain here until marriage; they spin and weave under the supervision of their mother. The boys walk to the fields with their father and exercise themselves in arms. The Romans are not an artistic people; they require no more of their children than that they know how to read, write, and reckon; neither music nor poetry is taught them. They are brought up to be sober, silent, modest in their demeanor, and obedient.

The Father of the Family.—The master of the house was called by the Romans the father of the family. The paterfamilias is at once the proprietor of the domain, the priest of the cult of the ancestors, and the sovereign of the family. He reigns as master in his house. He has the right of repudiating his wife, of rejecting his children, of selling them, and marrying them at his pleasure. He can take for himself all that belongs to them, everything that his wife brings to him, and everything that his children gain; for neither the wife nor the children may be proprietors. Finally he has over them all[1] the "right of life and death," that is to say, he is their only judge. If they commit crime, it is not the magistrate who punishes them, but the father of the family who condemns them. One day (186 B.C.) the Roman Senate decreed the penalty of death for all those who had participated in the orgies of the cult of Bacchus. The men were executed, but for all the women who were discovered among the guilty, it was necessary that the Senate should address itself to the fathers of families, and it was these who condemned to death their wives or their daughters. "The husband," said the elder Cato, "is the judge of the wife, he can do with her as he will; if she has committed any fault, he chastises her; if she has drunk wine, he condemns her; if she has been unfaithful to him, he kills her." When Catiline conspired against the Senate, a senator perceived that his own son had taken part in the conspiracy; he had him arrested, judged him, and condemned him to death.

The power of the father of the family endured as long as life; the son was never freed from it. Even if he became consul, he remained subject to the power of his father. When the father died, the sons became in turn fathers of families. As for the wife, she could never attain freedom; she fell under the power of the heir of her husband; she could, then, become subject to her own son.

[1] In the language of the Roman law the wife, children, and slaves "are not their own masters."

CHAPTER XIX

THE ROMAN CITY

FORMATION OF THE ROMAN PEOPLE

The Kings.—Tradition relates that Rome for two centuries and a half was governed by kings. They told not only the names of these kings and the date of their death, but the life of each.

They said there were seven kings. Romulus, the first king, came from the Latin city of Alba, founded the hamlet on the Palatine, and killed his brother who committed the sacrilege of leaping over the sacred furrow encircling the settlement; he then allied himself with Tatius, a Sabine king. (A legend of later origin added that he had founded at the foot of the hill-city a quarter surrounded with a palisade where he received all the adventurers who wished to come to him.)

Numa Pompilius, the second king, was a Sabine. It was he who organized the Roman religion, taking counsel with a goddess, the nymph Egeria who dwelt in a wood.

The third king, Tullus Hostilius, was a warrior. He made war on Alba, the capital of the Latin confederation, took and destroyed it.

Ancus Martius, the fourth king, was the grandson of Numa and built the wooden bridge over the Tiber and founded the port of Ostia through which commerce passed up the river to Rome.

The last three kings were Etruscans. Tarquin the Elder enlarged the territory of Rome and introduced religious ceremonies from Etruria. Servius Tullius organized the Roman army, admitting all the citizens without distinction of birth and separating them into centuries (companies) according to wealth. The last king, Tarquinius Superbus, oppressed the great families of Rome; some of the nobles conspired against him and succeeded in expelling him. Since this time there were no longer any kings. The Roman state, or as they said, the commonwealth (res publica) was governed by the consuls, two magistrates elected each year.

It is impossible to know how much truth there is in this tradition, for it took shape a long time after the Romans began to write their history, and it includes so many legends that we cannot accept it in its entirety.

Attempt has been made to explain these names of kings as symbols of a race or class. The early history of Rome has been reconstructed in a variety of ways, but the greater the labor applied to it, the less the agreement among students with regard to it.

The Roman People.—About the fifth century before Christ there were in Rome two classes of people, the patricians and the plebeians. The patricians were the descendants of the old families who had lived from remote antiquity on the little territory in the vicinity of the city; they alone had the right to appear in the assembly of the people, to assist in religious ceremonies, and to hold office. Their ancestors had founded the

Roman state, or as they called it, the Roman city (Civitas), and these had bequeathed it to them. And so they were the true people of Rome.

The Plebs.—The plebeians were descended from the foreigners[1] established in the city, and especially from the conquered peoples of the neighboring cities; for Rome had gradually subjected all the Latin cities and had forcibly annexed their inhabitants. Subjects and yet aliens, they obeyed the government of Rome, but they could have no part in it. They did not possess the Roman religion and could not participate in its ceremonies. They had not even the right of intermarrying with the patrician families. They were called the plebs (the multitude) and were not considered a part of the Roman people. In the old prayers we still find this formula: "For the welfare of the people and the plebs of Rome."

Strife between Patricians and Plebeians.—The people and the plebs were like two distinct peoples, one of masters, the other of subjects. And yet the plebeians were much like the patricians. Soldiers, like them, they served in the army at their own cost and suffered death in the service of the Roman people; peasants like them, they lived on their domains. Many of the plebeians were rich and of ancient family. The only difference was that they were descended from a great family of some conquered Latin city, while the patricians were the scions of an old family in the conquering city.

Tribunes of the Plebs.—One day, says the legend,

[1] Probably some of the plebeians originated in non-noble Roman families.—Ed.

the plebeians, finding themselves mistreated, withdrew under arms to a mountain, determined to break with the Roman people. The patricians in consternation sent to them Menenius Agrippa who told them the fable of the members and the stomach. The plebs consented to return but they made a treaty with the people. It was agreed that their chiefs (they called them tribunes of the plebs) should have the right of protecting the plebeians against the magistrates of the people and of prohibiting any measure against them. All that was necessary was to pronounce the word "Veto" (I forbid); this single word stopped everything; for religion prevented attacks on a tribune under penalty of being devoted to the infernal gods.

Triumph of the Plebs.—The strife between the two orders beginning at the end of the fifth century continued for two centuries (494 B.C. to about 300 B.C.).[1]

The plebeians, much more numerous and wealthy, ended by gaining the victory. They first secured the adoption of laws common to the two orders; afterward that marriage should be permitted between the patricians and the plebeians. The hardest task was to obtain the high magistracies, or, as it was said, "secure the honors." Religious scruple ordained, indeed, that before one could be named as a magistrate, the gods must be asked for their approval of the choice. This was determined by inspecting the flight of birds ("taking the auspices"). But the old Roman religion allowed the auspices to be taken only on the name

[1] We know the story of this contest only through Livy and Dionysius of Halicarnassus; their very dramatic account has become celebrated, but it is only a legend frequently altered by falsifiers.

of a patrician; it was not believed that the gods could accept a plebeian magistrate. But there were great plebeian families who were bent on being the equals of the patrician families in dignity, as they were in riches and in importance. They gradually forced the patricians to open to them all the offices, beginning with the consulship, and ending with the great pontifical office (Pontifex Maximus). The first plebeian consul was named in 366 B.C., the first plebeian pontifex maximus in 302 B.C.[1] Patricians and plebeians then coalesced and henceforth formed but one people.

THE ROMAN PEOPLE

The Right of Citizenship.—The *people* in Rome, as in Greece, is not the whole of the inhabitants, but the body of citizens. Not every man who lives in the territory is a citizen, but only he who has the right of citizenship. The citizen has numerous privileges:

1. He alone is a member of the body politic; he alone has the right of voting in the assemblies of the Roman people, of serving in the army, of being present at the religious ceremonials at Rome, of being elected a Roman magistrate. These are what were called public rights.

2. The citizen alone is protected by the Roman law; he only has the right of marrying legally, of becoming the father of a family, that is to say, of being master of his wife and his children, of making his will, of buying or selling. These were the private rights.

[1] The pontificate was opened to the plebeians by the Ogulnian Law of 300 B.C. The first plebeian pontifex maximus was in 254 B.C. Livy, Epitome, xviii.—ED.

Those who were not citizens were not only excluded from the army and the assembly, but they could not marry, could not possess the absolute power of the father, could not hold property legally, could not invoke the Roman law, nor demand justice at a Roman tribunal. Thus the citizens constituted an aristocracy amidst the other inhabitants of the city. But they were not equal among themselves; there were class differences, or, as the Romans said, ranks.

The Nobles.—In the first rank are the nobles. A citizen is noble when one of his ancestors has held a magistracy, for the magisterial office in Rome is an honor, it ennobles the occupant and also his posterity.

When a citizen becomes ædile, prætor, or consul, he receives a purple-bordered toga, a sort of throne (the curule chair), and the right of having an image made of himself. These images are statuettes, at first in wax, later in silver. They are placed in the atrium, the sanctuary of the house, near the hearth and the gods of the family; there they stand in niches like idols, venerated by posterity. When any one of the family dies, the images are brought forth and carried in the funeral procession, and a relative pronounces the oration for the dead. It is these images that ennoble a family that preserves them. The more images there are in a family, the nobler it is. The Romans spoke of those who were "noble by one image" and those who were "noble by many images."

The noble families of Rome were very few (they would not amount to 300), for the magistracies which conferred nobility were usually given to men who were already noble

The Knights.—Below the nobles were the knights. They were the rich who were not noble. Their fortune as inscribed on the registers of the treasury must amount to at least 400,000[1] sesterces. They were merchants, bankers, and contractors; they did not govern, but they grew rich. At the theatre they had places reserved for them behind the nobles.

If a knight were elected to a magistracy, the nobles called him a "new man" and his son became noble.

The Plebs.—Those who were neither nobles nor knights formed the mass of the people, the plebs. The majority of them were peasants, cultivating a little plat in Latium or in the Sabine country. They were the descendants of the Latins or the Italians who were subjugated by the Romans. Cato the Elder in his book on Agriculture gives us an idea of their manners: "Our ancestors, when they wished to eulogize a man, said 'a good workman,' 'a good farmer'; this encomium seemed the greatest of all."[2]

Hardened to work, eager for the harvest, steady and economical, these laborers constituted the strength of the Roman armies. For a long time they formed the assembly too, and dictated the elections. The nobles who wished to be elected magistrates came to the parade-ground to grasp the hand of these peasants ("prensare manus," was the common expression). A candidate, finding the hand of a laborer callous, ventured to ask him, "Is it because you walk on your

[1] This qualification was set in the last century of the republic. —Ed.

[2] He cites several of their old proverbs: "A bad farmer is one who buys what his land can raise." "It is bad economy to do in the day what can be done at night."

hands?" He was a noble of great family, but he was not elected.

The Freedmen.—The last of all the citizens are the freedmen, once slaves, or the sons of slaves. The taint of their origin remains on them; they are not admitted to service in the Roman army and they vote after all the rest.

THE GOVERNMENT OF THE REPUBLIC

The Comitia.—The government of Rome called itself a republic (Respublica), that is to say, a thing of the people. The body of citizens called the people was regarded as absolute master in the state. It is this body that elects the magistrates, votes on peace and war, and that makes the laws. "The law," say the jurisconsults, "is what the Roman people ordains." At Rome, as in Greece, the people do not appoint deputies, they pass on the business itself. Even after more than 500,000 men scattered over all Italy were admitted into the citizenship, the citizens had to go in person to Rome to exercise their rights. The people, therefore, meet at but one place; the assembly is called the Comitia.

A magistrate convokes the people and presides over the body. Sometimes the people are convoked by the blast of the trumpet and come to the parade-ground (the Campus Martius), ranging themselves by companies under their standards. This is the Comitia by centuries. Sometimes they assemble in the market-place (the forum) and separate themselves into thirty-five groups, called tribes. Each tribe in turn enters an enclosed space where it does its voting. This is the Comitia by tribes. The magistrate who convokes the assembly indicates the business on which the suffrages are to be taken, and when the assembly has voted, it dissolves. The people are sovereign, but accustomed to obey their chiefs.

The Magistrates.—Every year the people elect officials to govern them and to them they delegate absolute power. These are called magistrates (those who are masters). Lictors march before them bearing a bundle of rods and an axe, emblems of the magisterial powers of chastising and condemning to death. The magistrate has at once the functions of presiding over the popular assembly and the senate, of sitting in court, and of commanding the army; he is master everywhere. He convokes and dissolves the assembly at will, he alone renders judgment, he does with the soldiers as he pleases, putting them to death without even taking counsel with his officers. In a war against the Latins Manlius, the Roman general, had forbidden the soldiers leaving camp: his son, provoked by one of the enemy, went forth and killed him; Manlius had him arrested and executed him immediately.

According to the Roman expression, the magistrate has the power of a king; but this power is brief and divided. The magistrate is elected for but one year and he has a colleague who has the same power as himself. There are at once in Rome two consuls who govern the people and command the armies, and several prætors to serve as subordinate governors or commanders and to pronounce judgment. There are other magistrates, besides—two censors, four ædiles to supervise the public ways and the markets, ten tribunes of the plebs, and quæstors to care for the state treasure.

The Censors.—The highest of all the magistrates are the censors. They are charged with taking the census every five years, that is to say, the enumeration of the Roman people. All the citizens appear before them to declare under oath their name, the number of their children and their slaves, the amount of their fortune; all this is inscribed on the registers. It is their duty, too, to draw up the list of the senators, of the knights, and of the citizens, assigning to each his proper rank in the city. They are charged as a result with making the lustrum, a great ceremony of purification which occurs every five years.[1]

On that day all the citizens are assembled on the Campus Martius arranged in order of battle; thrice there are led around the assembly three expiatory victims, a bull, a ram, and a swine; these are killed and their blood sprinkled on the people; the city is purified and reconciled with the gods.

The censors are the masters of the registration and they rank each as they please; they may degrade a senator by striking him from the senate-list, a knight by not registering him among the knights, and a citizen by not placing his name on the registers of the tribes. It is for them an easy means of punishing those whom they regard at fault and of reaching those whom the law does not condemn. They have been known to degrade citizens for poor tillage of the soil and for having too costly an equipage, a senator because he

[1] After the completion of the census.—Ed.

possessed ten pounds of silver, another for having repudiated his wife. It is this overweening power that the Romans call the supervision of morals. It makes the censors the masters of the city.

The Senate.—The Senate is composed of about 300 persons appointed by the censor. But the censor does not appoint at random; he chooses only rich citizens respected and of high family, the majority of them former magistrates. Almost always he appoints those who are already members of the Senate, so that ordinarily one remains a senator for life. The Senate is an assembly of the principal men of Rome, hence its authority. As soon as business is presented, one of the magistrates convokes the senators in a temple, lays the question before them, and then asks "what they think concerning this matter." The senators reply one by one, following the order of dignity. This is what they call "consulting the Senate," and the judgment of the majority is a senatus consultum (decree of the Senate). This conclusion is only advisory as the Senate has no power to make laws; but Rome obeys this advice as if it were a law. The people have confidence in the senators, knowing that they have more experience than themselves; the magistrates do not dare to resist an assembly composed of nobles who are their peers. And so the Senate regulates all public business: it declares war and determines the number of the armies; it receives ambassadors and makes peace; it fixes the revenues and the expenses. The people ratify these measures and the magistrates execute them. In 200 B.C. the Senate decided on war with the king of Macedon, but the people in terror refused to approve it: the Senate then ordered a magistrate to convoke the comitia anew and to adopt a more persuasive speech. This time the people voted for the war. In Rome it was the people who reigned, just as is the case with the king in England, but it was the Senate that governed.

The Offices.—Being magistrate or senator in Rome is not a profession. Magistrates or senators spend their time and their money without receiving any salary. A magistracy in Rome is before all an honor. Entrance to it is to nobles, at most to knights, but always to the rich; but these come to the highest magistracies only after they have occupied all the others. The man who aims one day to govern Rome must serve in the army during ten campaigns. Then he may be elected quæstor and he receives the administration of the state treasury. After this he becomes ædile, charged with the policing of the city and with the provision of the corn supply. Later he is elected prætor and gives judgment in the courts. Later yet, elected consul, he commands an army and presides over the assemblies. Then only may he aspire to the censorship. This is the highest round of the ladder and may be reached hardly before one's fiftieth year. The same man has therefore, been financier, administrator, judge, general, and governor before arriving at this original function of censor, the political distribution of the Roman people. This series of offices is what is called the "order of the honors." Each of these functions lasts but one year, and to rise to the one next higher a new election is necessary. In the year which precedes the voting one must show one's self continually in the streets, "circulate" as the Romans say (*ambire:* hence the word "ambition"), to solicit the suffrages of the people. For all this time it is the custom to wear a white toga, the very sense of the word "candidate" (white garment).

CHAPTER XX

ROMAN CONQUEST

THE ROMAN ARMY

Military Service.—To be admitted to service in the Roman army one must be a Roman citizen. It is necessary to have enough wealth to equip one's self at one's own expense, for the state furnishes no arms to its soldiers; down to 402 B.C. it did not even pay them. And so only those citizens are enrolled who are provided with at least a small fortune. The poor (called the proletariat) are exempt from service, or rather, they have no right to serve. Every citizen who is rich enough to be admitted to the army owes the state twenty campaigns; until these are completed the man remains at the disposition of the consul and this from the age of seventeen to forty-six. In Rome, as in the Greek cities, every man is at once citizen and soldier. The Romans are a people of small proprietors disciplined in war.

The Levy.—When there was need of soldiers, the consul ordered all the citizens qualified for service to assemble at the Capitol. There the officers elected by the people chose as many men as were necessary to form the army. This was the enrolment (the Romans called it the Choice); then came the military oath. The officers first took the oath, and then the rank and file; they swore to obey their general, to follow him wherever he led them and to remain under the standards until he released them from their oath. One man pronounced the formula and each in turn advanced and said, "I also." From this time the army was bound to the general by the bonds of religion.

Legions and Allies.—The Roman army was at first called the Legion (levy). When the people increased in number, instead of one legion, several were formed.

The legion was a body of 4,200 to 5,000 men, all Roman citizens. The smallest army had always at least one legion, every army commanded by a consul had at least two. But the legions constituted hardly a half of the Roman army. All the subject peoples in Italy were required to send troops, and these soldiers, who were called allies, were placed under the orders of Roman officers. In a Roman army the allies were always a little more numerous than the citizens of the legions. Ordinarily with four legions (16,800 men) there were enrolled 20,000 archers and 40,000 horse from the allies. In the Second Punic War, in 218 B.C., 26,000 citizens and 45,000 allies were drawn for service. Thus the Roman people, in making war, made use of its subjects as well as of its citizens.

Military Exercises.—Rome had no gymnasium; the future soldiers exercised themselves on the parade-ground, the Campus Martius, on the other side of the Tiber. There the young man marched, ran, leaped under the weight of his arms, fenced with his sword, hurled the javelin, wielded the mattock, and then, covered with dust and with perspiration, swam across the Tiber. Often the older men, sometimes even the generals, mingled with the young men, for the Roman never ceased to exercise. Even in the campaign the rule was not to allow the men to be unoccupied; once a day, at least, they were required to take exercise, and when there was neither enemy to fight nor intrenchment to erect, they were employed in building roads, bridges, and aqueducts.

The Camp.—The Roman soldier carried a heavy burden—his arms, his utensils, rations for seventeen days, and a stake, in all sixty Roman pounds. The army moved more rapidly as it was not encumbered with baggage. Every time that a Roman army halted for camp, a surveyor traced a square enclosure, and along its lines the soldiers dug a deep ditch; the earth which was excavated, thrown inside, formed a bank which they fortified with stakes. The camp was thus defended by a ditch and a palisade. In this improvised fortress the soldiers erected their tents, and in the middle was set the Prætorium, the tent of the general. Sentinels mounted guard throughout the night, and so prevented the army from being surprised.

The Order of Battle.—In the presence of the enemy the soldiers did not form in a solid mass, as did the Greeks. The legion was divided into small bodies of 120 men, called maniples because they had for standards bundles of hay.[1] The maniples were ranged in quincunx form in three lines, each separated from the neighboring maniple in such a way as to manœuvre separately. The soldiers of the maniples of the first line hurled their javelins, grasped their swords, and began the battle. If they were repulsed, they withdrew to

[1] Wisps or bundles of hay were twisted around poles.—Ed.

the rear through the vacant spaces. The second line of the maniples then in turn marched to the combat. If it was repulsed, it fell back on the third line. The third line was composed of the best men of the legion and was equipped with lances. They received the others into their ranks and threw themselves on the enemy. The army was no longer a single mass incapable of manœuvring; the general could form his lines according to the nature of the ground. At Cynoscephalæ, where for the first time the two most renowned armies of antiquity met, the Roman legion and the Macedonian phalanx, the ground was bristling with hills; on this rugged ground the 16,000 Macedonion hoplites could not remain in order, their ranks were opened, and the Roman platoons threw themselves into the gaps and demolished the phalanx.

Discipline.—The Roman army obeyed a rude discipline. The general had the right of life and death over all his men. The soldier who quitted his post or deserted in battle was condemned to death; the lictors bound him to a post, beat him with rods, and cut off his head; or the soldiers may have killed him with blows of their staves. When an entire body of troops mutinied, the general separated the guilty into groups of ten and drew by lot one from every group to be executed. This was called decimation (from decimus, the tenth). The others were placed on a diet of barley-bread and made to camp outside the lines, always in danger of surprise from the enemy. The Romans never admitted that their soldiers were conquered or taken prisoners: after the battle of Cannæ the 3,000 soldiers who escaped the carnage were sent by the senate to serve in Sicily without pay and without honors until the enemy should be expelled from Italy; the 8,000 left in the camp were taken by Hannibal who offered to return them for a small ransom, but the senate refused to purchase them.

Colonies and Military Roads.—In the countries that were still only partially subject, Rome established a small garrison. This body of soldiers founded a town which served as a fortress, and around about it the lands were cut into small domains and distributed to the soldiers. This is what they called a Colony. The colonists continued to be Roman citizens and obeyed all commands from Rome. Quite different from a Greek colony which emancipated itself even to the point of making war on its mother city, the Roman colony remained a docile daughter. It was only a Roman garrison posted in the midst of the enemy. Almost all these military posts were in Italy, but there were others besides; Narbonne and Lyons were once Roman colonies.

To hold these places and to send their armies to a distance the Romans built military roads. These were causeways constructed in a straight line, of limestone, stone, and sand. The Romans covered their empire with them. In a land like France there is no part where one does not find traces of the Roman roads.

CHARACTER OF THE CONQUEST

War.—There was at Rome a temple consecrated to the god Janus whose gates remained open while the Roman people continued at war. For the five hundred years of the republic this temple was closed but once and that for only a few years. Rome, then, lived in a state of war. As it had the strongest army of the time, it finished by conquering all the other peoples and by overcoming the ancient world.

Conquest of Italy.—Rome began by subjecting her neighbors, the Latins, first, then the little peoples of the south, the Volscians, the Æquians, the Hernicans, later the Etruscans and the Samnites, and finally the Greek cities. This was the hardest and slowest of their conquests: beginning with the time of the kings, it did not terminate until 266, after four centuries of strife.[1]

The Romans had to fight against peoples of the same race as themselves, as vigorous and as brave as they. Some who were not content to obey they exterminated. The rich plains of the Volscians became a swampy wilderness, uninhabitable even to the present time, the gloomy region of the Pontine marshes.

In the land of the Samnites there were still recognizable, three hundred years after the war, the forty-five camps of Decius and the eighty-six of Fabius, less apparent by the traces of their intrenchments than by the solitude of the neighborhood.

The Punic Wars.—Come into Sicily, Rome antagonized Carthage. Then began the Punic wars (that is to say, against the Phœnicians). There were three of these wars. The first, from 264 to 241, was determined by naval battles; Rome became mistress of Sicily. It

[1] Regarding all these Italian wars the Romans had only a number of legends, most of them developed to glorify the heroism of some ancestor of a noble family—a Valerius, a Fabius, a Decius, or a Manlius.

was related that Rome had never had any war-ships, that she took as a model a Carthaginian galley cast ashore by accident on her coast and began by exercising her oarsmen in rowing on the land. This legend is without foundation for the Roman navy had long endured. This is the Roman account of this war: the Roman consul Duillius had vanquished the Carthaginian fleet at Mylæ (260); a Roman army had disembarked in Africa under the lead of Regulus, had been attacked and destroyed (255); Regulus was sent as a prisoner to Rome to conclude a peace, but persuading the Senate to reject it, he returned to Carthage where he perished by torture. The war was concentrated in Sicily where the Carthaginian fleet, at first victorious at Drepana, was defeated at the Ægates Islands; Hamilcar, besieged on Mount Eryx, signed the peace.

The second war (from 218 to 201) was the work of Hannibal.

The third war was a war of extermination: the Romans took Carthage by assault, razed it, and conquered Africa.

These wars had long made Rome tremble. Carthage had the better navy, but its warriors were armed adventurers fighting not for country but for pay, lawless, terrible under a general like Hannibal.

Hannibal.—Hannibal, who directed the whole of the second war and almost captured Rome, was of the powerful family of the Barcas. His father Hamilcar had commanded a Carthaginian army in the first Punic war and had afterwards been charged with the conquest of Spain. Hannibal was then but a child, but his father took him with him. The departure of an army was always accompanied by sacrifices to the gods of the country; it was said that Hamilcar after the sacrifice made his infant son swear eternal enmity to Rome.

Hannibal, brought up in the company of the soldiers, became the best horseman and the best archer of the army. War was his only aim in life; his only needs, therefore, were a horse and arms. He had made himself so popular that at the death of Hasdrubal who was in the command of the army, the soldiers elected him general without waiting for orders from the Carthaginian senate. Thus Hannibal found himself at the age of twenty-one at the head of an army which was obedient only to himself. He began war, regardless of the senate at Carthage, by advancing to the siege of Saguntum, a Greek colony allied with Rome; he took this and destroyed it.

The glory of Hannibal was that he did not wait for the Romans, but had the audacity to march into Italy to attack them. As he had no fleet, he resolved to advance by land, through the Pyrenees, crossing the Rhone and the Alps. He made sure of the alliance of the Gallic peoples and penetrated the Pyrenees with an army of 60,000 men, African and Spanish mercenaries, and with 37 war-elephants. A Gallic people wished to stop him at the Rhone, but he sent a detachment to pass the river some leagues farther up the stream and to attack the Gauls in the rear; the mass of the army crossed the river in boats, the elephants on great rafts.

He next ascended the valley of the Isère and arrived

at the Alps at the end of October; he crossed them regardless of the snow and the attacks of the mountaineers; many men and horses rolled down the precipices. But nine days were consumed in attaining the summits of the Alps. The descent was very difficult; the pass by which he had to go was covered with ice and he was compelled to cut a road out of the rock. When he arrived in the plain, the army was reduced to half its former number.

Hannibal met three Roman armies in succession, first at the Ticinus, next on the banks of the Trebia, and last near Lake Trasimenus in Etruria. He routed all of them. As he advanced, his army increased in number; the warriors of Cisalpine Gaul (northern Italy) joined him against the Romans. He took up position beyond Rome in Apulia, and it was here that the Roman army came to attack him. Hannibal had an army only half as large as theirs, but he had African cavalrymen mounted on swift horses; he formed his lines in the plain of Cannæ so that the Romans had the sun in their face and the dust driven by the wind against them; the Roman army was surrounded and almost annihilated (216). It was thought that Hannibal would march on Rome, but he did not consider himself strong enough to do it. The Carthaginian senate sent him no reënforcements. Hannibal endeavored to take Naples and to have Rome attacked by the king of Macedon; he succeeded only in gaining some towns which Rome besieged and destroyed. Hannibal remained nine years in south Italy; at last his brother Hasdrubal started with the army of Spain to assist him, and made his way almost to central

Italy. The two Carthaginian armies marched to unite their forces, each opposed by a Roman army under the command of a consul. Nero, facing Hannibal, had the audacity to traverse central Italy and to unite with his colleague who was intrenched against Hasdrubal. One morning Hasdrubal heard the trumpets sounding twice in the camp of the Romans, a sign that there were two consuls in the camp. He believed his brother was conquered and so retreated; the Romans pursued him, he was killed and his entire army massacred. Then Nero rejoined the army which he had left before Hannibal and threw the head of Hasdrubal into the Carthaginian camp (207). Hannibal, reduced to his own troops, remained in Calabria for five years longer. The descent of a Roman army on Africa compelled him to leave Italy; he massacred the Italian soldiers who refused to accompany him and embarked for Carthage (203). The battle of Zama (202) terminated the war. Hannibal had counted as usual on drawing the Romans within his lines and surrounding them; but Scipio, the Roman general, kept his troops in order and on a second attack threw the enemy's army into rout. Carthage was obliged to treat for peace; she relinquished everything she possessed outside of Africa, ceding Spain to the Romans. She bound herself further to surrender her navy and the elephants, to pay over $10,000,000 and to agree not to make war without the permission of Rome.

Hannibal reorganized Carthage for a new war. The Romans, disturbed at this, demanded that the Carthaginians put him to death. Hannibal fled to Antiochus, king of Syria, and proposed to him to incite a revolt in Italy against Rome; but Antiochus, following the counsel of his courtiers, distrusted Hannibal and invaded Greece, where his army was captured. Hannibal withdrew to the king of Bithynia. The Romans sent Flamininus thither to take him, but Hannibal, seeing his house surrounded, took the poison which he always had by him (183).

Conquests of the Orient.—The Greek kings, successors of the generals of Alexander, divided the Orient among themselves. The most powerful of these took up war against Rome; but they were defeated—Philip, the king of Macedon, in 197, his son Perseus in 168, Antiochus, the king of Syria, in 190. The Romans, having from this time a free field, conquered one by one all the lands which they found of use to them: Macedon (148), the kingdom of Pergamum (129), the rest of Asia (from 74 to 64) after the defeat of Mithradates, and Egypt (30).

With the exception of the Macedonians, the Orient opposed the Romans with mercenaries only or with undisciplined barbarians who fled at the first onset. In the great victory over Antiochus at Magnesia there were only 350 Romans killed. At Chæronea, Sulla was victorious with the loss of but twelve men. The other kings, now terrified, obeyed the Senate without resistance.

Antiochus the Great, king of Syria, having conquered a part of Egypt, was bidden by Popilius acting under the command of the Senate to abandon his conquest. Antiochus hesitated; but Popilius, taking a rod in his hand, drew a circle about the king, and said,

"Before you move from this circle, give answer to the Senate." Antiochus submitted, and surrendered Egypt. The king of Numidia desired of the Senate that it should regard his kingdom as the property of the Roman people. Prusias, the king of Bithynia, with shaved head and in the garb of a freedman, prostrated himself before the Senate. Mithradates alone, king of Pontus, endeavored to resist; but after thirty years of war he was driven from his states and compelled to take his life by poison.

Conquest of the Barbarian Lands.—The Romans found more difficult the subjection of the barbarous and warlike peoples of the west. A century was required to conquer Spain. The shepherd Viriathus made guerilla warfare on them in the mountains of Portugal (149-139), overwhelmed five armies, and compelled even a consul to treat for peace; the Senate got rid of him by assassination.

Against the single town of Numantia it was necessary to send Scipio, the best general of Rome.

The little and obscure peoples of Corsica, of Sardinia, and of the mountains of Genoa (the Ligurians) were always reviving the war with Rome.

But the most indomitable of all were the Gauls. Occupying the whole of the valley of the Po, they threw themselves on Italy to the south. One of their bands had taken Rome in 390. Their big white bodies, their long red mustaches, their blue eyes, their savage yells terrified the Roman soldiers. As soon as their approach was learned, consternation seized Rome, and the Senate proclaimed the levy of the whole army (they called this the "Gallic tumult"). These wars were the bloodiest but the shortest; the first (225-222) gave to the Romans all Cisalpine Gaul (northern Italy); the second (120), the Rhone lands (Languedoc, Provence, Dauphiné); the third (58-51), all the rest of Gaul.

ROMAN WARFARE

The Triumph.—When a general has won a great victory, the Senate permits him as a signal honor to celebrate the triumph. This is a religious procession to the temple of Jupiter. The magistrates and senators march at the head; then come the chariots filled with booty, the captives chained by the feet, and, at last, on a golden car drawn by four horses, the victorious general crowned with laurel. His soldiers follow him singing songs with the solemn refrain "Io, Triomphe."[1] The procession traverses the city in festal attire and ascends to the Capitol: there the victor lays down his laurel on the knees of Jupiter and thanks him for giving victory. After the ceremony the captives are imprisoned, or, as in the case of Vercingetorix, beheaded, or, like Jugurtha, cast into a dungeon to die of hunger. The triumph of Æmilius Paullus, conqueror of Macedon, lasted for three days. The first day witnessed a procession of 250 chariots bearing pictures and statues, the second the trophies of weapons and 25 casks of silver, the third the vases of gold and 120 sacrificial bulls. At the rear walked King Perseus, clad in black, surrounded by his followers in chains and his three young children who extended their hands to the people to implore their pity.

[1] These songs were mingled with coarse ribaldry at the expense of the general.—Ed.

Booty.—In the wars of antiquity the victor took possession of everything that had belonged to the vanquished, not only of the arms and camp-baggage, but of the treasure, the movable property, beasts of the hostile people, the men, women, and children. At Rome the booty did not belong to the soldiers but to the people. The prisoners were enslaved, the property was sold and the profits of the sale turned into the public chest. And so every war was a lucrative enterprise. The kings of Asia had accumulated enormous treasure and this the Roman generals transported to Rome. The victor of Carthage deposited in the treasury more than 100,000 pounds of silver; the conqueror of Antiochus 140,000 pounds of silver and 1,000 pounds of gold without counting the coined metals; the victor over Persia remitted 120,000,000 sesterces.

The Allies of Rome.—The ancient world was divided among a great number of kings, little peoples, and cities that hated one another. They never united for resistance and so Rome absorbed them one by one.

Those whom she did not attack remained neutral and indifferent; often they even united with the Romans. In the majority of her wars Rome did not fight alone, but had the assistance of allies: against Carthage, the king of Numidia; against the king of Macedon, the Ætolians; against the king of Syria, the Rhodians. In the east many kings proudly assumed the title of "Ally of the Roman People." In the countries divided into small states, some peoples called in the Romans against their neighbors, receiving the Roman army, furnishing it with provisions, and guiding it to the frontiers of the hostile country. And so in Gaul it was Marseilles that introduced the Romans into the valley of the Rhone; it was the people of Autun (the Ædui) who permitted them to establish themselves in the heart of the land.

Motives of Conquest.—The Romans did not from the first have the purpose to conquer the world. Even after winning Italy and Carthage they waited a century before subjecting the Orient which really laid itself at their feet. They conquered, it appears, without predetermined plan, and because they all had interest in conquest. The magistrates who were leaders of the armies saw in conquest a means of securing the honors of the triumph and the surest instrument for making themselves popular. The most powerful statesmen in Rome, Papirius, Fabius, the two Scipios, Cato, Marius, Sulla, Pompey, Cæsar, and Crassus, were victorious generals. The nobles who composed the Senate gained by the increase of Roman subjects, and with these they allied themselves as governors to receive their homage and their presents. For the knights—that is to say, the bankers, the merchants, and the contractors—every new conquest was a new land to exploit. The people itself profited by the booty taken from the enemy. After the treasure of the king of Macedon was deposited in the public chest, taxes were finally abolished. As for the soldiers, as soon as war was carried into rich lands, they received immense sums from their general, to say nothing of what they took from the vanquished. The Romans conquered the world less for glory than for the profits of war.

EFFECTS OF ROMAN CONQUEST

The Empire of the Roman People.—Rome subjected all the lands around the Mediterranean from Spain to Asia Minor. These countries were not annexed, their inhabitants did not become citizens of Rome, nor their territory Roman territory. They remained aliens entering simply into the Roman empire, that is, under the domination of the Roman people. In just the same way today the Hindoos are not citizens but subjects of England; India is a part, not of England, but of the British Empire.

The Public Domain.—When a conquered people asked peace, this is the formula which its deputies were expected to pronounce: "We surrender to you the people, the town, the fields, the waters, the gods of the boundaries, and movable property; all things which belonged to the gods and to men we deliver to the power of the Roman people." By this act, the Roman people became the proprietor of everything that the vanquished possessed, even of their persons. Sometimes it sold the inhabitants into slavery: Æmilius Paullus sold 150,000 Epeirots who surrendered to him. Ordinarily Rome left to the conquered their liberty, but their territory was incorporated into the *domain of the Roman people.* Of this land three equal parts were made:

1. A part of their lands was returned to the people, but on condition that they pay a tribute in money or in grain, and Rome reserved the right of recalling the land at will.

2. The fields and pastures were farmed out to publicans.

3. Some of the uncultivated land was resigned to the first occupant, every Roman citizen having the right of settling there and of cultivating it.

Agrarian Laws.—The Agrarian Laws which deeply agitated Rome were concerned with this public domain. No Roman had leave to expel the possessors, for the boundaries of these domains were gods (Termini) and religious scruple prevented them from being disturbed. By the Agrarian Laws the people resumed the lands of the public domain which they distributed to citizens as property. Legally the people had the right to do this, since all the domain belonged to them. But for some centuries certain subjects or citizens had been permitted to enjoy these lands; at last they regarded them as their own property; they bequeathed them, bought and sold them. To take these from the occupants would suddenly ruin a multitude of people. In Italy especially, if this were done, all the people of a city would be expelled. Thus Augustus deprived the inhabitants of Mantua of the whole of their territory; Vergil was among the victims, but, thanks to his verse, he obtained the return of his domain, while the other proprietors who were not poets remained in exile. These lands thus recovered were sometimes distributed to poor citizens of Rome, but most frequently to old soldiers. Sulla bestowed lands on 120,000 veterans at the expense of the people of Etruria. The Agrarian Laws were a menace to all the subjects of Rome, and it was one of the benefits conferred by the emperors that they were abolished.

CHAPTER XXI

THE CONQUERED PEOPLES

THE PROVINCIALS

The Provinces.—The inhabitants of conquered countries did not enter into Roman citizenship, but remained strangers (peregrini), while yet subjects of the Roman empire. They were to pay tribute—the tithe of their crops, a tax in silver, a capitation tax. They must obey Romans of every order. But as the Roman people could not itself administer the province, it sent a magistrate in its place with the mission of governing. The country subject to a governor was called *province* (which signifies mission).

At the end of the republic (in 46), there were seventeen provinces: ten in Europe, five in Asia, two in Africa—the majority of these very large. Thus the entire territory of Gaul constituted but four provinces, and Spain but two. "The provinces," said Cicero, "are the domains of the Roman people"—if it made all these peoples subjects, it was not for their advantage, but for its own. Its aim was not to administer, but to exploit them.

The Proconsuls.—For the administration of a province the Roman people always appointed a magistrate, consul or prætor, who was just finishing the term of his office, and whose prerogative it prolonged.[1] The

[1] In the smallest provinces the title of the governor was *proprætor*.

proconsul,. like the consul, had absolute power and he could exercise it to his fancy, for he was alone in his province;[1] there were no other magistrates to dispute the power with him, no tribunes of the people to veto his acts, no senate to watch him. He alone commanded the troops, led them to battle, and posted them where he wished. He sat in his tribunal (prætorium) condemning to fine, imprisonment, or death. He promulgated decrees which had the force of law. He was the sole authority over himself for he was in himself the incarnation of the Roman people.

Tyranny and Oppression of the Proconsuls.—This governor, whom no one resisted, was a true despot. He made arrests, cast into prison, beat with rods, or executed those who displeased him. The following is one of a thousand of these caprices of the governor as a Roman orator relates it: "At last the consul came to Termini, where his wife took a fancy to bathe in the men's bath. All the men who were bathing there were driven out. The wife of the consul complained that it had not been done quickly enough and that the baths were not well prepared. The consul had a post set up in a public place, brought to it one of the most eminent men of the city, stripped him of his garments, and had him beaten with rods."

The proconsul drew from the province as much money as he wanted; thus he regarded it as his private property. Means were not wanting to exploit it. He plundered the treasuries of the cities, removed the statues and jewels stored in the temples, and made

[1] In the oriental countries Rome left certain little kings (like King Herod in Judæa), but they paid tribute and obeyed the governor.

requisitions on the rich inhabitants for money or grain. As he was able to lodge troops where he pleased, the cities paid him money to be exempt from the presence of the soldiers. As he could condemn to death at will, individuals gave him security-money. If he demanded an object of art or even a sum of money, who would dare to refuse him? The men of his escort imitated his example, pillaging under his name, and even under his protection. The governor was in haste to accumulate his wealth as it was necessary that he make his fortune in one year. After he returned to Rome, another came who recommenced the whole process. There was, indeed, a law that prohibited every governor from accepting a gift, and a tribunal (since 149) expressly for the crime of extortion. But this tribunal was composed of nobles and Roman knights who would not condemn their compatriot, and the principal result of this system was, according to the remark of Cicero, to compel the governor to take yet more plunder from the province in order to purchase the judges of the tribunal.

It cannot surprise one that the term "proconsul" came to be a synonym for despot. Of these brigands by appointment the most notorious was Verres, proprætor of Sicily, since Cicero from political motives pronounced against him seven orations which have made him famous. But it is probable that many others were as bad as he.

The Publicans.—In every province the Roman people had considerable revenues—the customs, the mines, the imposts, the grain-lands, and the pastures. These were farmed out to companies of contractors who were called publicans. These men bought from the state the right of collecting the impost in a certain place, and the provincials had to obey them as the representatives of the Roman people. And so in every province there were many companies of publicans, each with a crowd of clerks and collectors. These people carried themselves as masters, extorted more than was due them, reduced the debtors to misery, sometimes selling them as slaves. In Asia they even exiled the inhabitants without any pretext. When Marius required the king of Bithynia to furnish him with soldiers, the king replied that, thanks to the publicans, he had remaining as citizens only women, children, and old people. The Romans were well informed of these excesses. Cicero wrote to his brother, then a governor, "If you find the means of satisfying the publicans without letting the provincials be destroyed, it is because you have the attributes of a god." But the publicans were judged in the tribunals and the proconsuls themselves obeyed them. Scaurus, the proconsul of Asia, a man of rigid probity,[1] wished to prevent them from pillaging his province; on his return to Rome they had him accused and condemned.

The publicans drove to extremities even the peaceable and submissive inhabitants of the Orient: in a single night, at the order of Mithradates, 100,000 Romans were massacred. A century later, in the time of Christ, the word "publican" was synonymous with thief.

The Bankers.—The Romans had heaped up at home the silver of the conquered countries. And so silver

[1] This estimate of the character of Scaurus is too favorable.—Ed.

was very abundant in Rome and scarce in the provinces. At Rome one could borrow at four or five per cent.; in the provinces not less than twelve per cent. was charged. The bankers borrowed money in Rome and loaned it in the provinces, especially to kings or to cities. When the exhausted peoples could not return the principal and the interest, the bankers imitated the procedure of the publicans. In 84 the cities of Asia made a loan to pay an enormous war-levy; fourteen years later, the interest alone had made the debt amount to six times the original amount. The bankers compelled the cities to sell even their objects of art; parents sold even their children. Some years later one of the most highly esteemed Romans of his time, Brutus, the Stoic, loaned to the city of Salamis in Cyprus a sum of money at forty-eight per cent. interest (four per cent. a month). Scaptius, his business manager, demanded the sum with interest; the city could not pay; Scaptius then went in search of the proconsul Appius, secured a squadron of cavalry and came to Salamis to blockade the senate in its hall of assembly; five senators died of famine.

Defencelessness of the Provincials.—The provincials had no redress against all these tyrants. The governor sustained the publicans, and the Roman army and people sustained the governor. Admit that a Roman citizen could enter suit against the plunderers of the provinces: a governor was inviolable and could not be accused until he had given up his office; while he held his office there was nothing to do but to watch him plunder. If he were accused on his return to Rome, he appeared before a tribunal of nobles and of publicans who were more interested to support him than to render justice to the provincials. If, perchance, the tribunal condemned him, exile exempted him from all further penalty and he betook himself to a city of Italy to enjoy his plunder. This punishment was nothing to him and was not even a loss to him. And so the provincials preferred to appease their governor by submission. They treated him like a king, flattered him, sent presents, and raised statues to him. Often, indeed, in Asia they raised altars to him,[1] built temples to him, and adored him as a god.

SLAVERY

The Sale of Slaves.—Every prisoner of war, every inhabitant of a captured city belonged to the victor. If they were not killed, they were enslaved. Such was the ancient custom and the Romans exercised the right to the full. Captives were treated as a part of the booty and were therefore either sold to slave-merchants who followed the army or, if taken to Rome, were put up at auction.[2] After every war thousands of captives, men and women, were sold as slaves. Children born of slave mothers would themselves be slaves. Thus it was the conquered peoples who furnished the slave-supply for the Romans.

Condition of the Slave.—The slave belonged to a

[1] Cicero speaks of the temples which were raised to him by the people of Cilicia, of which country he was governor.

[2] Every important town had its market for slaves as for cattle and horses. The slave to be sold was exhibited on a platform with a label about his neck indicating his age, his better qualities and his defects.

master, and so was regarded not as a person but as a piece of property. He had, then, no rights; he could not be a citizen or a proprietor; he could be neither husband nor father. "Slave marriages!" says a character in a Roman comedy;[1] "A slave takes a wife; it is contrary to the custom of every people." The master has full right over his slave; he sends him where he pleases, makes him work according to his will, even beyond his strength, ill feeds him, beats him, tortures him, kills him without accounting to anybody for it. The slave must submit to all the whims of his master; the Romans declare, even, that he is to have no conscience, his only duty is blind obedience. If he resists, if he flees, the state assists the master to subdue or recover him; the man who gives refuge to a fugitive slave renders himself liable to the charge of theft, as if he had taken an ox or a horse belonging to another.

Number of Slaves.—Slaves were far more numerous than free men. Rich citizens owned 10,000 to 20,000 of them,[2] some having enough of them to constitute a real army. We read of Cæcilius Claudius Isidorius who had once been a slave and came to possess more than 4,000 slaves. Horace, who had seven slaves, speaks of his modest patrimony. Having but three was in Rome a mark of poverty.

Urban Slaves.—The Roman nobles, like the Orientals of our day, delighted in surrounding themselves with a crowd of servants. In a great Roman house lived hundreds of slaves, organized for different services. There were slaves to care for the furniture, for

[1] In the Casina of Plautus.

[2] Athenæus, who makes this statement, is probably guilty of exaggeration.—Ed.

the silver plate, for the objects of art; slaves of the wardrobe, valets and chambermaids, the troop of cooks, the slaves of the bath, the master of the house and his aids, the slaves to escort the master and mistress on the street, the litter-carriers, coachmen and grooms, secretaries, readers, copyists, physicians, teachers, actors, musicians, artisans of every kind, for in every great house grain was ground, flax was spun, and garments were woven. Others, gathered in workshops, manufactured objects which the master sold to his profit. Others were hired out as masons or as sailors; Crassus had 500 carpenter-slaves. These classes of slaves were called "slaves of the city."

Rural Slaves.—Every great domain was tilled by a band of slaves. They were the laborers, the shepherds, the vine-dressers, the gardeners, the fishermen, grouped together in squads of ten. An overseer, himself a slave, superintended them. The proprietor made it a matter to produce everything on his lands: "He buys nothing; everything that he consumes he raises at home," this is the compliment paid to the rich. The Roman, therefore, kept a great number of country-slaves, as they were called. A Roman domain had a strong resemblance to a village; indeed it was called a "villa." The name has been preserved: what the French call "ville" since the Middle Ages is only the old Roman domain increased in size.

Treatment of Slaves.—The kind of treatment the slaves received depended entirely on the character of the master. Some enlightened and humane masters may be enumerated, such as Cicero, Seneca, and Pliny, who fed their slaves well, talked with them, sometimes had them sit at table with them, and permitted them to have families and small fortunes (the peculium).

But other masters are mentioned who treated their slaves as animals, punished them cruelly, and even had them put to death for a whim. Examples of these are not lacking. Vedius Pollio, a freedman of Augustus, used to keep some lampreys in his fish-pond: when one of his slaves carelessly broke a vase, he had him thrown into the fish-pond as food for the lampreys. The philosopher Seneca paints in the following words the violent cruelty of the masters: "If a slave coughs or sneezes during a meal, if he pursues the flies too slowly, if he lets a key fall noisily to the floor, we fall into a great rage. If he replies with too much spirit, if his countenance shows ill humor, have we any right to have him flogged? Often we strike too hard and shatter a limb or break a tooth." The philosopher Epictetus, who was a slave, had had his ankle fractured in this way by his master. Women were no more humane. Ovid, in a compliment paid to a woman, says, "Many times she had her hair dressed in my presence, but never did she thrust her needle into the arm of the serving-woman."

Public opinion did not condemn these cruelties. Juvenal represents a woman angry at one of her slaves. "Crucify him," says she. "By what crime has the slave merited this punishment? Blockhead! Is a slave, then, a man? It may be that he has done nothing. I wish it, I order it, my will is reason enough."

The law was no milder than custom. As late as the first century after Christ, when a master was assassinated in his house, all the slaves were put to death.

When some wished to aoolish this law, Thraseas, one of the philosophers of high repute, rose to address the Senate to demand that the law be maintained.

The Ergastulum.—A subterranean prison, lighted by narrow windows so high that they could not be reached by the hand, was called the ergastulum. The slaves who had displeased their master spent the night there; during the day they were sent to work loaded with heavy chains of iron. Many were branded with a red-hot iron.

The Mill.—The ancients had no mills run by machinery; they had the grain ground by slaves with hand-mills. It was the most difficult kind of work and was usually inflicted as a punishment. The mill of antiquity was like a convict-prison. "There," says Plautus, "moan the wicked slaves who are fed on polenta; there resound the noise of whips and the clanking of chains." Three centuries later, in the second century, Apuleius the novelist, depicts the interior of a mill as follows: "Gods! what poor shrunken up men! with white skin striped with blows of the whip, . . . they wear only the shreds of a tunic; bent forward, head shaved, the feet held in a chain, the body deformed by the heat of the fire, the eyelids eaten away by the fumes, everything covered with grain-dust."

Character of the Slaves.—Subjected to crushing labor or to enforced idleness, always under the threat of the whip or of torture, slaves became, according to their nature, either melancholy and savage, or lazy and subservient. The most energetic of them committed suicide; the others led a life that was merely mechanical. "The slave," said Cato the Elder, "ought always to work or to sleep." The majority of them lost all sense of honor. And so they used to call a mean act "servile," that is, like a slave.

Slave Revolts.—The slaves did not write and so we do not know from their own accounts what they thought of their masters. But the masters felt themselves surrounded by hate. Pliny the Younger, learning that a master was to be assassinated at the bath by his slaves, made this reflection, "This is the peril under which we all live." "More Romans," says another writer, "have fallen victims to the hate of their slaves than to that of tyrants."

At different times slave revolts flamed up (the servile wars), almost always in Sicily and south Italy where slaves were armed to guard the herds. The most noted of these wars was the one under Spartacus. A band of seventy gladiators, escaping from Capua, plundered a chariot loaded with arms, and set themselves to hold the country. The slaves escaped to them in crowds to unite their fortunes with theirs, and soon they became an army.

The slaves defeated three Roman armies sent in succession against them.

Their chief Spartacus wished to traverse the whole peninsula of Italy in order to return to Thrace, from which country he had been brought as a prisoner of war to serve as a gladiator. But at last these ill-disciplined bands were shattered by the army of Crassus. The revolutionists were all put to death. Rome now prohibited the slaves from carrying arms thereafter, and it is reported that a shepherd was once executed for having killed a boar with a spear.

Admission to Citizenship.—Rome treated its subjects and its slaves brutally, but it did not drive them out, as the Greek cities did.

The alien could become a Roman citizen by the will of the Roman people, and the people often accorded this favor, sometimes they even bestowed it upon a whole people at once. They created the Latins citizens at one stroke; in 89 it was the turn of the Italians; in 46 the people of Cisalpine Gaul entered the body of citizens. All the inhabitants of Italy thus became the equals of the Romans.

The slave could be manumitted by his master and soon became a citizen.

This is the reason why the Roman people, gradually exhausting themselves, were renewed by accessions from the subjects and the slaves. The number of the citizens was increased at every census; it rose from 250,000 to 700,000. The Roman city, far from emptying itself as did Sparta, replenished itself little by little from all those whom it had conquered.

CHAPTER XXII

TRANSFORMATION OF LIFE IN ROME

Greek and Oriental Influence.—Conquest gave the Romans a clearer view of the Greeks and Orientals. Thousands of foreigners brought to Rome as slaves, or coming thither to make their fortune, established themselves in the city as physicians, professors, diviners, or actors. Generals, officers and soldiers lived in the midst of Asia, and thus the Romans came to know the customs and the new beliefs and gradually adopted them. This transformation had its beginning with the first Macedonian war (about 200 B.C.), and continued until the end of the empire.

CHANGES IN RELIGION

The Greek Gods.—The Roman gods bore but a slight resemblance to the Greek gods, even in name; yet in the majority of the divinities of Rome the Greeks recognized or believed they recognized their own. The Roman gods up to that time had neither precise form nor history; this rendered confusion all the easier. Every Roman god was represented under the form of a Greek god and a history was made of the adventures of this god.

The Latin Jupiter was confounded with the Greek Zeus; Juno with Hera; Minerva, the goddess of memory, with Pallas, goddess of wisdom; Diana, female counterpart of Janus, unites with Artemis, the brilliant huntress; Hercules, the god of the enclosure, was assimilated to Herakles, the victor over monsters. Thus Greek mythology insinuated itself under Latin names, and the gods of Rome found themselves transformed into Greek gods. The fusion was so complete that we have preserved the custom of designating the Greek gods by their Latin names; we still call Artemis Diana, and Pallas Minerva.

The Bacchanals.—The Greeks had adopted an oriental god, Bacchus, the god of the vintage, and the Romans began to adore him also. The worshippers of Bacchus celebrated his cult at night and in secret. Only the initiated were admitted to the mysteries of the Bacchanals, who swore not to reveal any of the ceremonies. A woman, however, dared to denounce to the Senate the Bacchanalian ceremonies that occurred in Rome in 186. The Senate made an inquiry, discovered 7,000 persons, men and women, who had participated in the mysteries, and had them put to death.

Oriental Superstitions.—Already in 220 there was in Rome a temple of the Egyptian god Serapis. The Senate ordered it to be demolished. As no workman dared to touch it, the consul himself had to come and beat down the doors with blows of an axe.

Some years after, in 205, during the war with Hannibal, it was the Senate itself that sent an ambassador to Asia Minor to seek the goddess Cybele. The Great Mother (as she was called) was represented by a black stone, and this the envoys of the Senate brought in great pomp and installed in Rome. Her priests followed her and paced the streets to the sound of fifes and cymbals, clad in oriental fashion, and begging from door to door.

Later, Italy was filled with Chaldean sorcerers. The mass of the people were not the only ones to believe in these diviners. When the Cimbri menaced Rome (104), Martha, a prophetess of Syria, came to the Senate to offer it victory over the barbarians; the Senate drove her out, but the Roman women brought her to the camp, and Marius, the general in chief, kept her by him and consulted her to the end of the war. Sulla, likewise, had seen in vision the goddess of Cappadocia and it was on her advice that he took his way to Italy.

Sceptics.—Not only priests and diviners came to Rome, but also philosophers who scoffed at the old religion. The best known of these, Carneades, the ambassador of the Athenians, spoke in Rome in public, and the youth of Rome came in crowds to hear him. The Senate bade him leave the city. But the philosophers continued to teach in the schools of Athens and Rhodes, and it was the fashion to send the Roman youth thither for instruction. About the third century before Christ Euhemerus, a Greek, had written a book to prove that there were no gods; the gods, he said, were only men of ancient times who had been deified; Jupiter himself had been a king of Crete. This book had a great success and was translated into Latin by the poet Ennius. The nobles of Rome were accustomed to mock at their gods, maintaining only the cult of the old religion. The higher Roman society was for a century at once superstitious and sceptical.

CHANGES IN MANNERS

The Old Customs.—The old Romans had for centuries been diligent and rude husbandmen, engaged in cultivating their fields, in fighting, and in fulfilling the ceremonies of their religion. Their ideal was the *grave* man. Cincinnatus, they said, was pushing his plough when the deputies of the Senate came to offer him the dictatorship. Fabricius had of plate only a cup and a salt-cellar of silver. Curius Dentatus, the conqueror of the Samnites, was sitting on a bench eating some beans in a wooden bowl when the envoys of the Samnites presented themselves before him to offer him a bribe.[1] "Go and tell the Samnites," said he, "that Curius prefers commanding those who have gold to having it himself." These are some of the anecdotes that they used to tell about the generals of the olden time. True or false, these legends exhibit the ideas that were current in Rome at a later time regarding the ancient Romans.

Cato the Elder.—At the time when manners were changing, one man made himself notable by his attachment to the "customs of the fathers." This was Cato. He was born in 232[2] in the little village of Tusculum and had spent his youth in manual labor. Entering the army, according to the usage of the time, at the age of seventeen, he fought in all the campaigns against Hannibal. He was not noble, but he made

[1] Another version is that he was sitting at the hearth roasting turnips.—ED.

[2] 232 and 234 are both given as the date of Cato's birth. The latter is the more probable.—ED.

himself popular by his energy, his probity, and his austerity. He passed through the whole course of political honors—quæstor, ædile, prætor, consul, and censor. He showed himself everywhere, like the old Romans, rude, stern, and honest. As quæstor he remonstrated with the consul about his expenses; but the consul, who was Scipio, replied to him, "I have no need of so exact a quæstor." As prætor in Sardinia, he refused the money that was offered him by the province for the expenses of entertainment. As consul, he spoke with vigor for the Oppian law which prohibited Roman women from wearing costly attire; the women put it off, and the law was abrogated. Sent to command the army of Spain, Cato took 400 towns, securing immense treasure which he turned into the public chest; at the moment of embarking, he sold his horse to save the expenses of transportation. As censor, he erased from the senate-list many great persons on the ground of their extravagance; he farmed the taxes at a very high price and taxed at ten times their value the women's habits, jewels, and conveyances. Having obtained the honor of a triumph, he withdrew to the army in Macedonia as a simple officer.

All his life he fought with the nobles of the new type, extravagant and elegant. He "barked" especially at the Scipios, accusing them of embezzling state moneys. In turn he was forty-four times made defendant in court, but was always acquitted.

On his farm Cato labored with his slaves, ate with them, and when he had to correct them, beat them with his own hand. In his treatise on Agriculture, written for his son, he has recorded all the old axioms of the

Roman peasantry.[1] He considered it to be a duty to become rich. "A widow," he said, "can lessen her property; a man ought to increase his. He is worthy of fame and inspired of the gods who gains more than he inherits." Finding that agriculture was not profitable enough, he invested in merchant ships; he united with fifty associates and all together constructed fifty ships of commerce, that each might have a part in the risks and the profits. A good laborer, a good soldier, a foe to luxury, greedy of gain, Cato was the type of the Roman of the old stock.

The New Manners.—Many Romans on the contrary, especially the nobles, admired and imitated the foreigners. At their head were the generals who had had a nearer view of Greece and the Orient—Scipio, conqueror of the king of Syria, Flamininus and Æmilius Paullus, victors over the kings of Macedon, later Lucullus, conqueror of the king of Armenia. They were disgusted with the mean and gross life of their ancestors, and adopted a more luxurious and agreeable mode of living. Little by little all the nobles, all the rich followed their example; one hundred and fifty years later in Italy all the great were living in Greek or oriental fashion.

Oriental Luxury.—In the East the Romans found models in the royal successors of Alexander, possessors of enormous wealth; for all the treasure that was not employed in paying mercenaries was squandered by the court. These oriental kings indulged their vanity by displaying gleaming robes, precious stones, furniture

[1] Nearly all Romans of Cato's time were husbandmen, tilling the soil with their own hands.—Ed.

of silver, golden plate; by surrounding themselves with a multitude of useless servants, by casting money to the people who were assembled to admire them.[1]

The Romans, very vain and with artistic tastes but slightly developed, had a relish for this species of luxury. They had but little regard for beauty or for comfort, and had thought for nothing else than display. They had houses built with immense gardens adorned with statues, sumptuous villas projecting into the sea in the midst of enormous gardens. They surrounded themselves with troops of slaves. They and their wives substituted for linen garments those of gauze, silk, and gold. At their banquets they spread embroidered carpets, purple coverings, gold and silver plate. Sulla had one hundred and fifty dishes of silver; the plate of Marcus Drusus weighed 10,000 pounds. While the common people continued to sit at table in accordance with old Italian custom, the rich adopted the oriental usage of reclining on couches at their meals. At the same time was introduced the affected and costly cookery of the East—exotic fishes, brains of peacocks, and tongues of birds.

From the second century the extravagance was such that a consul who died in 152 could say in his will: "As true glory does not consist in vain pomp but in the merits of the dead and of one's ancestors, I bid my children not to spend on my funeral ceremonies more than a million as" ($10,000).

Greek Humanity.—In Greece the Romans saw the monuments, the statues, and the pictures which had

[1] This taste for useless magnificence is exhibited in the stories of the Thousand and One Nights.

crowded their cities for centuries; they came to know their learned people and the philosophers. Some of the Romans acquired a taste for the beautiful and for the life of the spirit. The Scipios surrounded themselves with cultivated Greeks. Æmilius Paullus asked from all the booty taken by him from Macedon only the library of King Perseus; he had his children taught by Greek preceptors. It was then the fashion in Rome to speak, and even to write in Greek.[1] The nobles desired to appear connoisseurs in painting and in sculpture; they imported statues by the thousand, the famous bronzes of Corinth, and they heaped these up in their houses. Thus Verres possessed a whole gallery of objects of art which he had stolen in Sicily. Gradually the Romans assumed a gloss of Greek art and literature. This new culture was called "humanity," as opposed to the "rusticity" of the old Roman peasants.

It was little else than gloss; the Romans had realized but slightly that beauty and truth were to be sought for their own sakes; art and science always remained objects of luxury and parade. Even in the time of Cicero the soldier, the peasant, the politician, the man of affairs, the advocate were alone regarded as truly occupied. Writing, composing, contributing to science, philosophy, or criticism—all this was called "being at leisure."[2] Artists and scholars were never regarded at Rome as the equals of the rich merchant.

[1] Cato the Elder had a horror of the Greeks. He said to his son: "I will tell what I have seen in Athens. This race is the most perverse and intractable. Listen to me as to an oracle: whenever this people teaches us its arts it will corrupt everything."

[2] "Schola," from which we derive "school," signified leisure.

Lucian, a Greek writer, said, "If you would be a Pheidias, if you would make a thousand masterpieces, nobody will care to imitate you, for as skilful as you are, you will always pass for an artisan, a man who lives by the work of his hands."

Lucullus.—Lucullus, the type of the new Roman, was born in 145 of a noble and rich family; thus he entered without difficulty into the course of political honors. From his first campaigns he was notable for his magnanimity to the vanquished. Become consul, he was placed at the head of the army against Mithradates. He found the inhabitants of Asia exasperated by the brigandage and the cruelties of the publicans, and gave himself to checking these excesses; he forbade, too, his soldiers pillaging conquered towns. In this way he drew to him the useless affection of the Asiatics and the dangerous hate of the publicans and the soldiers. They intrigued to have him recalled; he had then defeated Mithradates and was pursuing him with his ally, the king of Armenia; he came with a small army of 20,000 men to put to rout an immense multitude of barbarians. His command was taken from him and given to Pompey, the favorite of the publicans.

Lucullus then retired to enjoy the riches that he had accumulated in Asia. He had in the neighborhood of Rome celebrated gardens, at Naples a villa constructed in part in the sea, and at Tusculum a summer palace with a whole museum of objects of art. He spent the beautiful season at Tusculum surrounded by his friends, by scholars and men of letters, reading Greek authors, and discussing literature and philosophy.

Many anecdotes are told of the luxury of Lucullus. One day, being alone at dinner, he found his table simpler than ordinary and reproached the cook, who excused himself by saying there was no guest present. "Do you not know," replied his master, "that Lucullus dines today with Lucullus?" Another day he invited Cæsar and Cicero to dine, who accepted on condition that he would make no change from his ordinary arrangements. Lucullus simply said to a slave to have dinner prepared in the hall of Apollo. A magnificent feast was spread, the guests were astonished. Lucullus replied he had given no order, that the expense of his dinners was regulated by the hall where he gave them; those of the hall of Apollo were to cost not less than $10,000. A prætor who had to present a grand spectacle asked Lucullus if he would lend him one hundred purple robes; he replied by tendering two hundred.

Lucullus remained the representative of the new manners, as Cato of the old customs. For the ancients Cato was the virtuous Roman, Lucullus the degenerate Roman. Lucullus, in effect, discarded the manners of his ancestors, and so acquired a broader, more elevated, and more refined spirit, more humanity toward his slaves and his subjects.

The New Education.—At the time when Polybius lived in Rome (before 150) the old Romans taught their children nothing else than to read.[1] The new Romans provided Greek instructors for their children. Some Greeks opened in Rome schools of poesy, rhetoric, and music. The great families took sides be-

[1] Also to write and reckon, as previously stated.—Ed.

tween the old and new systems. But there always remained a prejudice against music and the dance; they were regarded as arts belonging to the stage, improper for a man of good birth. Scipio Æmilianus, the protector of the Greeks, speaks with indignation of a dancing-school to which children and young girls of free birth resorted: "When it was told me, I could not conceive that nobles would teach such things to their children. But when some one took me to the dancing-school, I saw there more than 500 boys and girls and, among the number a twelve-year-old child, a candidate's son, who danced to the sound of castanets." Sallust, speaking of a Roman woman of little reputation, says, "She played on the lyre and danced better than is proper for an honest woman."

The New Status of Women.—The Roman women gave themselves with energy to the religions and the luxury of the East. They flocked in crowds to the Bacchanals and the mysteries of Isis. Sumptuary laws were made against their fine garments, their litters, and their jewels, but these laws had to be abrogated and the women allowed to follow the example of the men. Noble women ceased to walk or to remain in their homes; they set out with great equipages, frequented the theatre, the circus, the baths, and the places of assembly. Idle and exceedingly ignorant, they quickly became corrupt. In the nobility, women of fine character became the exception. The old discipline of the family fell to the ground. The Roman law made the husband the master of his wife; but a new form of marriage was invented which left the woman under the authority of her father and gave no power to her husband. To make their daughter still more independent, her parents gave her a dower.

Divorce.—Sometimes the husband alone had the right to repudiate his wife, but the custom was that this right should be exercised only in the gravest circumstances. The woman gained the right of leaving her husband, and so it became very easy to break a marriage. There was no need of a judgment, or even of a motive. It was enough for the discontented husband or wife to say to the other, "Take what belongs to you, and return what is mine." After the divorce either could marry again.

In the aristocracy, marriage came to be regarded as a passing union; Sulla had five wives, Cæsar four, Pompey five, and Antony four. The daughter of Cicero had three husbands. Hortensius divorced his wife to give her to a friend. "There are noble women," says Seneca, "who count their age not by the years of the consuls, but by the husbands they have had; they divorce to marry again, they marry to divorce again."

But this corruption affected hardly more than the nobles of Rome and the upstarts. In the families of Italy and the provinces the more serious manners of the old time still prevailed; but the discipline of the family gradually slackened and the woman slowly freed herself from the despotism of her husband.

CHAPTER XXIII

FALL OF THE REPUBLIC

DECADENCE OF REPUBLICAN INSTITUTIONS

Destruction of the Peasantry.—The old Roman people consisted of small proprietors who cultivated their own land. These honest and robust peasants constituted at once the army and the assembly of the people. Though still numerous in 221 and during the Second Punic War, in 133 there were no more of them. Many without doubt had perished in the foreign wars; but the special reason for their disappearance was that it had become impossible for them to subsist.

The peasants lived by the culture of grain. When Rome received the grain of Sicily and Africa, the grain of Italy fell to so low a price that laborers could not raise enough to support their families and pay the military tax. They were compelled to sell their land and this was bought by a rich neighbor. Of many small fields he made a great domain; he laid the land down to grazing, and to protect his herds or to cultivate it he sent shepherds and slave laborers. On the soil of Italy at that time there were only great proprietors and troops of slaves. "Great domains," said Pliny the Elder, "are the ruin of Italy."

It was, in fact, the great domains that drove the free

peasants from the country districts. The old proprietor who sold his land could no longer remain a farmer; he had to yield the place to slaves, and he himself wandered forth without work. "The majority of these heads of families," says Varro in his treatise on agriculture, "have slipped within our walls, leaving the scythe and the plough; they prefer clapping their hands at the circus to working in their fields and their vineyards." Tiberius Gracchus, a tribune of the plebs, exclaimed in a moment of indignation, "The wild beasts of Italy have at least their lairs, but the men who offer their blood for Italy have only the light and the air that they breathe; they wander about without shelter, without a dwelling, with their wives and their children. Those generals do but mock them who exhort them to fight for their tombs and their temples. Is there one of them who still possesses the sacred altar of his house and the tomb of his ancestors? They are called the masters of the world while they have not for themselves a single foot of earth."

The City Plebs.—While the farms were being drained, the city of Rome was being filled with a new population. They were the descendants of the ruined peasants whom misery had driven to the city; besides these, there were the freedmen and their children. They came from all the corners of the world—Greeks, Syrians, Egyptians, Asiatics, Africans, Spaniards, Gauls—torn from their homes, and sold as slaves; later freed by their masters and made citizens, they massed themselves in the city. It was an entirely new people that bore the name Roman. One day Scipio, the conqueror of Carthage and of Numantia, haranguing the people in the forum, was interrupted by the cries of the mob. "Silence! false sons of Italy," he cried; "do as you like; those whom I brought to Rome in chains will never frighten me even if they are no longer slaves." The populace preserved quiet, but these "false sons of Italy," the sons of the vanquished, had already taken the place of the old Romans.

This new plebeian order could not make a livelihood for itself, and so the state had to provide food for it. A beginning was made in 123 with furnishing corn at half price to all citizens, and this grain was imported from Sicily and Africa. Since the year 63[1] corn was distributed gratuitously and oil was also provided. There were registers and an administration expressly for these distributions, a special service for furnishing provisions (the Annona). In 46 Cæsar found 320,000 citizens enrolled for these distributions.

Electoral Corruption.—This miserable and lazy populace filled the forum on election days and made the laws and the magistrates. The candidates sought to win its favors by giving shows and public feasts, and by dispensing provisions. They even bought votes. This sale took place on a large scale and in broad day; money was given to distributers who divided it among the voters. Once the Senate endeavored to stop this trade; but when Piso, the consul, proposed a law to prohibit the sale of suffrages, the distributers excited a riot and drove the consul from the forum. In the time of Cicero no magistrate could be elected without enormous expenditures.

[1] The Lex Clodia of 58 B.C. made these distributions legal. —ED.

Corruption of the Senate.—Poverty corrupted the populace who formed the assemblies; luxury tainted the men of the old families who composed the Senate. The nobles regarded the state as their property and so divided among themselves the functions of the state and intrigued to exclude the rest of the citizens from them. When Cicero was elected magistrate, he was for thirty years the first "new man" to enter the succession of offices.

Accustomed to exercise power, some of the senators believed themselves to be above the law. When Scipio was accused of embezzlement, he refused even to exonerate himself and said at the tribune, "Romans, it was on this day that I conquered Hannibal and the Carthaginians. Follow me to the Capitol to render thanks to the gods and to beseech them always to provide generals like myself."

To support their pretensions at home, the majority of the nobles required a large amount of money. Many used their power to get it for themselves: some sent as governors plundered the subjects of Rome; others compelled foreign or hostile kings to pay for the peace granted them, or even for letting their army be beaten. It was in this way that Jugurtha bribed a Roman general. Cited to Rome to answer for a murder, he escaped trial by buying up a tribune who forbade him to speak. It was related that in leaving Rome he had said, "O city for sale, if thou only couldst find a purchaser!"

Corruption of the Army.—The Roman army was composed of small proprietors who, when a war was finished, returned to the cultivation of their fields. In becoming soldiers they remained citizens and fought only for their country. Marius began to admit to the legions poor citizens who enrolled themselves for the purpose of making capital from their campaigns. Soon the whole army was full of adventurers who went to war, not to perform their service, but to enrich themselves from the vanquished. One was no longer a soldier from a sense of duty, but as a profession.

The soldiers enrolled themselves for twenty years; their time completed, they reëngaged themselves at higher pay and became veterans. These people knew neither the Senate nor the laws; their obedience was only to their general. To attach them to himself, the general distributed to them the money taken from the vanquished. During the war against Mithradates Sulla lodged his men with the rich inhabitants of Asia; they lived as they chose, they and their friends, receiving each sixteen drachmas a day. These first generals, Marius and Sulla, were still Roman magistrates. But soon rich individuals like Pompey and Crassus drew the soldiers to their pay. In 78 at the death of Sulla there were four armies, levied entirely and commanded by simple citizens. From that time there was no further question of the legions of Rome, there were left only the legions of Pompey or Cæsar.

THE REVOLUTION

Necessity of the Revolution.—The Roman people was no longer anything but an indigent and lazy multitude, the army only an aggregation of adventurers. Neither the assembly nor the legions obeyed the Senate, for the corrupt nobles had lost all moral authority, so that there was left but one real power—the army; there were no men of influence beside the generals, and the generals had no longer any desire to obey. The government by the Senate, now no longer practicable, gave place to the government of the general.

The Civil Wars.—The revolution was inevitable, but it did not come at one stroke; it required more than a hundred years to accomplish it. The Senate resisted, but too weak itself to govern, it was strong enough to prevent domination by another power. The generals fought among themselves to see who should remain master. For a century the Romans and their subjects lived in the midst of riot and civil war.

The Gracchi.—The first civil discord that blazed up in Rome was the contest of the Gracchi against the Senate. The two brothers, Tiberius and Gaius Gracchus, were of one of the noblest families of Rome, but both endeavored to take the government from the nobles who formed the Senate by making themselves tribunes of the plebs. There was at that time, either in Rome or in Italy, a crowd of citizens without means who desired a revolution; even among the rich the majority were of the class of the knights, who complained that they had no part in the government. Tiberius Gracchus had himself named tribune of the plebs and sought to gain control of the government. He proposed to the people an agrarian law. All the lands of the public domain occupied by individuals were to be resumed by the state (with the exception of 500 acres for each one); these lands taken by the state were to be distributed in small lots to poor citizens.

The law was voted. It caused general confusion regarding property, for almost all of the lands of the empire constituted a part of the public domain, but they had been occupied for a long time and the possessors were accustomed to regard themselves as proprietors. Further, as the Romans had no registry of the lands, it was often very difficult to ascertain whether a domain were private or public property. To direct these operations, Tiberius had three commissioners named on whom the people conferred absolute authority; they were Tiberius, his brother, and his father-in-law, and it was uncertain whether Tiberius had acted in the interest of the people, or simply to have a pretext for having power placed in his hands. For a year he was master of Rome; but when he wished to be elected tribune of the plebs for the succeeding year, his enemies protested, as this was contrary to custom. A riot followed. Tiberius and his friends seized the Capitol; the partisans of the Senate and their slaves, armed with clubs and fragments of benches, pursued them and despatched them (133).

Ten years later Gaius, the younger of the Gracchi, elected tribune of the plebs (123), had the agrarian law voted anew, and established distributions[1] of corn to the poor citizens. Then, to destroy the power of the nobles, he secured a decree that the judges should be taken from among the knights. For two years Gaius dominated the government, but while he was absent from the city conducting a colony of Roman citizens to Carthage the people abandoned him. On his return he could not be reëlected. The consul armed

[1] At a very low price.—Ed.

the partisans of the Senate and marched against Gaius and his friends who had fled to the Aventine Hill. Gaius had himself killed by a slave; his followers were massacred or executed in prison; their houses were razed and their property confiscated.

Marius and Sulla.—The contests of the Gracchi and the Senate had been no more than riots in the streets of Rome, terminating in a combat between bands hastily armed. The strife that followed was a succession of real wars between regular armies, wars in Italy, wars in all the provinces. From this time the party chiefs were no other than the generals.

The first to use his army to secure obedience in Rome was Marius. He was born in Arpinum, a little town in the mountains, and was not of noble descent. He had attained reputation as an officer in the army, and had been elected tribune of the plebs, then prætor, with the help of the nobles. He turned against them and was elected consul and commissioned with the war against Jugurtha, king of Numidia, who had already fought several Roman armies. It was then that Marius enrolled poor citizens for whom military service became a profession. With his army Marius conquered Jugurtha and the barbarians, the Cimbri and Teutones, who had invaded the empire. He then returned to Rome where he had himself elected consul for the sixth time and now exercised absolute power. Two parties now took form in Rome who called themselves the party of the people (the party of Marius), and the party of the nobles (that of the Senate).

The partisans of Marius committed so many acts of

violence that they ended by making him unpopular. Sulla, a noble, of the great family of the Cornelii, profited by this circumstance to dispute the power of Marius; Sulla was also a general. When the Italians rose against Rome to secure the right of citizenship and levied great armies which marched almost to the gates of the city, it was Sulla who saved Rome by fighting the Italians.

He became consul and was charged with the war against Mithradates, king of Pontus, who had invaded Asia Minor and massacred all the Romans (88). Marius in jealousy excited a riot in the city; Sulla departed, joined his army which awaited him in south Italy, then returned to Rome. Roman religion prohibited soldiers entering the city under arms; the consul even before passing the gates had to lay aside his mantle of war and assume the toga. Sulla was the first general who dared to violate this restriction. Marius took flight.

But when Sulla had left for Asia, Marius came with an army of adventurers and entered Rome by force (87). Then commenced the proscriptions.

The principal partisans of Sulla were outlawed, and command was given to kill them anywhere they were met and to confiscate their goods. Marius died some months later; but his principal partisan, Cinna, continued to govern Rome and to put to death whomever he pleased.

During this time Sulla had conquered Mithradates and had assured the loyalty of his soldiers by giving them the free pillage of Asia. He returned with his army (83) to Italy. His enemies opposed him with five armies, but these were defeated or they deserted. Sulla entered Rome, massacred his prisoners and overthrew the partisans of Marius. After some days of slaughter he set himself to proceed regularly: he posted three lists of those whom he wished killed. "I have posted now all those whom I can recall; I have forgotten many, but their names will be posted as the names occur to me." Every proscribed man—that is to say, every man whose name was on the list, was marked for death; the murderer who brought his head was rewarded. The property of the proscribed was confiscated. Proscription was not the result of any trial but of the caprice of the general, and that too without any warning. Sulla thus massacred not only his enemies but the rich whose property he coveted. It is related that a citizen who was unaccustomed to politics glanced in passing at the list of proscriptions and saw his own name inscribed at the top of the list. "Alas!" he cried, "my Alban house has been the death of me!" Sulla is said to have proscribed 1800[1] knights.

After having removed his enemies, he endeavored to organize a government in which all power should be in the hands of the Senate. He had himself named Dictator, an old title once given to generals in moments of danger and which conferred absolute power. Sulla used the office to make laws which changed the entire constitution. From that time all the judges were to be taken from the Senate, no law could be discussed before it had been accepted by the Senate, the right of

[1] 1600, according to Mommsen, "History of Rome," Bk. IV, ch. x.—ED.

proposing laws was taken from the tribunes of the plebs.

After these reforms Sulla abdicated his functions and retired to private life (79). He knew he had nothing to fear, for he had established 100,000 of his soldiers in Italy.

Pompey and Cæsar.—The Senate had recovered its power because Sulla saw fit to give it this, but it had not the strength to retain it if a general wished again to seize it. The government of the Senate endured, however, in appearance for more than thirty years; this was because there were several generals and each prevented a rival from gaining all power.

At the death of Sulla four armies took the field: two obeyed the generals who were partisans of the Senate, Crassus and Pompey; two followed generals who were adversaries of the Senate, Lepidus in Italy, and Sertorius in Spain. It is very remarkable that no one of these armies was regular, no one of the generals was a magistrate and therefore had the right to command troops; down to this time the generals had been consuls, but now they were individuals—private persons; their soldiers came to them not to serve the interests of the state, but to profit at the expense of the inhabitants.

The armies of the enemies of the Senate were destroyed, and Crassus and Pompey, left alone, joined issues to control affairs. They had themselves elected consuls and Pompey received the conduct of two wars. He went to Asia with a devoted army and was for several years the master of Rome; but as he was more the possessor of offices than of power, he changed nothing in the government. It was during this time that Cæsar, a young noble, made himself popular. Pompey, Crassus, and Cæsar united to divide the power between themselves. Crassus received the command of the army sent to Asia against the Parthians and was killed (53). Pompey remained at Rome. Cæsar went to Gaul where he stayed eight years subjecting the country and making an army for himself.

Pompey and Cæsar were now the only persons on the stage. Each wished to be master. Pompey had the advantage of being at Rome and of dominating the Senate; Cæsar had on his side his army, disciplined by eight years of expeditions. Pompey secured a decree of the Senate that Cæsar should abandon his army and return to Rome. Cæsar decided then to cross the boundary of his province (the river Rubicon), and to march on Rome. Pompey had no army in Italy to defend himself, and so with the majority of the senators took flight to the other side of the Adriatic. He had several armies in Spain, in Greece, and in Africa. Cæsar defeated them, one after another—that of Spain first (49), then that of Greece at Pharsalus (48), at last, that of Africa (46). Pompey, vanquished at Pharsalus, fled to Egypt where the king had him assassinated.

On his return to Rome Cæsar was appointed dictator for ten years and exercised absolute power. The Senate paid him divine honors, and it is possible that Cæsar desired the title of king. He was assassinated by certain of his favorites who aimed to reëstablish the sovereignty of the Senate (44).

End of the Republic.—The people of Rome, who loved Cæsar, compelled Brutus and Cassius, the chiefs of the assassins, to flee. They withdrew to the East where they raised a large army. The West remained in the hand of Antony, who with the support of the army of Cæsar, governed Rome despotically.

Cæsar in his will had adopted a young man of eighteen years, his sister's son,[1] Octavian, who according to Roman usage assumed the name of his adoptive father and called himself from that time Julius Cæsar Octavianus. Octavian rallied to his side the soldiers of Cæsar and was charged by the Senate with the war against Antony. But after conquering him he preferred to unite with him for a division of power; they associated Lepidus with them, and all three returned to Rome where they secured absolute power for five years under the title of triumvirs for organizing public affairs. They began by proscribing their adversaries and their personal enemies. Antony secured the death of Cicero (43). Then they left for the East to destroy the army of the conspirators. After they had divided the empire among themselves it was impossible to preserve harmony and war was undertaken in Italy. It was the soldiers who compelled them to make terms of peace. A new partition was made; Antony took the East and Octavian the West (39). For some years peace was preserved; Antony resigned himself to the life of an oriental sovereign in company with Cleopatra, queen of Egypt; Octavian found it necessary to fight a campaign against the sons of Pompey. The two leaders came at last to an open breach, and then flamed up the last of the civil wars. This was a war between the East and West. It was

[1] Grandson.—Ed.

decided by the naval battle of Actium; Antony, abandoned by the fleet of Cleopatra, fled to Egypt and took his own life. Octavian, left alone, was absolute master of the empire. The government of the Senate was at an end.

Need of Peace.—Everybody had suffered by these wars. The inhabitants of the provinces were plundered, harassed, and massacred by the soldiers; each of the hostile generals forced them to take sides with him, and the victor punished them for supporting the vanquished. To reward the old soldiers the generals promised them lands, and then expelled all the inhabitants of a city to make room for the veterans.

Rich Romans risked their property and their life; when their party was overthrown, they found themselves at the mercy of the victor. Sulla had set the example for organized massacres (81). Forty years later (in 43) Octavian and Antony again drew up lists of proscription.

The populace suffered. The grain on which they lived came no longer to Rome with the former regularity, being intercepted either by pirates or by the fleet of an enemy.

After a century of this régime all the Romans and provincials, rich and poor, had but one desire—peace.

The Power of the Individual.—It was then that the heir of Cæsar, his nephew[1] Octavian, one of the triumvirs, after having conquered his two colleagues presented himself to the people now wearied with civil discord. "He drew to himself all the powers of the people, of the Senate, and of the magistrates;" for

[1] Grand-nephew.—ED.

twelve years he was emperor without having the title. No one dreamed of resisting him; he had closed the temple of Janus and given peace to the world, and this was what everybody wished. The government of the republic by the Senate represented only pillage and civil war. A master was needed strong enough to stop the wars and revolutions. Thus the Roman empire was founded.

CHAPTER XXIV

THE EMPIRE AT ITS HEIGHT

THE TWELVE CÆSARS

The Emperor.—In the new régime absolute authority was lodged in a single man; he was called the emperor (imperator—the commander). In himself alone he exercised all those functions which the ancient magistrates distributed among themselves: he presided over the Senate; he levied and commanded all the armies; he drew up the lists of senators, knights, and people; he levied taxes; he was supreme judge; he was pontifex maximus; he had the power of the tribunes. And to indicate that this authority made him a superhuman being, it was decreed that he should bear a religious surname: Augustus (the venerable).

The empire was not established by a radical revolution. The name of the republic was not suppressed and for more than three centuries the standards of the soldiers continued to bear the initials S. P. Q. R. (senate and people of Rome). The emperor's power was granted to him for life instead of for one year, as with the old magistrates. The emperor was the only and lifelong magistrate of the republic. In him the Roman people was incarnate; this is why he was absolute.

Apotheosis of the Emperor.—As long as the emperor lived he was sole master of the empire, since the Roman people had conveyed all its power to him. But at his death the Senate in the name of the people reviewed his life and passed judgment upon it. If he were condemned, all the acts which he had made were nullified, his statues thrown down, and his name effaced from the monuments.[1] If, on the contrary, his acts were ratified (which almost always occurred), the Senate at the same time decreed that the deceased emperor should be elevated to the rank of the gods. The majority of the emperors, therefore, became gods after their death. Temples were raised to them and priests appointed to render them worship. Throughout the empire there were temples dedicated to the god Augustus and to the goddess Roma, and persons are known who performed the functions of flamen (priest) of the divine Claudius, or of the divine Vespasian. This practice of deifying the dead emperor was called Apotheosis. The word is Greek; the custom probably came from the Greeks of the Orient.

The Senate and the People.—The Roman Senate remained what it had always been—the assembly of the richest and most eminent personages of the empire. To be a senator was still an eagerly desired honor; in speaking of a great family one would say, "a senatorial family." But the Senate, respected as it was, was now powerless, because the emperor could dispense with it. It was still the most distinguished body in the state, but it was no longer the master of the government. The emperor often pretended to consult it, but he was not bound by its advice.

The people had lost all its power since the assemblies

[1] Inscriptions have been found where the name of Domitian has thus been cut away.

(the Comitia) were suppressed in the reign of Tiberius. The population of 2,000,000 souls crowded into Rome was composed only of some thousands of great lords with their slaves and a mob of paupers. Already the state had assumed the burden of feeding the latter; the emperors continued to distribute grain to them, and supplemented this with donations of money (the congiarium). Augustus thus donated $140 apiece in nine different distributions, and Nero $50 in three. At the same time to amuse this populace shows were presented. The number of days regularly appointed for the shows under the republic had already amounted to 66 in the year; it had increased in a century and a half, under Marcus Aurelius, to 135, and in the fourth century to 175 (without counting supplementary days). These spectacles continued each day from sunrise to sunset; the spectators ate their lunch in their places. This was a means used by the emperors for the occupation of the crowd. "It is for your advantage, Cæsar," said an actor to Augustus, "that the people engage itself with us." It was also a means for securing popularity. The worst emperors were among the most popular; Nero was adored for his magnificent spectacles; the people refused to believe that he was dead, and for thirty years they awaited his return.[1]

[1] Suetonius ("Lives of the Twelve Cæsars," Nero, ch. lvii.) relates that the king of the Parthians, when he sent ambassadors to the Senate to renew his alliance with the Roman people, earnestly requested that due honor should be paid to the memory of Nero. The historian continues, "When, twenty years afterwards, at which time I was a young man, some person of obscure birth gave himself out for Nero, that name secured him so favorable a reception from the Parthians that he was very zealously supported, and it was with much difficulty that they were persuaded to give him up."—Ed.

The multitude of Rome no longer sought to govern; it required only to be amused and fed: in the forceful expression of Juvenal—to be provided with bread and the games of the circus (panem et circenses).

The Prætorians.—Under the republic a general was prohibited from leading his army into the city of Rome. The emperor, chief of all the armies, had at Rome his military escort (prætorium), a body of about 10,000 men quartered in the interior of the city. The prætorians, recruited among the veterans, received high pay and frequent donatives. Relying on these soldiers, the emperor had nothing to fear from malcontents in Rome. But the danger came from the prætorians themselves; as they had the power they believed they had free rein, and their chief, the prætorian prefect, was sometimes stronger than the emperor.

The Freedmen of the Emperor.—Ever since the monarchy had superseded the republic, there was no other magistrate than the emperor. All the business of the empire of 80,000,000 people originated with him. For this crushing task he required assistants. He found them, not among the men of great family whom he mistrusted, but among the slaves of whom he felt sure. The secretaries, the men of trust, the ministers of the emperor were his freedmen, the majority of them foreigners from Greece or the Orient, pliant people, adepts in flattery, inventiveness, and loquacity. Often the emperor, wearied with serious matters, gave the government into their hands, and, as occurs in absolute monarchies, instead of aiding their master, they supplemented him. Pallas and Narcissus, the freedmen of Claudius, distributed offices and pronounced judgments; Helius, Nero's freedman, had knights and senators executed without even consulting his master. Of all the freedmen Pallas was the most powerful, the richest, and the most insolent; he gave his orders to his underlings only by signs or in writing. Nothing so outraged the old noble families of Rome as this. "The princes," said a Roman writer, "are the masters of citizens and the slaves of their freedmen." Among the scandals with which the emperors were reproached, one of the gravest was governing Roman citizens by former slaves.

Despotism and Disorder.—This régime had two great vices:

1. *Despotism.*—The emperor was invested for life with a power unlimited, extravagant, and hardly conceivable; according to his fancy he disposed of persons and their property, condemned, confiscated, and executed without restraint. No institution, no law fettered his will. "The decree of the emperor has the force of law," say the jurisconsults themselves. Rome recognized then the unlimited despotism that the tyrants had exercised in the Greek cities, no longer circumscribed within the borders of a single city, but gigantic as the empire itself. As in Greece some honorable tyrants had presented themselves, one sees in Rome some wise and honest monarchs (Augustus, Vespasian, Titus). But few men had a head strong enough to resist vertigo when they saw themselves so elevated above other men. The majority of the emperors profited by their tremendous power only to make their names proverbial: Tiberius, Nero, Domitian by their cruelty, Vitellius by his gluttony, Claudius by

his imbecility. One of them, Caligula, was a veritable fool; he had his horse made consul and himself worshipped as a god. The emperors persecuted the nobles especially to keep them from conspiring against them, and the rich to confiscate their goods.

2. *Disorder.*—This overweening authority was, moreover, very ill regulated; it resided entirely in the person of the emperor. When he was dead, everything was in question. It was well known that the world could not continue without a master, but no law nor usage determined who was to be this master. The Senate alone had the right of nominating the emperor, but almost always it would elect under pressure the one whom the preceding emperor had designated or the man who was pleasing to the soldiers.

After the death of Caligula, some prætorians who were sacking the palace discovered, concealed behind the tapestry, a poor man trembling with fear. This was a relative of Caligula; the prætorians made him emperor (it was the emperor Claudius). After the death of Nero, the Senate had elected Galba; the prætorians did not find him liberal enough and so they massacred him to set up in his place Otho, a favorite of Nero. In their turn the soldiers on the frontier wished to make an emperor: the legions of the Rhine entered Italy, met the prætorians at Bedriac near Cremona, and overthrew them in so furious a battle that it lasted all night; then they compelled the Senate to elect Vitellius, their general, as emperor. During this time the army of Syria had elected its chief Vespasian, who in turn defeated Vitellius and was named in his place; thus in two years three emperors had been created and three overthrown by the soldiers. The new emperor often undid what his predecessor had done; imperial despotism had not even the advantage of being stable.

The Twelve Cæsars.—This régime of oppression interrupted by violence endured for more than a century (31 B.C. to 96 A.D.).

The twelve emperors who came to the throne during this time are called the Twelve Cæsars, although only the first six were of the family of Augustus. It is difficult to judge them equitably. Almost all of them persecuted the noble families of Rome of whom they were afraid, and it is the writers of these families that have made their reputation. But it is quite possible that in the provinces their government was mild and just, superior to that of the senators of the republic.

THE CENTURY OF THE ANTONINES

The Antonines.—The five emperors succeeding the twelve Cæsars, Nerva, Trajan, Hadrian, Antoninus, and Marcus Aurelius (96-180), have left a reputation for justice and wisdom. They were called the Antonines, though this name properly belongs only to the last two. They were not descended from the old families of Rome; Trajan and Hadrian were Spaniards, Antoninus was born at Nîmes in Gaul. They were not princes of imperial family, destined from their birth to rule. Four emperors came to the throne without sons and so the empire could not be transmitted by inheritance. On each occasion the prince chose among his generals and his governors the man most capable of succeeding him; he adopted him as his son and sought his confirmation by the Senate. Thus there came to the empire only experienced men, who without confusion assumed the throne of their adoptive fathers.

Government of the Antonines.—This century of the Antonines was the calmest that the ancient world had ever known. Wars were relegated to the frontier of the empire. In the interior there were still military seditions, tyranny, and arbitrary condemnations. The Antonines held the army in check, organized a council of state of jurisconsults, established tribunals, and replaced the freedmen who had so long irritated the Romans under the twelve Cæsars by regular functionaries taken from among the men of the second class—that is, the knights. The emperor was no longer a tyrant served by the soldiers; he was truly the first magistrate of the republic, using his authority only for the good of the citizens. The last two Antonines especially, Antoninus and Marcus Aurelius, honored the empire by their integrity. Both lived simply, like ordinary men, although they were very rich, without anything that resembled a court or a palace, never giving the impression that they were masters. Marcus Aurelius consulted the Senate on all state business and regularly attended its sessions.

Marcus Aurelius.—Marcus Aurelius has been termed the Philosopher on the Throne. He governed from a sense of duty, against his disposition, for he loved solitude; and yet he spent his life in administration and the command of armies. His private journal (his "Thoughts") exhibits the character of the Stoic—virtuous, austere, separated from the world, and yet mild and good. "The best form of vengeance on the wicked is not to imitate them; the gods themselves do good to evil men; it is your privilege to act like the gods."

Conquests of the Antonines.—The emperors of the first century had continued the course of conquest; they had subjected the Britons of England, the Germans on the left bank of the Rhine, and in the provinces had reduced several countries which till then had retained their kings—Mauretania, Thrace, Cappadocia. The Rhine, the Danube, and the Euphrates were the limits of the empire.

The emperors of the second century were almost all generals; they had the opportunity of waging numerous wars to repel the hostile peoples who sought to invade the empire. The enemies were in two quarters especially:

1. On the Danube were the Dacians, barbarous people, who occupied the country of mountains and forests now called Transylvania.

2. On the Euphrates was the great military monarchy of the Parthians which had its capital at Ctesiphon, near the ruins of Babylon, and which extended over all Persia.

Trajan made several expeditions against the Dacians, crossed the Danube, won three great battles, and took the capital of the Dacians (101-102). He offered them peace, but when they reopened the war he resolved to end matters with them: he had a stone bridge built over the Danube, invaded Dacia and reduced it to a Roman province (106). Colonies were transferred thither, cities were built, and Dacia became a Roman province where Latin was spoken and Roman customs were assimilated. When the Roman armies withdrew at the end of the third century, the Latin language remained and continued throughout the Middle Ages, notwithstanding the invasions of the barbarian Slavs. It is from Transylvania (ancient Dacia) that the peoples came from the twelfth to the fourteenth century who now inhabit the plains to the north of the Danube. It has preserved the name of Rome (Roumania) and speaks a language derived from the Latin, like the French or Spanish. Trajan made war on the Parthians also. He crossed the Euphrates, took Ctesiphon, the capital, and advanced into Persia, even to Susa, whence he took away the massive gold throne of the kings of Persia. He constructed a fleet on the Tigris, descended the stream to its mouth and sailed into the Persian Gulf; he would have delighted, like Alexander, in the conquest of India. He took from the Parthians the country between the Euphrates and the Tigris—Assyria and Mesopotamia—and erected there two Roman provinces.

To commemorate his conquests Trajan erected monuments which still remain. The Column of Trajan on the Roman Forum is a shaft whose bas-reliefs represent the war against the Dacians. The arch of triumph of Benevento recalls the victories over the Parthians.

Of these two conquests one alone was permanent, that of Dacia. The provinces conquered from the Parthians revolted after the departure of the Roman army. The emperor Hadrian retained Dacia, but returned their provinces to the Parthians, and the Roman empire again made the Euphrates its eastern frontier.

To escape further warfare with the highlanders of Scotland, Hadrian built a wall in the north of England (the Wall of Hadrian) extending across the whole island. There was no need of other wars save against the revolting Jews; these people were overthrown and expelled from Jerusalem, the name of which was changed to obliterate the memory of the old Jewish kingdom.

Marcus Aurelius, the last of the Antonines, had to resist the invasion of several barbarous peoples of Germany who had crossed the Danube on the ice and had penetrated even to Aquileia, in the north of Italy. In order to enroll a sufficient army he had to enlist slaves and barbarians (172). The Germans retreated, but while Marcus was occupied with a general uprising in Syria, they renewed their attacks on the empire, and the emperor died on the banks of the Danube (180). This was the end of conquest.

IMPERIAL ADMINISTRATION

Extent of the Empire in the Second Century.—The Roman emperors were but little bent on conquest. But to occupy their army and to secure frontiers which might be easily defended, they continued to conquer barbarian peoples for more than a century. When the course of conquest was finally arrested after Trajan, the empire extended over all the south of Europe, all the north of Africa and the west of Asia; it was limited only by natural frontiers—the ocean to the west; the mountains of Scotland, the Rhine, the Danube, and the Caucasus to the north; the deserts of the Euphrates and of Arabia to the east; the cataracts of the Nile and the great desert to the south. The empire, therefore, embraced the countries which now constitute England, Spain, Italy, France, Belgium, Switzerland, Bavaria, Austria, Hungary, European Turkey, Morocco, Algiers, Tunis, Egypt, Syria, Palestine, and Asiatic Turkey. It was more than double the extent of the empire of Alexander.

This immense territory was subdivided into forty-eight provinces,[1] unequal in size, but the majority of them very large. Thus Gaul from the Pyrenees to the Rhine formed but seven provinces.

The Permanent Army.—In the provinces of the interior there was no Roman army, for the peoples of the empire had no desire to revolt. It was on the frontier that the empire had its enemies, foreigners always ready to invade: behind the Rhine and the Danube the barbarian Germans; behind the sands of Africa the nomads of the desert; behind the Euphrates the Persian army. On this frontier which was constantly threatened it was necessary to have soldiers always in readiness. Augustus had understood this, and so created a permanent army. The soldiers of the empire were no longer proprietors transferred from their fields to serve during a few campaigns, but poor men who made war a profession. They enlisted for sixteen or twenty years and often reënlisted. There were, then, thirty legions of citizens—that is, 180,000 legionaries, and, according to Roman usage, a slightly larger number of auxiliaries—in all about 400,000 men. This number was small for so large a territory.

[1] Italy was not included among the provinces.

Each frontier province had its little army, garrisoned in a permanent camp similar to a fortress. Merchants came to establish themselves in the vicinity, and the camp was transformed into a city; but still the soldiers, encamped in the face of the enemy, preserved their valor and their discipline. There were for three centuries severe wars, especially on the banks of the Rhine and of the Danube, where Romans fought fierce barbarians in a swampy country, uncultivated, covered with forests and bogs. The imperial army exhibited, perhaps, as much bravery and energy in these obscure wars as the ancient Romans in the conquest of the world.

Deputies and Agents of the Emperor.—All the provinces belonged to the emperor[1] as the representative of the Roman people. He is there the general of all the soldiers, master of all persons, and proprietor of all lands.[2] But as the emperor could not be everywhere at once, he sent deputies appointed by himself. To each province went a lieutenant (called a deputy of Augustus with the function of prætor); this official governed the country, commanded the army, and went on circuit through his province to judge important cases, for he, like the emperor, had the right of life and death.

The emperor sent also a financial agent to levy the taxes and return the money to the imperial chest. This official was called the "procurator of Augustus." These two men represented the emperor, governing his

[1] A few provinces, the less important, remained to the Senate, but the emperor was almost always master in these as well.

[2] The jurisconsult Gaius says, "On provincial soil we can have possession only; the emperor owns the property."

subjects, commanding his soldiers, and exploiting his domain. The emperor always chose them among the two nobilities of Rome, the prætors from the senators, the procurators from the knights. For them, as for the magistrates of old Rome, there was a succession of offices: they passed from one province to another, from one end of the empire to the other,[1] from Syria to Spain, from Britain to Africa. In the epitaphs of officials of this time we always find carefully inscribed all the posts which they have occupied; inscriptions on their tombs are sufficient to construct their biographies.

Municipal Life.—Under these omnipotent representatives of the emperor the smaller subject peoples continued to administer their own government. The emperor had the right of interfering in their local affairs, but ordinarily he did not exercise this right. He only demanded of them that they keep the peace, pay their taxes regularly, and appear before the tribunal of the governor. There were in every province several of these little subordinate governments; they were called, just as at other times the Roman state was called, "cities," and sometimes municipalities. A city in the empire was copied after the Roman city: it also had its assembly of the people, its magistrates elected for a year and grouped into colleges of two members, its senate called a curia, formed of the great proprietors, people rich and of old family. There, as at Rome, the assembly of the people was hardly more than a form; it is the senate—that is to say, the nobility, that governs.

[1] "Great personages," says Epictetus, "cannot root themselves like plants; they must be much on the move in obedience to the commands of the emperor."

The centre of the provincial city was always a town, a Rome in miniature, with its temples, its triumphal arches, its public baths, its fountains, its theatres, and its arenas for the combats. The life led there was that of Rome on a small scale: distributions of grain and money, public banquets, grand religious ceremonies, and bloody spectacles. Only, in Rome, it was the money of the provinces that paid the expenses; in the municipalities the nobility itself defrayed the costs of government and fêtes. The tax levied for the treasury of the emperor went entirely to the imperial chest; it was necessary, then, that the rich of the city should at their own charges celebrate the games, heat the baths, pave the streets, construct the bridges, aqueducts, and circuses. They did this for more than two centuries, and did it generously; monuments scattered over the whole of the empire and thousands of inscriptions are a witness to this.

The Imperial Régime.—After the conquest three or four hundred families of the nobility of Rome governed and exploited the rest of the world. The emperor deprived them of the government and subjected them to his tyranny. The Roman writers could groan over their lost liberty. The inhabitants of the provinces had nothing to regret; they remained subject, but in place of several hundreds of masters, ceaselessly renewed and determined to enrich themselves, they had now a single sovereign, the emperor, interested to spare them. Tiberius stated the imperial policy in the following words: "A good shepherd shears his sheep, but does not flay them." For more than two centuries the emperors contented themselves with shearing the people of the empire; they took much of their money, but they protected them from the enemy without, and even against their own agents. When the provincials had grounds of complaint on account of the violence or the robbery of their governor, they could appeal to the emperor and secure justice. It was known that the emperor received complaints against his subordinates; this was sufficient to frighten bad governors and reassure subjects. Some emperors, like Marcus Aurelius, came to recognize that they had duties to their subjects. The other emperors at least left their subjects to govern themselves when they had no interest to prevent this.

The imperial régime was a loss for the Romans, but a deliverance for their subjects: it abased the conquerors and raised the vanquished, reconciling them and preparing them for assimilation in the empire.

SOCIAL LIFE UNDER THE EMPIRE

Moral Decay Continues at Rome.—Seneca in his Letters and Juvenal in his Satires have presented portraits of the men and women of their time so striking that the corruption of the Rome of the Cæsars has remained proverbial. They were not only the disorders left over from the republic—the gross extravagance of the rich, the ferocity of masters against their slaves, the unbridled frivolity of women. The evil did not arise with the imperial régime, but resulted from the excessive accumulation of the riches of the world in the hands of some thousands of nobles or upstarts, under whom lived some hundreds of free men in poverty, and slaves by millions subjected to an unrestrained oppression. Each of these great proprietors lived in the midst of his slaves like a petty prince, indolent and capricious. His house at Rome was like a palace; every morning the hall of honor (the atrium) was filled with clients, citizens who came for a meagre salary to salute the master[1] and escort him in the street. For fashion required that a rich man should never appear in public unless surrounded by a crowd; Horace ridicules a prætor who traversed the streets of Tibur with only five slaves in his following. Outside Rome the great possessed magnificent villas at the sea-shore or in the mountains; they went from one to the other, idle and bored.

These great families were rapidly extinguished. Alarmed at the diminishing number of free men, Augustus had made laws to encourage marriage and to punish celibacy. As one might expect, his laws did not remedy the evil. There were so many rich men who had not married that it had become a lucrative trade to flatter them in order to be mentioned in their will; by having no children one could surround himself with a crowd of flatterers. "In the city," says a Roman story-teller, "all men divide themselves into two classes, those who fish, and those who are angled for." "Losing his children augments the influence of a man."

The Shows.—In the life of this idle people of Rome the spectacles held a place that we are now hardly able

[1] A client's task was a hard one; the poet Martial, who had served thus, groans about it. He had to rise before day, put on his toga which was an inconvenient and cumbersome garment, and wait a long time in the ante-room.

to conceive. They were, as in Greece, games, that is to say, religious ceremonies. The games proceeded throughout the day and again on the following day, and this for a week at least. The amphitheatre was, as it were, the rendezvous of the whole free population; it was there that they manifested themselves. Thus, in 196, during the civil wars, all the spectators cried with one voice, "Peace!" The spectacle was the passion of the time. Three emperors appeared in public, Caligula as a driver, Nero as an actor, Commodus as a gladiator.

The Theatre.—There were three sorts of spectacles: the theatre, the circus, and the amphitheatre.

The theatre was organized on Greek models. The actors were masked and presented plays imitated from the Greek. The Romans had little taste for this recreation which was too delicate for them. They preferred the mimes, comedies of gross character, and especially the pantomimes in which the actor without speaking expressed by his attitudes the sentiments of the character.

The Circus.—Between the two hills of the Aventine and the Palatine extended a field filled with race courses surrounded by arcades and tiers of seats rising above them. This was the Circus Maximus. After Nero enlarged it it could accommodate 250,000 spectators; in the fourth century its size was increased to provide sittings for 385,000 people.

Here was presented the favorite spectacle of the Roman people, the four-horse chariot race (quadrigæ); in each race the chariot made a triple circuit of the circus and there were twenty-five races in a single day. The drivers belonged to rival companies whose colors they wore; there were at first four of these colors, but they were later reduced to two—the Blue and the Green, notorious in the history of riots. At Rome there was the same passion for chariot-races that there is now for horse-races; women and even children talked of them. Often the emperor participated and the quarrel between the Blues and the Greens became an affair of state.

The Amphitheatre.—At the gates of Rome the emperor Vespasian had built the Colosseum, an enormous structure of two stories, accommodating 87,000 spectators. It was a circus surrounding an arena where hunts and combats were represented.

For the hunts the arena was transformed into a forest where wild beasts were released and men armed with spears came into combat with them. Variety was sought in this spectacle by employing the rarest animals—lions, panthers, elephants, bears, buffaloes, rhinoceroses, giraffes, tigers, and crocodiles. In the games presented by Pompey had already appeared seventeen elephants and five hundred lions; some of the emperors maintained a large menagerie.

Sometimes instead of placing armed men before the beasts, it was found more dramatic to let loose the animals on men who were naked and bound. The custom spread into all cities of the empire of compelling those condemned to death to furnish this form of entertainment for the people. Thousands of persons of both sexes and of every age, and among them Christian martyrs, were thus devoured by beasts under the eyes of the multitude.

The Gladiators.—But the national spectacle of the Romans was the fight of gladiators (men armed with swords). Armed men descended into the arena and fought a duel to the death. From the time of Cæsar[1] as many as 320 pairs of gladiators were fought at once; Augustus in his whole life fought 10,000 of them, Trajan the same number in four months. The vanquished was slain on the field unless the people wished to show him grace.

Sometimes the condemned were compelled to fight, but more often slaves and prisoners of war. Each victory thus brought to the amphitheatre bands of barbarians who exterminated one another for the delight of the spectators.[2] Gladiators were furnished by all countries—Gauls, Germans, Thracians, and sometimes negroes. These peoples fought with various weapons, usually with their national arms. The Romans loved to behold these battles in miniature.

There were also, among these contestants in the circus, some who fought from their own choice, free men who from a taste for danger submitted to the terrible discipline of the gladiator, and swore to their chief "to allow themselves to be beaten with rods, be burned with hot iron, and even be killed." Many senators enrolled themselves in these bands of slaves and adventurers, and even an emperor, Commodus, descended into the arena.

[1] Cæsar gave also a combat between two troops, each composed of 500 archers, 300 knights (30 knights according to Suetonius; Julius, ch. 39), and 20 elephants.

[2] In an official discourse an orator thanks the emperor Constantine who had given to the amphitheatre an entire army of barbarian captives, "to bring about the destruction of these men for the amusement of the people. What triumph," he cried, "could have been more glorious?"

These bloody games were practised not only at Rome, but in all the cities of Italy, Gaul, and Africa. The Greeks always opposed their adoption. An inscription on a statue raised to one of the notables in the little city of Minturnæ runs as follows: "He presented in four days eleven pairs of gladiators who ceased to fight only when half of them had fallen in the arena. He gave a hunt of ten terrible bears. Treasure this in memory, noble fellow-citizens." The people, therefore, had the passion for blood,[1] which still manifests itself in Spain in bull-fights. The emperor, like the modern king of Spain, must be present at these butcheries. Marcus Aurelius became unpopular in Rome because he exhibited his weariness at the spectacles of the amphitheatre by reading, speaking, or giving audiences instead of regarding the games. When he enlisted gladiators to serve against the barbarians who invaded Italy, the populace was about to revolt. "He would deprive us of our amusements," cried one, "to compel us to become philosophers."

The Roman Peace.—But there was in the empire something else than the populace of Rome. To be just to the empire as a whole one must consider events in the provinces. By subjecting all peoples, the Romans had suppressed war in the interior of their empire. Thus was established the Roman Peace which a Greek author describes in the following language: "Every man can go where he will; the harbors are full of ships, the mountains are safe for travellers just as the towns for their inhabitants. Fear has everywhere

[1] St. Augustine in his "Confessions" describes the irresistible attraction of these sanguinary spectacles.

ceased. The land has put off its old armor of iron and put on festal garments. You have realized the word of Homer, 'the earth is common to all.'" For the first time, indeed, men of the Occident could build their houses, cultivate their fields, enjoy their property and their leisure without fearing at every moment being robbed, massacred, or thrown into slavery—a security which we can hardly appreciate since we have enjoyed it from infancy, but which seemed very sweet to the men of antiquity.

The Fusion of Peoples.—In this empire now at peace travel became easy. The Romans had built roads in every direction with stations and relays; they had also made road-maps of the empire. Many people, artisans, traders, journeyed from one end of the empire to the other.[1] Rhetors and philosophers penetrated all Europe, going from one city to another giving lectures. In every province could be found men from the most remote provinces. Inscriptions show us in Spain professors, painters, Greek sculptors; in Gaul, goldsmiths and Asiatic workmen. Everybody transported and mingled customs, arts, and religion. Little by little they accustomed themselves to speak the language of the Romans. From the third century the Latin had become the common language of the West, as the Greek since the successors of Alexander had been the language of the Orient. Thus, as in Alexandria, a common civilization was developed. This has been called by the name Roman, though it was this hardly more than in name and in language. In reality, it was

[1] A Phrygian relates in an inscription that he had made seventy-two voyages from Asia to Italy.

the civilization of the ancient world united under the emperor's authority.

Superstitions.—Religious beliefs were everywhere blended. As the ancients did not believe in a single God, it was easy for them to adopt new gods. All peoples, each of whom had its own religion, far from rejecting the religions of others, adopted the gods of their neighbors and fused them with their own. The Romans set the example by raising the Pantheon, a temple to "all the gods," where each deity had his sanctuary.

Everywhere there was much credulity. Men believed in the divinity of the dead emperors; it was believed that Vespasian had in Egypt healed a blind man and a paralytic. During the war with the Dacians the Roman army was perishing of thirst; all at once it began to rain, and the sudden storm appeared to all as a miracle; some said that an Egyptian magician had conjured Hermes, others believed that Jupiter had taken pity on the soldiers; and on the column of Marcus Aurelius Jupiter was represented, thunderbolt in hand, sending the rain which the soldiers caught in their bucklers.

When the apostles Barnabas and Paul came to the city of Lystra in Asia Minor, the inhabitants invoked Barnabas as Jupiter and Paul as Mercury; they were met by a procession, with priests at the head leading a bull which they were about to sacrifice.

Cultured people were none the less credulous.[1] The Stoic philosophers admitted omens. The emperor Au-

[1] There were some sceptical writers, like Lucian, but they were isolated.

gustus regarded it as a bad sign when he put on the wrong shoe. Suetonius wrote to Pliny the Younger, begging him to transfer his case to another day on account of a dream which he had had. Pliny the Younger believed in ghosts.

Among peoples ready to admit everything, different religions, instead of going to pieces, fused into a common religion. This religion, at once Greek, Roman, Egyptian, and Asiatic, dominated the world at the second century of our era; and so the Christians called it the religion of the nations; down to the fourth century they gave the pagans the name of "gentiles" (men of the nations); at the same time the common law was called the Law of Nations.

CHAPTER XXV

THE ARTS AND SCIENCES IN ROME

LETTERS

Imitation of the Greeks.—The Romans were not artists naturally. They became so very late and by imitating the Greeks. From Greece they took their models of tragedy, comedy, the epic, the ode, the didactic poem, pastoral poetry, and history. Some writers limited themselves to the free translation of a Greek original (as Horace in his Odes). All borrowed from the Greeks at least their ideas and their forms. But they carried into this work of adaptation their qualities of patience and vigor, and many came to a true originality.

The Age of Augustus.—There is common agreement in regarding the fifty years of the government of Augustus as the most brilliant period in Latin literature. It is the time of Vergil, Horace, Ovid, Tibullus, Propertius, and Livy. The emperor, or rather his friend Mæcenas, personally patronized some of these poets, especially Horace and Vergil, who sang the glory of Augustus and of his time. But this Augustan Age was preceded and followed by two centuries that perhaps equalled it. It was in the preceding century,[1] the first before Christ, that the most original Roman

[1] Sometimes called the Age of Cicero.

poet[1] appeared, Cæsar the most elegant prose-writer, and Cicero the greatest orator. It was in the following age that Seneca, Lucan, Tacitus, Pliny, and Juvenal wrote. Between Lucretius and Tacitus there were for three centuries many great writers in Rome. One might also add another century by recurring to the time of Plautus, the second century before Christ.

Of these great authors a few had their origin in Roman families; but the majority of them were Italians. Many came from the provinces, Vergil from Mantua, Livy from Padua (in Cisalpine Gaul), while Seneca was a Spaniard.

Orators and Rhetors.—The true national art at Rome was eloquence. Like the Italians of our day, the Romans loved to speak in public. In the forum where they held the assemblies of the people was the rostrum, the platform for addressing the people, so named from the prows of captured ships that ornamented it like trophies of war. Thither the orators came in the last epoch of the republic to declaim and to gesticulate before a tumultuous crowd.

The tribunals, often composed of a hundred judges, furnished another occasion for eloquent advocates. The Roman law permitted the accused to have an advocate speak in his place.

There were orators in Rome from the second century. Here, as in Athens, the older orators, such as Cato and the Gracchi, spoke simply, too simply for the taste of Cicero. Those who followed them in the first century learned in the schools of the Greek rhetors the long oratorical periods and pompous style. The great-

[1] Lucretius.—Ed.

est of all was Cicero, the only one whose works have come down to us in anything but fragments; and yet we have his speeches as they were left by him and not as they were delivered.[1]

With the fall of the republic the assemblies and the great political trials ceased. Eloquence perished for the want of matter, and the Roman writers remarked this with bitterness.[2] Then the rhetors commenced to multiply, who taught the art of speaking well.[3] Some of these teachers had their pupils compose as exercises pleas on imaginary rhetorical subjects. The rhetor Seneca has left us many of these oratorical themes; they discuss stolen children, brigands, and romantic adventures.

Then came the mania for public lectures. Pollio, a favorite of Augustus, had set the example. For a century it was the fashion to read poems, panegyrics, even tragedies before an audience of friends assembled to applaud them. The taste for eloquence that had once produced great orators exhibited in the later centuries only finished declaimers.

Importance of the Latin Literature and Language.—Latin literature profited by the conquests of Rome; the Romans carried it with their language to their barbarian subjects of the West. All the peoples of Italy, Gaul, Spain, Africa, and the Danubian lands discarded their language and took the Latin. Having no national

[1] One of the most noted, the plea for Milo, was written much later. Cicero at the time of the delivery was distracted and said almost nothing.

[2] See the "Dialogue of the Orators," attributed to Tacitus.

[3] The word "rhetor" signified in Greek simply orator; the Romans used the word in a mistaken sense to designate the men who made a profession of speaking.

literature, they adopted that of their masters. The empire was thus divided between the two languages of the two great peoples of antiquity: the Orient continued to speak Greek; almost the entire Occident acquired the Latin. Latin was not only the official language of the state functionaries and of great men, like the English of our day in India; the people themselves spoke it with greater or less correctness—in fact, so well that today eighteen centuries after the conquest five languages of Europe are derived from the Latin—the Italian, Spanish, Portuguese, French, and Roumanian.

With the Latin language the Latin literature extended itself over all the West. In the schools of Bordeaux and Autun in the fifth century only Latin poets and orators were studied. After the coming of the barbarians, bishops and monks continued to write in Latin and they carried this practice among the peoples of England and Germany who were still speaking their native languages. Throughout almost the whole mediæval period, acts, laws, histories, and books of science were written in Latin. In the convents and the schools they read, copied, and appreciated only works written in Latin; beside books of piety only the Latin authors were known—Vergil, Horace, Cicero, and Pliny the Younger. The renaissance of the fifteenth and sixteenth centuries consisted partly in reviving the forgotten Latin writers. More than ever it was the fashion to know and to imitate them.

As the Romans constructed a literature in imitation of the Greeks, the moderns have taken the Latin writers for their models. Was this good or bad? Who would venture to say? But the fact is indisputable. Our romance languages are daughters of the Latin, our literatures are full of the ideas and of the literary methods of the Romans. The whole western world is impregnated with the Latin literature.

THE ARTS

Sculpture and Painting.—Great numbers of Roman statues and bas-reliefs of the time of the empire have come to light. Some are reproductions and almost all are imitations of Greek works, but less elegant and less delicate than the models. The most original productions of this form of art are the bas-reliefs and the busts.

Bas-reliefs adorned the monuments (temples, columns, and triumphal arches), tombs, and sarcophagi. They represent with scrupulous fidelity real scenes, such as processions, sacrifices, combats, and funeral ceremonies and so give us information about ancient life. The bas-reliefs which surround the columns of Trajan and Marcus Aurelius bring us into the presence of the great scenes of their wars. One may see the soldiers fighting against the barbarians, besieging their fortresses, leading away the captives; the solemn sacrifices, and the emperor haranguing the troops.

The busts are especially those of the emperors, of their wives and their children. As they were scattered in profusion throughout the empire, so many have been found that today all the great museums of Europe have collections of imperial busts. They are real portraits, probably very close resemblances, for each emperor had a well-marked physiognomy, often of a striking ugliness that no one attempted to disguise.

In general, Roman sculpture holds itself much more close to reality than does the Greek; it may be said that the artist is less concerned with representing things beautifully than exactly.

Of Roman painting we know only the frescoes painted on the walls of the rich houses of Pompeii and of the house of Livy at Rome. We do not know but these were the work of Greek painters; they bear a close resemblance to the paintings on Greek vases, having the same simple and elegant grace.

Architecture.—The true Roman art, because it operated to satisfy a practical need, is architecture. In this too the Romans imitated the Greeks, borrowing the column from them. But they had a form that the Greeks never employed—the arch, that is to say, the art of arranging cut stones in the arc of a circle so that they supported one another. The arch allowed them to erect buildings much larger and more varied than those of the Greeks. The following are the principal varieties of Roman monuments:

1. The *Temple* was sometimes similar to a Greek temple with a broad vestibule, sometimes vaster and surmounted with a dome. Of this sort is the Pantheon built in Rome under Augustus.

2. The *Basilica* was a long low edifice, covered with a roof and surrounded with porticos. There sat the judge with his assistants about him; traders discussed the price of goods; the place was at once a bourse and a tribunal. It was in the basilicas that the assemblies of the Christians were later held, and for

several centuries the Christian churches preserved the name and form of basilicas.

3. The *Amphitheatre* and the *Circus* were constructed of several stories of arcades surrounding an arena; each range of arcades supported many rows of seats. Such were the Colosseum at Rome and the arenas at Arles and Nîmes.

4. The *Arch of Triumph* was a gate of honor wide enough for the passage of a chariot, adorned with columns and surmounted with a group of sculpture. The Arch of Titus is an example.

5. The *Sepulchral Vault* was an arched edifice provided with many rows of niches, in each of which were laid the ashes of a corpse. It was called a Columbarium (pigeon-house) from its shape.

6. The *Thermæ* were composed of bathing-halls furnished with basins. The heat was provided by a furnace placed in an underground chamber. The Thermæ in a Roman city were what the gymnasium was in a Greek city—a rendezvous for the idle. Much more than the gymnasium it was a labyrinth of halls of every sort: there were a cool hall, warm apartments, a robing-room, a hall where the body was anointed with oil, parlors, halls for exercise, gardens, and the whole surrounded by an enormous wall. Thus the Thermæ of Caracalla covered an immense area.

7. The *Bridge* and the *Aqueduct* were supported by a range of arches thrown over a river or over a valley. Examples are the bridge of Alcantara and the Pont du Gard.

8. The *House* of a rich Roman was a work of art. Unlike our modern houses, the ancient house had no

façade; the house was turned entirely toward the interior; on the outside it showed only bare walls.

The rooms were small, ill furnished, and dark; they were lighted only through the atrium. In the centre was the great hall of honor (the atrium) where the statues of the ancestors were erected and where visitors were received. It was illuminated by an opening in the roof.

Behind the atrium was the peristyle, a garden surrounded by colonnades, in which were the dining halls, richly ornamented and provided with couches, for among the rich Romans, as among the Asiatic Greeks, guests reclined on couches at the banquets. The pavement was often made of mosaic.

Character of the Roman Architecture.—The Romans,[1] unlike the Greeks, did not always build in marble. Ordinarily they used the stone that they found in the country, binding this together with an indestructible mortar which has resisted even dampness for eighteen hundred years. Their monuments have not the wonderful grace of the Greek monuments, but they are large, strong, and solid—like the Roman power. The soil of the empire is still covered with their débris. We are astonished to find monuments almost intact as remote as the deserts of Africa. When it was planned to furnish a water-system for the city of Tunis, all that had to be done was to repair a Roman aqueduct.

Rome and Its Monuments.—Rome at the time of the

[1] The same reserve must be maintained with regard to the arts as to the literature. The builders of the Roman monuments were not Romans, but provincials, often slaves; the only Roman would be the master for whom the slaves worked.

emperors was a city of 2,000,000 inhabitants.[1] This population was herded in houses of five and six stories, poorly built and crowded together. The populous quarters were a labyrinth of tortuous paths, steep, and ill paved. Juvenal who frequented them leaves us a picture of them which has little attractiveness. At Pompeii, a city of luxury, it may be seen how narrow were the streets of a Roman city. In the midst of hovels monuments by the hundred would be erected. The emperor Augustus boasted of having restored more than eighty temples. "I found a city of bricks," said he; "I leave a city of marble." His successors all worked to embellish Rome. It was especially about the Forum that the monuments accumulated. The Capitol with its temple of Jupiter became almost like the Acropolis at Athens. In the same quarter many monumental areas were constructed—the forum of Cæsar, the forum of Augustus, the forum of Nerva, and, most brilliant of all, the forum of Trajan. Two villas surrounded by a park were situated in the midst of the city; the most noted was the Golden House, built for Nero

THE LAW

The Twelve Tables.—The Romans, like all other ancient peoples, had at first no written laws. They followed the customs of the ancestors—that is to say, each generation did in everything just as the preceding generation did.

In 450 ten specially elected magistrates, the decem-

[1] This estimate is too liberal. 1,500,000 is probably nearer the truth. See Friedlaender, Sittengeschichte Roms, i., 25.—Ed.

virs, made a series of laws that they wrote on twelve tables of stone. This was the Law of the Twelve Tables, codified in short, rude, and trenchant sentences —a legislation severe and rude like the semi-barbarous people for whom it was made. It punished the sorcerer who by magical words blasted the crop of his neighbor. It pronounced against the insolvent debtor, "If he does not pay, he shall be cited before the court; if sickness or age deter him, a horse shall be furnished him, but no litter; he may have thirty days' delay, but if he does not satisfy the debt in this time, the creditor may bind him with straps or chains of fifteen pounds weight; at the end of sixty days he may be sold beyond the Tiber; if there are many creditors, they may cut him in parts, and if they cut more or less, there is no wrong in the act." According to the word of Cicero, the Law of the Twelve Tables was "the source of all the Roman law." Four centuries after it was written down the children had to learn it in the schools.

The Symbolic Process.—In the ancient Roman law it was not enough in buying, selling, or inheriting that this was the intention of the actor; to obtain justice in the Roman tribunal it was not sufficient to present the case; one had to pronounce certain words and use certain gestures. Consider, for example, the manner of purchasing. In the presence of five citizens who represent an assembly and of a sixth who holds a balance in his hand, the buyer places in the balance a piece of brass which represents the price of the thing sold. If it be an animal or a slave that is sold, the purchaser touches it with his hand saying, "This is mine by the law of the Romans, I have bought it with this brass duly weighed." Before the tribunal every process is a pantomime: to reclaim an object one seizes it with the hand; to protest against a neighbor who has erected a wall, a stone is thrown against the wall. When two men claim proprietorship in a field, the following takes place at the tribunal: the two adversaries grasp hands and appear to fight; then they separate and each says, "I declare this field is mine by the law of the Romans; I cite you before the tribunal of the prætor to debate our right at the place in question." The judge orders them to go to the place. "Before these witnesses here present, this is your road to the place; go!" The litigants take a few steps as if to go thither, and this is the symbol of the journey. A witness says to them, "Return," and the journey is regarded as completed. Each of the two presents a clod of earth, the symbol of the field. Thus the trial commences;[1] then the judge alone hears the case. Like all primitive peoples, the Romans comprehended well only what they actually saw; the material acts served to represent to them the right that could not be seen.

The Formalism of Roman Law.—The Romans scrupulously respected their ancient forms. In justice, as in religion, they obeyed the letter of the law, caring nothing for its sense. For them every form was sacred and ought to be strictly applied. In cases before the courts their maxim was: "What has already been pronounced ought to be the law." If an advocate made a mistake in one word in reciting the for-

[1] Cicero describes this juridical comedy which was still in force in his time.

mula, his case was lost. A man entered a case against his neighbor for having cut down his vines: the formula that he ought to use contained the word "arbor," he replaced it with the word "vinea," and could not win his case.

This absolute reverence for the form allowed the Romans some strange accommodations. The law said that if a father sold his son three times, the son should be freed from the power of the father; when, therefore, a Roman wished to emancipate his son, he sold him three times in succession, and this comedy of sale sufficed to emancipate him.

The law required that before beginning war a herald should be sent to declare it at the frontier of the enemy. When Rome wished to make war on Pyrrhus, king of Epirus, who had his kingdom on the other side of the Adriatic, they were much embarrassed to execute this formality. They hit on the following: a subject of Pyrrhus, perhaps a deserter, bought a field in Rome; they then assumed that this territory had become territory of Epirus, and the herald threw his javelin on this land and made his solemn declaration. Like all other immature peoples, the Romans believed that consecrated formulas had a magical virtue.

Jurisprudence.—The Law of the Twelve Tables and the laws made after them were brief and incomplete. But many questions presented themselves that had no law for their solution. In these embarrassing cases it was the custom at Rome to consult certain persons who were of high reputation for their knowledge of questions of law. These were men of eminence, often old consuls or pontiffs; they gave their advice in writing, and their replies were called the Responses of the Wise. Usually these responses were authoritative according to the respect had for the sages. The emperor Augustus went further: he named some of them whose responses should have the force of law. Thus Law began to be a science and the men versed in law formulated new rules which became obligatory. This was Jurisprudence.

The Prætor's Edict.—To apply the sacred rules of law a supreme magistrate was needed at Rome. Only a consul or a prætor could direct a tribunal and, according to the Roman expression, "say the law." The consuls engaged especially with the army ordinarily left this care to the prætors.

There were always at Rome at least two prætors as judges: one adjudicated matters between citizens and was called the prætor of the city (prætor urbanus); the other judged cases between citizens and aliens and was called prætor of the aliens (prætor peregrinus), or, more exactly, prætor between aliens and citizens. There was need of at least two tribunals, since an alien could not be admitted to the tribunal of the citizens. These prætors, thanks to their absolute power, adjusted cases according to their sense of equity; the prætor of the aliens was bound by no law, for the Roman laws were made only for Roman citizens. And yet, since each prætor was to sit and judge for a year, on entering upon his office he promulgated a decree in which he indicated the rules that he expected to follow in his tribunal; this was the Prætor's Edict. At the end of the year, when the prætor left his office, his ordinance was no longer in force, and his successor had the right to make an entirely different one. But it came to be the custom for each prætor to preserve the edicts of his predecessors, making a few changes and some additions. Thus accumulated for centuries the ordinances of the magistrates. At last the emperor Hadrian in the second century had the Prætorian Edict codified and gave it the force of law.

Civil Law and the Law of Nations.—As there were two separate tribunals, there developed two systems of rules, two different laws. The rules applied to the affairs of citizens by the prætor of the city formed the Civil Law—that is to say, the law of the city. The rules followed by the prætor of aliens constituted the Law of Nations—that is to say, of the peoples (alien to Rome). It was then perceived that of these two laws the more human, the more sensible, the simpler—in a word, the better, was the law of aliens. The law of citizens, derived from the superstitious and strict rules of the old Romans, had preserved from this rude origin troublesome formulas and barbarous regulations. The Law of Nations, on the contrary, had for its foundation the dealings of merchants and of men established in Rome, dealings that were free from every formula, from every national prejudice, and were slowly developed and tried by the experience of several centuries. And so it may be seen how contrary to reason the ancient law was. "Strict law is the highest injustice," is a Roman proverb. The prætors of the city set themselves to correct the ancient law and to judge according to equity or justice. They came gradually to apply to citizens the same rules that the prætor of the aliens followed in his tribunal. For example, the Roman law ordained that only relatives on the male side should be heirs; the prætor summoned the relatives on the female side also to participate in the succession.

The old law required that a man to become a proprietor must perform a complicated ceremony of sale; the prætor recognized that it was sufficient to have paid the price of the sale and to be in possession of the property. Thus the Law of Nations invaded and gradually superseded the Civil Law.

"Written Reason."—It was especially under the emperors that the new Roman law took its form. The Antonines issued many ordinances (edicts) and rescripts (letters in which the emperor replied to those who consulted him). Jurisconsults who surrounded them assisted them in their reforms. Later, at the beginning of the third century, under the bad emperors as under the good, others continued to state new rules and to rectify the old. Papinian, Ulpian, Modestinus, and Paullus were the most noted of these lawyers; their works definitively fixed the Roman law.

This law of the third century has little resemblance to the old Roman law, so severe on the weak. The jurisconsults adopt the ideas of the Greek philosophers, especially of the Stoics. They consider that all men have the right of liberty: "By the law of nature all men are born free," which is to say that slavery is contrary to nature. They also admit that a slave could claim redress even against his master, and that the master, if he killed his slave, should be punished as a murderer. Likewise they protect the child against the tyranny of the father.

It is this new law that was in later times called Written Reason. In fact, it is a philosophical law such as reason can conceive for all men. And so there remains no longer an atom of the strict and gross law of the Twelve Tables. The Roman law which has for a long time governed all Europe, and which today is preserved in part in the laws of several European states is not the law of the old Romans. It is constructed, on the contrary, of the customs of all the peoples of antiquity and the maxims of Greek philosophers fused together and codified in the course of centuries by Roman magistrates and jurisconsults.

CHAPTER XXVI

THE CHRISTIAN RELIGION

ORIGIN OF CHRISTIANITY

The Christ.—He whom the Jews were expecting as their liberator and king, the Messiah, appeared in Galilee, a small province of the North, hardly regarded as Jewish, and in a humble family of carpenters. He was called Jesus, but his Greek disciples called him the Christ (the anointed), that is to say, the king consecrated by the holy oil. He was also called the Master, the Lord, and the Saviour. The religion that he came to found is that we now possess. We all know his life: it is the model of every Christian. We know his instructions by heart; they form our moral law. It is sufficient, then, to indicate what new doctrines he disseminated in the world.

Charity.—Before all, Christ commended love. "Thou shalt love the Lord thy God with all thy heart and with all thy mind and thy neighbor as thyself. . . . On these two commandments hang all the law and the prophets." The first duty is to love others and to benefit them. When God will judge men, he will set on his right hand those who have fed the hungry, given drink to those who were thirsty, and have clad those that were naked. To those who would follow him the Christ said at the beginning: "Go, . . . sell all that ye have and give to the poor."

For the ancients the good man was the noble, the rich, the brave. Since the time of Christ the word has changed its sense: the good man is he who loves others. Doing good is loving others and seeking to be of service to them. Charity (the Latin name of love) from that time has been the cardinal virtue. Charitable becomes synonymous with beneficent. To the old doctrine of vengeance the Christ formally opposes his doctrine of charity. "Ye have heard that it was said, An eye for an eye and a tooth for a tooth; but I say unto you . . . whosoever shall smite thee on thy right cheek, turn to him the other also. . . . Ye have heard that it hath been said, Thou shalt love thy neighbor and hate thine enemy; but I say unto you love your enemies, do good to them that hate you, and pray for them that persecute you, . . . that ye may be the children of your Father who is in heaven, who maketh his sun to rise on the evil and the good, and sendeth rain on the just and the unjust." He himself on the cross prayed for his executioners, "Father, forgive them, for they know not what they do."

Equality.—The Christ loved all men; he died not for one people only, but for all humanity. He never made a difference between men; all are equal before God. The ancient religions, even the Jewish, were religions of peoples who kept them with jealous care, as a treasure, without wishing to communicate them to other peoples. Christ said to his disciples, "Go, and teach all nations." And the apostle Paul thus formulated the doctrine of Christian equality: "There is neither Greek nor Jew, circumcision nor uncircumcision, barbarian, bond nor free." Two centuries later

Tertullian, a Christian writer, said, "The world is a republic, the common land of the human race."

Poverty and Humility.—The ancients thought that riches ennobled a man and they regarded pride as a worthy sentiment. "Blessed are the poor," said Christ, "for theirs is the kingdom of heaven." He that would not renounce all that he had could not be his disciple. He himself went from city to city, possessing nothing, and when his disciples were preoccupied with the future, he said, "Be not anxious for what ye shall eat, nor for what ye shall put on. Behold the birds of the heaven, they sow not neither do they reap, yet your heavenly Father feedeth them."

The Christian was to disdain riches, and more yet, worldly honors. One day when his disciples were disputing who should have the highest rank in heaven, he said, "He that is greatest among you shall be your servant." "Whosoever exalteth himself shall be abased, and he that humbleth himself shall be exalted." Till our day the successor of Saint Peter calls himself "Servant of the servants of God." Christ drew to himself by preference the poor, the sick, women, children,—in a word, the weak and the helpless. He took all his disciples from among the populace and bade them be "meek and lowly of heart."

The Kingdom of God.—Christ said that he had come to the earth to found the kingdom of God. His enemies believed that he wished to be a king, and when he was crucified, they placed this inscription on his cross, "Jesus of Nazareth, king of the Jews." This was a gross mistake. Christ himself had declared, "My kingdom is not of this world." He did not come to overturn governments nor to reform society. To him who asked if he should pay the Roman tax, he replied, "Render unto Cæsar the things that are Cæsar's, and to God the things that are God's." And so the Christian accepted what he found established and himself worked to perfect it, not to remodel society. To make himself pleasing to God and worthy of his kingdom it was not necessary to offer him sacrifices or to observe minute formulas as the pagans did: "True worshippers shall worship the Father in spirit and truth." Their moral law is contained in this word of Christ: "Be ye therefore perfect even as your Father which is in heaven is perfect."

THE FIRST CENTURIES OF THE CHURCH

Disciples and Apostles.—The twelve disciples who associated with Christ received from him the mission to preach his doctrine to all peoples. From that time they were called Apostles. The majority of them lived in Jerusalem and preached in Judæa; the first Christians were still Jews. It was Saul, a new convert, who carried Christianity to the other peoples of the Orient. Paul (for he took this name) spent his life visiting the Greek cities of Asia, Greece, and Macedonia, inviting to the new religion not only the Jews, but also and especially the Gentiles: "You were once without Christ," said he to them, "strangers to the covenant and to the promises; but you have been brought nigh by the blood of Christ, for it is he who of two peoples hath made both one." From this time it was no longer necessary to be a Jew if one would become a Christian. The other nations, disregarded by the law of Moses, are brought near by the law of Christ. This fusion was the work of St. Paul, also called the Apostle to the Gentiles.

The religion of Christ spread very slowly, as he himself had announced: "The kingdom of heaven is like a grain of mustard-seed . . . which is the least of all seeds; but when it is grown, it is the greatest among herbs . . . and the birds of the air lodge under its branches."

The Church.—In every city where Christians were found they assembled to pray together, to sing the praises of God, and to celebrate the mystery of the Lord's Supper. Their meeting was called Ecclesia (assembly). Usually the Christians of the same assembly regarded themselves as brothers; they contributed of their property to support the widows, the poor, and the sick. The most eminent directed the community and celebrated the religious ceremonies. These were the Priests (their name signifies "elders"). Others were charged with the administration of the goods of the community, and were called Deacons (servants). Besides these officers, there was in each city a supreme head—the Bishop (overseer).

Later the functions of the church became so exacting that the body of Christians was divided into two classes of people: the clergy, who were the officials of the community; the rest, the faithful, who were termed the laity.

Each city had its independent church; thus they spoke of the church of Antioch, of Corinth, of Rome; and yet they all formed but one church, the church of

Christ, in which all were united in one faith. The universal or Catholic faith was regarded as the only correct body of belief; all conflicting opinions (the heresies) were condemned as errors.

The Sacred Books.—The sacred scripture of the Jews, the Old Testament, remained sacred for the Christians, but they had other sacred books which the church had brought into one structure (the New Testament). The four Gospels recount the life of Christ and the "good news" of salvation which he brought. The Acts of the Apostles describes how the gospel was disseminated in the world. The Epistles are the letters addressed by the apostles to the Christians of the first century. The Apocalypse (Revelation) is the revelation made through St. John to the seven churches of Asia. Many other pseudo-sacred books were current among the Christians, but the church has rejected all of these, and has termed them apocryphal.

The Persecutions.—The Christian religion was persecuted from its birth. Its first enemies were the Jews, who forced the Roman governor of Judæa to crucify Christ; who stoned St. Stephen, the first martyr, and so set themselves against St. Paul that they almost compassed his death.

Then came the persecution by the Pagans. The Romans tolerated all the religions of the East because the devotees of Osiris, of Mithra, and of the Good Goddess recognized at the same time the Roman gods. But the Christians, worshippers of the living God, scorned the petty divinities of antiquity. More serious still in the eyes of the Romans, they refused to adore the emperor as a god and to burn incense on the altar of the goddess Roma. Several emperors promulgated edicts against the Christians, bidding the governors arrest them and put them to death. A letter of Pliny the Younger, then governor in Asia, to the emperor Trajan, shows the procedure against them. "Up to this time, regarding the people who have been denounced as Christians, I have always operated as follows: I asked them if they were Christians; if they confessed it, I put the question to them a second time, and then a third time, threatening them with the penalty of death. When they persisted, I had them put to death, convinced that, whatever their fault that they avowed, their disobedience and their resolute obstinacy merited punishment. Many who have been denounced in anonymous writings have denied that they were Christians, have repeated a prayer that I pronounced before them, have offered wine and incense to your statue, which I had set forth for this purpose together with the statues of the gods, and have even reviled the name of Christ. All these are things which it is not possible to compel any true Christians to do. Others have confessed that they were Christians, but they affirm that their crime and their error consisted only in assembling on certain days before sunrise to adore Christ as God, to sing together in his honor, and to bind themselves by oath to commit no crime, to perpetrate no theft, murder, adultery, nor to violate their word. I have believed it necessary in order to secure the truth to put to the torture two female slaves whom they called deaconesses; but I have discovered only an absurd and exaggerated superstition."

The Roman government was a persecutor,[1] but the populace were severer yet. They could not endure these people who worshipped another god than theirs and contemned their deities. Whenever famine or epidemic occurred, the well-known cry was heard, "To the lions with the Christians!" The people forced the magistrates to hunt and persecute the Christians.

The Martyrs.—For the two centuries and a half that the Christians were persecuted, throughout the empire there were thousands of victims, of every age, sex, and condition. Roman citizens, like St. Paul, were beheaded; the others were crucified, burned, most often sent to the beasts in the amphitheatre. If they were allowed to escape with their lives, they were set at forced labor in the mines. Sometimes torture was aggravated by every sort of invention. In the great execution at Lyons, in 177, the Christians, after being tortured and confined in narrow prison quarters, were brought to the arena. The beasts mutilated without killing them. They were then seated in iron chairs heated red by fire. Blandina, a young slave, who survived all these torments was bound with cords and exposed to the fury of a bull. The Christians joyfully suffered these persecutions which gave them entrance to heaven. The occasion presented an opportunity for rendering public testimony to Christ. And so they did not call themselves victims, but martyrs (witnesses); their torture was a testimony. They compared it to the combat of the Olympian games; like the victor in the athletic contests, they spoke of the

[1] The church counted ten persecutions, the first under Nero, the last under Diocletian.

palm or the crown. Even now the festal day of a martyr is the day of his death.

Frequently a Christian who was present at the persecution would draft a written account of the martyrdom—he related the arrest, the examination, the tortures, and the death. These brief accounts, filled with edifying details, were called The Acts of the Martyrs. They were circulated in the remotest communities; from one end of the empire to the other they published the glory of the martyrs and excited a desire to imitate them. Thousands of the faithful, seized by a thirst for martyrdom, pressed forward to incriminate themselves and to demand condemnation. One day a governor of Asia had decreed persecutions against some Christians: all the Christians of the city presented themselves in his tribunal and demanded to be persecuted. The governor, exasperated, had some of them executed and sent away the others. "Begone, you wretches! If you are so bent on death, you have precipices and ropes." Some of the faithful, to be surer of torture, entered the temples and threw down the idols of the gods. It was several times necessary for even the church to prohibit the solicitation of martyrdom.

The Catacombs.—The ancient custom of burning the dead was repugnant to the Christians. Like the Jews, they interred their dead wrapped with a shroud in a sarcophagus. Cemeteries[1] were therefore required. At Rome where land was very high in price the Christians went below ground, and in the brittle tufa on which Rome was built may be seen long galleries and

[1] The word is Greek and signifies place of repose.

subterranean chambers. There, in niches excavated along the passages, they laid the bodies of their dead. As each generation excavated new galleries, there was formed at length a subterranean city, called the Catacombs ("to the tombs"). There were similar catacombs in several cities—Naples, Milan, Alexandria, but the most celebrated were those in Rome. These have been investigated in our day and thousands of Christian tombs and inscriptions recovered. The discovery of this subterranean world gave birth to a new department of historical science—Christian Epigraphy and Archæology.

The sepulchral halls of the catacombs do not resemble those of the Egyptians or those of the Etruscans; they are bare and severe. The Christians knew that a corpse had no bodily wants and so they did not adorn the tombs. The most important halls are decorated with very simple ornaments and paintings which almost always represent the same scenes. The most common subjects are the faithful in prayer, and the Good Shepherd, symbolical of Christ. Some of these halls were like chapels. In them were interred the bodies of the holy martyrs and the faithful who wished to lie near them; every year Christians came here to celebrate the mysteries. During the persecutions of the third century the Christians of Rome often took refuge in these subterranean chapels to hold their services of worship, or to escape from pursuit. The Christians could feel safe in this bewildering labyrinth of galleries whose entrance was usually marked by a pagan tomb.

THE MONKS OF THE THIRD CENTURY

The Solitaries.—It was an idea current among Christians, especially in the East, that one could not become a perfect Christian by remaining in the midst of other men. Christ himself had said, "If any man come to me and hate not his father, and mother, and wife, and children, and brethren, and sisters . . . he cannot be my disciple." The faithful man or woman who thus withdrew from the world to work out his salvation the more surely, was termed an Anchorite (the man who is set apart), or a Monk (solitary). This custom began in the East in the middle of the third century. The first anchorites established themselves in the deserts and the ruins of the district of Thebes in Upper Egypt, which remained the holy land of the solitaries.

Paul (235-340), the oldest of the monks, lived to his ninetieth year in a grotto near a spring and a palm-tree which furnished him with food and clothing. The model of the monks was St. Anthony.[1] At the age of twenty he heard read one day the text of the gospel, "If thou wilt be perfect, sell all thy goods and give to the poor." He was fine looking, noble, and rich, having received an inheritance from his parents. He sold all his property, distributed it in alms and buried himself in the desert of Egypt. He first betook himself to an empty tomb, then to the ruins of a fortress; he was clad in a hair-shirt, had for food only the bread that was brought to him every six months, fasted, starved

[1] See his biography in the "Lives of the Fathers of the Desert," by Rufinus.

himself, prayed day and night. Often sunrise found him still in prayer. "O sun," cried he, "why hast thou risen and prevented my contemplating the true light?" He felt himself surrounded by demons, who, under every form, sought to distract him from his religious thoughts. When he became old and revered by all Egypt, he returned to Alexandria for a day to preach against the Arian heretics, but soon repaired to the desert again. They besought him to remain: he replied, "The fishes die on land, the monks waste away in the city; we return to our mountains like the fish to the water."

Women also became solitaries. Alexandra, one of these, shut herself in an empty tomb and lived there for ten years without leaving it to see anybody.

Asceticism.—These men who had withdrawn to the desert to escape the world thought that everything that came from the world turned the soul from God and placed it in the peril of losing salvation. The Christian ought to belong entirely to God; he should forget everything behind him. "Do you not know," said St. Nilus later, "that it is a trap of Satan to be too much attached to one's family?" The monk Poemen had withdrawn to the desert with his brothers, and their mother came to visit them. As they refused to appear, she waited a little until they were going to the church; but on seeing her, they fled and would not consent to speak to her unless they were concealed. She asked to see them, but they consoled her by saying, "You will see us in the other world."

But the world is not the only danger for the monk. Every man carried about with himself an enemy from whom he could not deliver himself as he had delivered himself from the world—that is, his own body. The body prevented the soul from rising to God and drew it to worldly pleasures that came from the devil. And so the solitaries applied themselves to overcoming the body by refusing to it everything that it loved. They subsisted only on bread and water; many ate but twice a week, some went to the mountains to cut herbs which they ate raw. They dwelt in grottoes, ruins, and tombs, lying on the earth or on a mat of rushes. The most zealous of them added other tortures to mortify, or kill, the body. St. Pachomius for fifteen years slept only in an erect position, leaning against a wall. Macarius remained six months in a morass, the prey of mosquitoes "whose stings would have penetrated the hide of a wild boar." The most noted of these monks was St. Simeon, surnamed Stylites (the man of the column). For forty years he lived in the desert of Arabia on the summit of a column, exposed to the sun and the rain, compelling himself to stay in one position for a whole day; the faithful flocked from afar to behold him; he gave them audience from the top of his column, bidding creditors free their debtors, and masters liberate their slaves; he even sent reproaches to ministers and counsellors of the emperor. This form of life was called Asceticism (exercise).

The Cenobites.—The solitaries who lived in the same desert drew together and adopted a common life for the practice of their austerities. About St. Anthony were already assembled many anchorites who gave him their obedience. St. Pachomius (272-348) in this way assembled 3,000. Their establishment was at

Tabenna, near the first cataract of the Nile. He founded many other similar communities, either of men or women. In 256 a traveller said he had seen in a single city of Egypt 10,000 monks and 20,000 vowed to a religious life. There were more of them in Syria, in Palestine, in all the Orient. The monks thus united in communities became Cenobites (people who live in common). They chose a chief, the abbot (the word signifies in Syriac "father"), and they implicitly obeyed him. Cassian relates that in one community in Egypt he had seen the abbot before the whole refectory give a cenobite a violent blow on the head to try his obedience.

The primitive monks renounced all property and family relations; the cenobites surrendered also their will. On entering the community they engaged to possess nothing, not to marry, and to obey. "The monks," says St. Basil, "live a spiritual life like the angels." The first union among the cenobites was the construction of houses in close proximity. Later each community built a monastery, a great edifice, where each monk had his cell. A Christian compares these cells "to a hive of bees where each has in his hands the wax of work, in his mouth the honey of psalms and prayers." These great houses needed a written constitution; this was the Monastic Rule. St. Pachomius was the first to prepare one. St. Basil wrote another that was adopted by almost all the monasteries of the Orient.

CHAPTER XXVII

THE LATER EMPIRE

THE REVOLUTIONS OF THE THIRD CENTURY

Military Anarchy.—After the reigns of the Antonines the civil wars commenced. There were in the empire, beside the prætorian guard in Rome, several great armies on the Rhine, on the Danube, in the East, and in England. Each aimed to make its general emperor. Ordinarily the rivals fought it out until there was but one left; this one then governed for a few years, after which he was assassinated,[1] or if, by chance, he could transmit his power to his son, the soldiers revolted against the son and the war recommenced. The following, for example, is what occurred in 193. The prætorians had massacred the emperor Pertinax, and the army conceived the notion of putting up the empire at auction; two purchasers presented themselves, Sulpicius offering each soldier $1,000 and Didius more than $1,200. The prætorians brought the latter to the Senate and had him named emperor; later, when he did not pay them, they murdered him. At the same time the great armies of Britain, Illyricum, and Syria proclaimed each its own

[1] Of the forty-five emperors from the first to the third century, twenty-nine died by assassination.

general as emperor and the three rivals marched on Rome. The Illyrian legions arrived first, and their general Septimius Severus was named emperor by the Senate. Then commenced two sanguinary wars, the one against the legions of Syria, and the other against the legions of Britain. At the end of two years the emperor was victorious. It is he who states his policy as follows, "My son, content the soldiers and you may despise the rest." For a century there was no other form of government than the will of the soldiers. They killed the emperors who displeased them and replaced them by their favorites.

Strange emperors, therefore, occupied the throne: Elagabalus, a Syrian priest, who garbed himself as a woman and had his mother assemble a senate of women; Maximin, a soldier of fortune, a rough and bloodthirsty giant, who ate, it was said, thirty pounds of food and drank twenty-one quarts of wine a day. Once there were twenty emperors at the same time, each in a corner of the empire (260-278). These have been called the Thirty Tyrants.

The Cult of Mithra.—This century of wars is also a century of superstitions. The deities of the Orient, Isis, Osiris, the Great Mother, have their devotees everywhere. But, more than all the others, Mithra, a Persian god, becomes the universal god of the empire. Mithra is no other than the sun. The monuments in his honor that are found in all parts of the empire represent him slaughtering a bull, with this inscription: "To the unconquerable sun, to the god Mithra." His cult is complicated, sometimes similar to the Christian worship; there are a baptism, sacred feasts, an anointing, penances, and chapels. To be admitted to this one must pass through an initiatory ceremony, through fasting and certain fearful tests.

At the end of the third century the religion of Mithra was the official religion of the empire. The Invincible God was the god of the emperors; he had his chapels everywhere in the form of grottoes with altars and bas-reliefs; in Rome, even, he had a magnificent temple erected by the emperor Aurelian.

The Taurobolia.—One of the most urgent needs of this time was reconciliation with the deity; and so ceremonies of purification were invented.

The most striking of these was the Taurobolia. The devotee, clad in a white robe with ornaments of gold, takes his place in the bottom of a ditch which is covered by a platform pierced with holes. A bull is led over this platform, the priest kills him and his blood runs through the holes of the platform upon the garments, the face, and the hair of the worshipper. It was believed that this "baptism of blood" purified one of all sins. He who had received it was born to a new life; he came forth from the ditch hideous to look upon, but happy and envied.

Confusion of Religions.—In the century that preceded the victory of Christianity, all religions fell into confusion. The sun was adored at once under many names (Sol, Helios, Baal, Elagabal, and Mithra). All the cults imitated one another and sometimes copied Christian forms. Even the life of Christ was copied. The Asiatic philosopher, Apollonius of Tyana, who lived in the first century (3-96), became in legend a kind of prophet, son of a god, who went about surrounded by his disciples, expelling demons, curing sicknesses, raising the dead. He had come, it was said, to reform the doctrine of Pythagoras and Plato. In the third century an empress had the life of Apollonius of Tyana written, to be, as it were, a Pythagorean gospel opposed to the gospel of Christ. The most remarkable example of this confusion in religion was given by Alexander Severus, a devout emperor, mild and conscientious: he had in his palace a chapel where he adored the benefactors of humanity—Abraham, Orpheus, Jesus, and Apollonius of Tyana.

THE GOVERNMENT OF THE LATER EMPIRE

Reforms of Diocletian and Constantine.—After a century of civil wars emperors were found who were able to stop the anarchy. They were men of the people, rude and active, soldiers of fortune rising from one grade to another to become generals-in-chief, and then emperors. Almost all arose in the semi-barbarous provinces of the Danube and of Illyria; some in their infancy had been shepherds or peasants. They had the simple manners of the old Roman generals. When the envoys of the king of Persia asked to see the emperor Probus, they found a bald old man clad in a linen cassock, lying on the ground, who ate peas and bacon. It was the story of Curius Dentatus repeated after five centuries.

Severe with their soldiers, these emperors reëstablished discipline in the army, and then order in the empire. But a change had become necessary. A single man was no longer adequate to the government and defence of this immense territory; and so from this time each emperor took from among his relatives or his friends two or three collaborators, each charged with a part of the empire. Usually their title was that of Cæsar, but sometimes there were two equal emperors, and both had the title of Augustus. When the emperor died, one of the Cæsars succeeded him; it was no longer possible for the army to create emperors. The provinces were too great, and Diocletian divided them. The prætorians of Rome being dangerous, Diocletian replaced them with two legions. The Occident was in ruins and depopulated and hence the Orient had become the important part of the empire; Diocletian, therefore, abandoned Rome and established his capital at Nicomedia in Asia Minor.[1] Constantine did more and founded a new Rome in the East—Constantinople.

Constantinople.—On a promontory where Europe is separated from Asia only by the narrow channel of the Bosporus, in a country of vineyards and rich harvests, under a beautiful sky, Greek colonists had founded the town of Byzantium. The hills of the vicinity made the place easily defensible; its port, the Golden Horn, one of the best in the world, could shelter 1,200 ships, and a chain of 820 feet in length was all that was necessary to exclude a hostile fleet. This was the site of Constantine's new city, Constantinople (the city of Constantine).

Around the city were strong walls; two public squares surrounded with porticos were constructed; a

[1] Other considerations also led to the change of capital.—Ed.

palace was erected, a circus, theatres, aqueducts, baths, temples, and a Christian church. To ornament his city Constantine transferred from other cities the most celebrated statues and bas-reliefs. To furnish it with population he forced the people of the neighboring towns to remove to it, and offered rewards and honors to the great families who would come hither to make their home. He established, as in Rome, distributions of grain, of wine, of oil, and provided a continuous round of shows. This was one of those rapid transformations, almost fantastic, in which the Orient delights. The task began the 4th of November, 326; on the 11th of May, 330, the city was dedicated. But it was a permanent creation. For ten centuries Constantinople resisted invasions, preserving always in the ruins of the empire its rank of capital. Today it is still the first city of the East.

The Palace.—The emperors who dwelt in the East[1] adopted the customs of the Orient, wearing delicate garments of silk and gold and for a head-dress a diadem of pearls. They secluded themselves in the depths of their palace where they sat on a throne of gold, surrounded by their ministers, separated from the world by a crowd of courtiers, servants, functionaries and military guards. One must prostrate one's self before them with face to the earth in token of

[1] There were often two emperors, one in the East, the other in the West, but there was but one empire. The two emperors, though they may have resided, one in Constantinople and the other in Italy, were considered as being but one person. In addressing one of them the word "you" (in the plural) was used, as if both were addressed at the same time. This was the first use of the pronoun of the second person in the plural for such a purpose; for throughout antiquity even kings and emperors were addressed in the singular.

adoration; they were called Lord and Majesty; they were treated as gods. Everything that touched their person was sacred, and so men spoke of the sacred palace, the sacred bed-chamber, the sacred Council of State, even the sacred treasury.

The régime of this period has been termed that of the Later Empire as distinguished from that of the three preceding centuries, which we call the Early Empire.

The life of an emperor of the Early Empire (from the first to the third century) was still that of a magistrate and a general; the palace of an emperor of the Later Empire became similar to the court of the Persian king.

The Officials.—The officials often became very numerous. Diocletian found the provinces too large and so made several divisions of them. In Gaul, for example, Lugdunensis (the province about Lyons) was partitioned into four, Aquitaine into three. In place of forty-six governors there were from this time 117.[1]

At the same time the duties of the officials were divided. Besides the governors and the deputies in the provinces there were in the border provinces military commanders—the dukes and the counts. The emperor had about him a small picked force to guard the palace, body-guards, chamberlains, assistants, domestics, a council of state, bailiffs, messengers, and a whole body of secretaries organized in four bureaus.

All these officials did not now receive their orders

[1] The number under Diocletian was 101; under Constantine (Bury's Gibbon, ii., 170), 116.—Ed.

directly from the emperor; they communicated with him only through their superior officers. The governors were subordinate to the two prætorian prefects, the officials of public works to the two prefects of the city, the collectors of taxes to the Count of the Sacred Largesses, the deputies to the Count of the Domains, all the officers of the palace to the Master of the Offices, the domestics of the court to the Chamberlain. These heads of departments had the character of ministers.

This system is not very difficult for us to comprehend. We are accustomed to see officials, judges, generals, collectors, and engineers, organized in distinct departments, each with his special duty, and subordinated to the commands of a chief of the service. We even have more ministers than there were in Constantinople; but this administrative machine which has become so familiar to us because we have been acquainted with it from our infancy, is none the less complicated and unnatural. It is the Later Empire that gave us the first model of this; the Byzantine empire preserved it and since that time all absolute governments have been forced to imitate it because it has made the work of government easier for those who have it to do.

Society in the Later Empire.—The Later Empire is a decisive moment in the history of civilization. The absolute power of the Roman magistrate is united to the pompous ceremonial of the eastern kings to create a power unknown before in history. This new imperial majesty crushes everything beneath it; the inhabitants of the empire cease to be citizens and from the fourth century are called in Latin "subjects" and in

Greek "slaves." In reality all are slaves of the emperor, but there are different grades of servitude. There are various degrees of nobility which the master confers on them and which they transmit to their posterity. The following is the series:[1]

1. The *Nobilissimi* (the very noble); these are the imperial family;

2. The *Illustres* (the notable)—the chief ministers of departments;

3. The *Spectabiles* (the eminent)—the high dignitaries;

4. The *Clarissimi* (most renowned)—the great officials, also sometimes called senators;

5. The *Perfectissimi* (very perfect).[2]

Every important man has his rank, his title, and his functions.[3] The only men who are of consequence are the courtiers and officials; it is the régime of titles and of etiquette. A clearer instance has never been given of the issue of absolute power united with the mania for titles and with the purpose to regulate everything. The Later Empire exhibits the completed type of a society reduced to a machine and of a government absorbed by a court. It realized the ideal that is proposed today by the partisans of absolute power; and for a long time the friends of liberty must fight against the traditions which the Later Empire has left to us.

[1] Without counting the ancient titles of consul and prætor, which were still preserved, and the new title of patrician which was given by special favor.

[2] Of inferior rank.

[3] We know the whole system by an official almanac of about the year 419, entitled Notitia Dignitatum, a list of all the civil and military dignities and powers in the East and West. Each dignitary has a special section preceded by an emblem which represents his honors.

THE CHURCH AND THE STATE

Triumph of Christianity.—During the first two centuries of our era the Christians occupied but a small place in the empire. Almost all of them were of the lower classes, workmen, freedmen, slaves, who lived obscure lives in the multitude of the great cities. For a long time the aristocracy ignored the Christians; even in the second century Suetonius in his "Lives of the Twelve Cæsars" speaks of a certain Chrestus who agitated the populace of Rome. When the religion first concerned the world of the rich and cultivated people, they were interested simply to deride it as one only for the poor and ignorant. It was precisely because it addressed the poor of this world in providing a compensation in the life to come that Christianity made so many proselytes. Persecution, far from suppressing it, gave it more force. "The blood of the martyrs," said the faithful, "is the seed of the church." During the whole of the third century conversions continued, not only among the poor, but among the aristocracy as well. At the first of the fourth century all the East had become Christian. Helena, the mother of Constantine, was a Christian and has been canonized by the church. When Constantine marched against his rival, he took for his ensign a standard (the labarum), which bore the cross and the monogram of Christ. His victory was the victory of the Christians. He allowed them now to perform their religious rites freely (by the edict of 313), and later he favored them openly.

Yet he did not break with the ancient religion: while he presided at the great assembly of the Christian bishops, he continued to hold the title of Pontifex Maximus; he carried in his helmet a nail of the true cross and on his coins he still had the sun-god represented. In his city of Constantinople he had a Christian church built, but also a temple to Victory. For a half-century it was difficult to know what was the official religion of the empire.

Organization of the Church.—The Christians even under persecution had never dreamed of overthrowing the empire. As soon as persecution ceased, the bishops became the allies of the emperors. Then the Christian church was organized definitively, and it was organized on the model of the Later Empire, in the form that it preserves to this day. Each city had a bishop who resided in the city proper and governed the people of the territory; this territory subject to the bishop was termed a Diocese. In any country in the Later Empire, there were as many bishops and dioceses as there were cities. This is why the bishops were so numerous and dioceses so many in the East and in Italy where the country was covered with cities. In Gaul, on the contrary, there were but 120 dioceses between the Rhine and the Pyrenees, and the most of these, save in the south, were of the size of a modern French department. Each province became an ecclesiastical province; the bishop of the capital (metropolis) became the metropolitan, or as he was later termed, the archbishop.

The Councils.—In this century began the councils, the great assemblies of the church. There had already been some local councils at which the bishops and priests of a single province had been present. For the first time, in 324,[1] Constantine convoked a General Assembly of the World (an ecumenical council) at Nicæa, in Asia Minor; 318 ecclesiastics were in attendance. They discussed questions of theology and drew up the Nicene Creed, the Catholic confession of faith. Then the emperor wrote to all the churches, bidding them "conform to the will of God as expressed by the council." This was the first ecumenical council, and there were three others[2] of these before the arrival of the barbarians made an assembly of the whole church impossible. The decisions reached by these councils had the force of law for all Christians: the decisions are called Canons[3] (rules). The collection of these regulations constitutes the Canon Law.

The Heretics.—From the second century there were among the Christians heretics who professed opinions contrary to those of the majority of the church. Often the bishops of a country assembled to pronounce the new teaching as false, to compel the author to abjure, and, if he refused, to separate him from the communion of Christians. But frequently the author of the heresy had partisans convinced of the truth of his teaching who would not submit and continued to profess the condemned opinions. This was the cause of hatred and violent strife between them and the faithful who were attached to the creed of the church (the

[1] It met in 325.—ED.

[2] It is to be noted that the author is speaking of ecumenical or world councils. The three referred to are Constantinople (381), Ephesus (431), and Chalcedon (451).—ED.

[3] Today, even, the word "canonical" signifies "in accordance with rule."

orthodox). As long as the Christians were weak and persecuted by the state, they fought among themselves only with words and with books; but when all society was Christian, the contests against the heretics turned into persecutions, and sometimes into civil wars.

Almost all of the heresies of this time arose among the Greeks of Asia or Egypt, peoples who were subtle, sophistical, and disputatious. The heresies were usually attempts to explain the mysteries of the Trinity and of the Incarnation. The most significant of these heresies was that of Arius; he taught that Christ was created by God the Father and was not equal to him. The Council of Nicæa condemned this view, but his doctrine, called Arianism, spread throughout the East. From that time for two centuries Catholics and Arians fought to see who should have the supremacy in the church; the stronger party anathematized, exiled, imprisoned, and sometimes killed the chiefs of the opposition. For a long time the Arians had the advantage; several emperors took sides with them; then, too, as the barbarians entered the empire, they were converted to Arianism and received Arian bishops. More than two centuries had passed before the Catholics had overcome this heresy.

Paganism.—The ancient religion of the Gentiles did not disappear at a single stroke. The Orient was quickly converted; but in the Occident there were few Christians outside the cities, and even there many continued to worship idols. The first Christian emperors did not wish to break with the ancient imperial religion; they simultaneously protected the bishops of the Christians and the priests of the gods; they presided over councils and yet remained pontifex maximus. One of them, Julian (surnamed the Apostate), openly returned to the ancient religion. The emperor Gratian in 384[1] was the first to refuse the insignia of the pontifex maximus. But as intolerance was general in this century, as soon as the Roman religion ceased to be official, men began to persecute it. The sacred fire of Rome that had burned for eleven centuries was extinguished, the Vestals were removed, the Olympian games were celebrated for the last time in 394. Then the monks of Egypt issued from their deserts to destroy the altars of the false gods and to establish relics in the temples of Anubis and Serapis. Marcellus, a bishop of Syria, at the head of a band of soldiers and gladiators sacked the temple of Jupiter at Apamæa and set himself to scour the country for the destruction of the sanctuaries; he was killed by the peasants and raised by the church to the honor of a saint.

Soon idolatry persisted only in the rural districts where it escaped detection; the idolaters were peasants who continued to adore sacred trees and fountains and to assemble in proscribed sanctuaries.[2] The Christians commenced to call "pagans" (the peasants) those whom up to this time they had called Gentiles. And this name has still clung to them. Paganism thus led an obscure existence in Italy, in Gaul, and in Spain down to the end of the sixth century.

Theodosius.—The incursions of the Germanic peoples into the empire continued for two centuries until the Huns, a people of Tartar horsemen, came from the

[1] Probably 375; Gratian died in 383.—Ed.

[2] Several saints, like St. Marcellus, found martyrdom at the hands of peasants exasperated at the destruction of their idols.

steppes of Asia, and threw themselves on the Germans, who occupied the country to the north of the Danube. In that country there was already a great German kingdom, that of the Goths, who had been converted to Christianity by Ulfilas, an Arian. To escape the Huns, a part of this people, the West Goths (Visigoths), fled into Roman territory, defeated the Roman armies, and overspread the country even to Greece. Valens, the emperor of the East, had perished in the defeat of Adrianople (378); Gratian, the emperor of the West, took as colleague a noble Spaniard, Theodosius by name, and gave him the title of Augustus of the East (379). Theodosius was able to rehabilitate his army by avoiding a great battle with the Visigoths and by making a war of skirmishes against them; this decided them to conclude a treaty. They accepted service under the empire, land was given them in the country to the south of the Danube, and they were charged with preventing the enemies of the empire from crossing the river.

Theodosius, having reëstablished peace in the East, came to the West where Gratian had been killed by order of the usurper Maximus (383). This Maximus was the commander of the Roman army of Britain; he had crossed into Gaul with his army, abandoning the Roman provinces of Britain to the ravages of the highland Scotch, had defeated Gratian, and invaded Italy. He was master of the West, Theodosius of the East. The contest between them was not only one between persons; it was a battle between two religions: Theodosius was Catholic and had assembled a council at Constantinople to condemn the heresy of

Arius (381); Maximus was ill-disposed toward the church. The engagement occurred on the banks of the Save; Maximus was defeated, taken, and executed.

Theodosius established Valentinian II, the son of Gratian, in the West and then returned to the East. But Arbogast, a barbarian Frank, the general of the troops of Valentinian, had the latter killed, and without venturing to proclaim himself emperor since he was not a Roman, had his Roman secretary Eugenius made emperor. This was a religious war: Arbogast had taken the side of the pagans; Theodosius, the victor, had Eugenius executed and himself remained the sole emperor. His victory was that of the Catholic church.

In 391 the emperor Theodosius promulgated the Edict of Milan. It prohibited the practice of the ancient religion: whoever offered a sacrifice, adored an idol, or entered a temple should be condemned to death as a state criminal, and his goods should be confiscated to the profit of the informer. All the pagan temples were razed to the ground or converted into Christian churches. And so Theodosius was extolled by ecclesiastical writers as the model for emperors.

Theodosius gave a rare example of submission to the church. The inhabitants of Thessalonica had risen in riot, had killed their governor, and overthrown the statues of the emperor. Theodosius in irritation ordered the people to be massacred; 7,000 persons suffered death. When the emperor presented himself some time after to enter the cathedral of Milan, Ambrose, the bishop, charged him with his crime before all the people, and declared that he could not give entrance to the church to a man defiled with so many murders. Theodosius confessed his sin, accepted the public penance which the bishop imposed upon him, and for eight months remained at the door of the church.

APPENDIX

REFERENCES FOR SUPPLEMENTARY READING

PREHISTORIC TIMES

Lubbock: Prehistoric Times. Appleton, 1878.
Lubbock: Origin of Civilization. Appleton, 1881.
Hoernes: Primitive Man. Temple Primers. Macmillan, 1901.
Lyell: Antiquity of Man. London: Murray, 1863.
Keary: Dawn of History. Scribners.
Tylor: Anthropology. Appleton, 1881.
McLennan: Studies in Ancient History. Macmillan, 1886.
Ripley: Races of Europe. 2 v. Appleton, 1899.
Sergi: The Mediterranean Race. Scribners, 1901.
Maine: Ancient Law. Holt, 1883.
Mason: Woman's Share in Primitive Culture. Appleton, 1894.

General Works of Reference—
Ploetz: Epitome of Universal History. Houghton, Mifflin & Co., 1883.
Ranke: Universal History, edited by Prothero. Harpers, 1885.
Andrews: Institutes of General History. Silver, 1887.
Haydn: Dictionary of Dates. Putnams, 1889.
Larned: History for Ready Reference. Nichols.

Atlases—
Spruner-Sieglin: Atlas Antiquus. Gotha.
Kiepert: Atlas Antiquus. Leach, Shewell, and Sanborn.
Putzger: Historischer Schul-atlas. Lemcke and Buechner, 1902.
Droysen: Allgemeiner Historischer Hand-atlas. Leipsic, 1885.
Freeman: Historical Geography of Europe. Edited by Bury. 2 v. Longmans, 1903.
Schrader: Atlas de Géographie Historique. Paris: Hachette.

General Histories of the East—
Sayce: Ancient Empires of the East. Scribners, 1886.
Lenormant and Chevallier: Ancient History of the East. 2 v. Lippincott, 1875.
Duncker: History of Antiquity. 6 v. London: Bentley 1877–82.

Rawlinson: Manual of Ancient History. American Book Co., 1871.
Clarke: Ten Great Religions. Houghton, Mifflin & Co., 1894.
Cunningham: Western Civilization in Its Economic Aspects. Cambridge (England), 1898.

EGYPT

SOURCES—

Records of the Past. 6 v. London: Bagster, 1888–92. 4*s.* 6*d.* each. Old Series, 1875–8. 12 v.
Herodotus: Book II. Rawlinson's edition. 2 v. Scribners, 1897.
Book of the Dead. Translated by Budge. 3 v. Open Court, 1901.

LITERATURE—

Rawlinson: Ancient Egypt. Putnams, 1887.
Flinders-Petrie: History of Egypt. 6 v. London: Scribners, 1899.
Breasted: History of Egypt. Scribners, 1905.
Erman, Life in Ancient Egypt. Macmillan, 1894.
Maspero: Dawn of Civilization. Appleton, 1896.
Maspero: Life in Ancient Egypt and Assyria. Appleton, 1892.
Wilkinson: Manners and Customs of the Ancient Egyptians. 3 v. Dodd.
Perrot and Chipiez: History of Art in Ancient Egypt. 2 v. Armstrong, 1882.
Flinders-Petrie: Egyptian Decorative Art. London: Methuen, 1895.

BABYLON AND ASSYRIA

SOURCES—

Records of the Past.

LITERATURE—

Ragozin: Chaldea. Putnams, 1886.
Ragozin: Assyria. Putnams, 1887.
Sayce: Assyria: Its Princes, Priests, and People. S. P. C. K., 1890.
Sayce: Social Life among the Assyrians and Babylonians. S. P. C. K., 1893.
Sayce: Fresh Light from Ancient Monuments. S. P. C. K., 1883.
Sayce: Babylonians and Assyrians. Scribners, 1889.
Goodspeed: History of the Babylonians and Assyrians. Scribners, 1902.
Layard: Discoveries among the Ruins of Nineveh and Babylon. Barnes, 1875.

Maspero: Dawn of Civilization. Appleton, 1896.
Maspero: Life in Ancient Egypt and Assyria. Appleton, 1892.
Maspero: Struggle of the Nations. Appleton, 1897.
Maspero: Passing of the Empires. Appleton, 1899.
Perrot and Chipiez: History of Art in Chaldea and Assyria. 2 v. Armstrong, 1884.

INDIA

SOURCES—

Sacred Books of the East.

LITERATURE—

Wheeler: Primer of Indian History. Macmillan, 1890
Smith, V. A.: Early History of India. Oxford, 1904.
Ragozin: Vedic India. Putnams, 1895.
Davids: Buddhist India. Putnams, 1903.
Rhys-Davids: Buddhism. Putnams, 1899.
Lane-Poole: Mediæval India under Mohammedan Rule. Putnams, 1903.
Monier-Williams: Buddhism, Brahmanism, and Hinduism. London: Murray, 1889.
Monier-Williams: Indian Wisdom. London: Allen, 1875–6.
Frazer: Literary History of India. Scribners, 1898.
Maine: Early History of Institutions. Holt, 1875.

PERSIA

SOURCES—

Records of the Past.
Herodotus.
Church: Stories of the East (from Herodotus). Dodd, Mead & Co., 1883.

LITERATURE—

Benjamin: Persia. Putnams, 1887.
Markham: General Sketch of the History of Persia. London: Longmans, 1874.
Vaux: Persia from the Monuments. Young, 1878.
Jackson: Zoroaster, Prophet of Ancient Iran. Macmillan, 1899.
Perrot and Chipiez: History of Art in Persia, Phrygia, etc. 2 v. Armstrong, 1895.

THE PHŒNICIANS

SOURCES—

The Old Testament.
Voyage of Hanno, translated by Falconer.

LITERATURE—
Rawlinson: Phœnicia. Putnams, 1889.
Maspero: Struggle of the Nations. Appleton, 1897.
Paton: Early History of Syria and Palestine. Scribners, 1901.
Taylor: The Alphabet. 2 v. Scribners, 1899.
Perrot and Chipiez: History of Art in Phœnicia and Cyprus. 2 v. Armstrong, 1885.

THE HEBREWS

SOURCES—
The Old Testament.
The Talmud.
Josephus: Antiquities of the Jews; Wars of the Jews; Whiston's translation. 4 v. London, 1825. New edition of Whiston by Shilleto. 5 v. Macmillan, 1889–90.

LITERATURE—
Hosmer: The Jews. Putnams, 1885.
Sayce: Early History of the Hebrews. Macmillan, 1897.
Kent: History of the Hebrew People. 2 v. Scribners, 1899.
Kent: History of the Jewish People. 2 v. Scribners, 1899.
Milman: History of the Jews. 3 v. Armstrong, 1870.
Stanley: History of the Jewish Church. 3 v. Scribners, 1884.
McCurdy: History, Prophecy, and the Monuments. Macmillan, 1901. 3 v.
Graetz: History of the Jews. 6 v. Jewish Publishing Co., 1891–98.
Perrot and Chipiez: History of Art in Sardinia, Judea, Syria and Asia Minor. 2 v. Armstrong, 1890.
Day: Social Life of the Hebrews. Scribners, 1901.
Rosenau: Jewish Ceremonial Institutions and Customs. Baltimore: Friedenwald, 1903.
Leroy-Boileau: Israel among the Nations; translated by Hellman. Putnams, 1900.
Cheyne: Jewish Religious Life after the Exile. Putnams, 1898.

GREECE

GENERAL HISTORIES—
Grote: History of Greece. 10 v. Harpers, 1851–6.
Holm: History of Greece. 4 v. Macmillan, 1894–8.
Duruy: History of Greece. 8 v. Estes, 1890–2.
Abbott: History of Greece. 3 v. Putnams, 1888–99.
One-volume histories of Greece are: Bury (Macmillan, 1902). Oman (Longmans, 1901). Botsford (Macmillan, 1899). Myers (Ginn, 1895). Cox (London, 1883).

GREEK ANTIQUITIES—
Smith: Dictionary of Greek and Roman Antiquities. London: Murray, 1890–1. 2 v.

Gardner and Jevons: Manual of Greek Antiquities. Scribners, 1895.
Schömann: The Antiquities of Greece. London, Rivingtons, 1880. A new and improved edition in the German.
Harpers' Classical Literature and Antiquities. Harpers, 1896.

GREEK HISTORICAL SOURCES (translated into English).
Homer: Iliad. Translated by Lang, Leaf, and Myers. Macmillan.
Homer: Odyssey. Translated by Butcher and Lang. Macmillan.
Herodotus: Translated by Rawlinson. Appleton, 1880. 4 v. Text of same with abridged notes: Scribners, 2 v. 1897.
Herodotus: Translated by Macaulay. 2 v. Macmillan, 1890.
Thucydides: Translated by Jowett. 2 v. Lothrop, 1883.
Xenophon: Dakyns' edition. 4 v. Macmillan, 1890–7.
Demosthenes: Works translated by Kennedy. 5 v. Macmillan.
Arrian: Translated in Bohn Library. Macmillan.
Pausanias: Description of Greece. 2 v. Macmillan, 1886.
Pausanias: Description of Greece. Frazer's edition. Macmillan, 6 v.
Polybius: Shuckburgh's edition. 2 v. Macmillan, 1889.
Plutarch: Lives. Translated by Stewart and Long. 4 v. Macmillan, 1880.
Plutarch: Lives. North's translation. 10 v. Macmillan.

SOURCE MATERIAL IN GREEK HISTORY (published in pamphlet form).
Fling: "Studies in European History." Chicago, Ainsworth. 5c. each.
The Homeric Age.
The Athenian Constitution.
Spartan Life.
Alexander's Methods of Warfare.
Achæan League.
Indiana University "Extracts from the Sources." Bloomington, Ind. 3c. each.
Funeral Oration of Pericles.
Demosthenes' Third Philippic.
Philip's Letter to the Athenians.
Typical Passage from the Apology of Socrates.
Cassell's National Library. Cassell, New York. 10c. each.
Plutarch translated in several volumes.
Plato's Crito and Phædo.
Xenophon's Memorable Thoughts of Socrates.
Herodotus, Egypt and Scythia.

PERIODS OF GREEK HISTORY—
Tsountas-Manatt: Mycenæan Age. Houghton, Mifflin & Co., 1896.

Ridgeway: The Early Age in Greece. 2 v. Cambridge, 1901.
Freeman: Studies of Travel: Greece. Putnams, 1893.
Clerke: Familiar Studies in Homer. Longmans, 1892.
Jebb: Introduction to Homer. Ginn & Co., 1887.
Allcroft and Mason: Early Grecian History. Hinds & Noble, 1898.
Benjamin: Troy. Scribners, 1880.
Allcroft and Mason: Making of Athens. Hinds & Noble, 1898.
Cox: Greeks and Persians. Scribners, 1876.
Grundy: The Great Persian War. Scribners, 1901
Cox: Athenian Empire. Scribners, 1877.
Lloyd: Age of Pericles. 2 v. Macmillan, 1875.
Abbott: Pericles. Putnams, 1895.
Grant: Greece in the Age of Pericles. Scribners, 1893.
Allcroft and Mason: Peloponnesian War. Hinds & Noble, 1898.
Freeman: Sicily. Putnams, 1892.
Allcroft and Mason: Sparta and Thebes. Hinds & Noble, 1898.
Sankey: Spartan and Theban Supremacies. Scribners, 1877.
Allcroft and Mason: Decline of Hellas. Hinds & Noble, 1898.
Curteis: Rise of the Macedonian Empire. Scribners, 1878.
Hogarth: Philip and Alexander. Scribners, 1897.
Wheeler: Alexander the Great. Putnams, 1900.
Dodge: Alexander. Houghton, Mifflin & Co., 1890.
Mahaffy: Alexander's Empire. Putnams, 1887.
Mahaffy: Problems in Greek History. Macmillan, 1892.
Bevan: House of Seleucus. 2 v. Longmans, 1902.
Mahaffy: Empire of Egypt under the Ptolemies. 2 v. Macmillan, 1899.
Mahaffy: Greek Life and Thought. Macmillan, 1887.

GREEK POLITICAL DEVELOPMENT—
Fowler: City-State of the Greeks and Romans. Macmillan, 1893.
Greenidge: Greek Constitutional History. Macmillan, 1896.
Schömann: Antiquities of Greece. London, 1880.
Cox: Lives of Greek Statesmen. 2 v. Harpers, 1886.
Gilbert: Constitutional Antiquities of Athens and Sparta. Macmillan, 1895.
Botsford: Athenian Constitution. Macmillan, 1893.
Whibley: Greek Oligarchies. Macmillan, 1896.
Whibley: Political Parties in Athens in the Peloponnesian War. Macmillan, 1889.
Freeman: History of Federal Government. Macmillan, 1863.

SOCIAL LIFE OF THE GREEKS—
Blümner: Home Life of the Ancient Greeks. Cassell, 1893.
Mahaffy: Social Life in Greece. Macmillan, 1887.
Mahaffy: A Survey of Greek Civilization. Macmillan, 1899.

Guhl and Koner: Life of the Greeks and Romans. Scribners, 1877.
Becker: Charicles. Longmans.
Cunningham: Western Civilization in Its Economic Aspects. Cambridge, 1898.
Davidson: Education of the Greek People. Appleton, 1894.
Mahaffy: Old Greek Education. Harpers, 1882.

HISTORIES OF GREEK LITERATURE—
Mahaffy: History of Classical Greek Literature. 2 v. Macmillan, 1880.
Murray: Ancient Greek Literature. Appleton, 1897.
Jevons: History of Greek Literature. Scribners, 1886.
Jebb: Primer of Greek Literature. American Book Co., 1878.
Jebb: Classical Greek Poetry. Houghton, Mifflin & Co.
Symonds: The Greek Poets. 2 v. Macmillan.
Warr: The Greek Epic. Young, 1895.
Jebb: The Attic Orators. 2 v. Macmillan, 1876.
Pater: Greek Studies. Macmillan, 1895.

HISTORIES OF ART—
Reber: History of Ancient Art. Harpers, 1882.
Lübke: Outlines of the History of Art. 2 v. Dodd, 1881.
Perrot and Chipiez: History of Art in Primitive Greece. 2 v. Armstrong, 1895.
Tarbell: History of Greek Art. Macmillan, 1896.
Fergusson: History of Architecture. 2 v. Dodd, 1875.
Gardner: Handbook of Greek Sculpture. Macmillan, 1896–7.
Harrison and Verall: Mythology and Monuments of Ancient Athens. Macmillan, 1894.
Harrison: Introductory Studies in Greek Art. Macmillan, 1892.
Gardner: Ancient Athens. Macmillan, 1902.

GREEK ARCHÆOLOGY—
Collignon: Manual of Greek Archæology. Cassell, 1886.
Murray: Handbook of Greek Archæology. Scribners, 1892.
Schuckardt: Schliemann's Excavations. Macmillan, 1891.
Diehl: Excursions in Greece. Lemcke & Buechner, 1893.
Gardner: New Chapters in Greek History. Putnams, 1892.

GREEK PHILOSOPHY—
Mayor: Sketch of Ancient Philosophy. Macmillan, 1881.
Marshall: Short History of Greek Philosophy. Macmillan, 1891.
Plato: Translated by Jowett. 4 v. Scribners.
Aristotle: Translated in Bohn's Library. Macmillan.
Zeller: Outlines of the History of Greek Philosophy. Holt, 1890.

GRECIAN MYTHOLOGY—
Gayley: Classic Myths. Ginn, 1893.
Guerber: Myths of Greece and Rome. American Book Co., 1893.
Bulfinch: Age of Fable. Lee & Shepard, 1881.

ROME

GENERAL HISTORIES—
Mommsen: History of Rome. 5 v. Scribners, 1895.
Ihne: History of Rome. 5 v. London: Longmans, 1871–82.
Duruy: History of Rome. 8 v. Boston: Jewett, 1884–5.
Long: Decline of the Roman Republic. 5 v. London: Bell, 1864–74.
Greenidge: History of Rome During the Latin Republic. I. Methuen, 1904.
Shuckburgh: History of Rome. Macmillan, 1894.
How and Leigh: History of Rome. Longmans, 1896.
Pelham: Outlines of Roman History. Putnams, 1893.
Botsford: History of Rome. Macmillan, 1903.
Merivale: History of the Romans under the Empire. 6 v. Appleton, 1875.
Gibbon: Decline and Fall of the Roman Empire, Bury's edition. 7 v. London: Methuen, 1900–2.

SOURCES OF ROMAN HISTORY (translated into English).
Livy: History and Epitome, translated by Spillan. 4 v. Macmillan, 1887–90.
Polybius: Histories, translated by Shuckburgh. 2 v. Macmillan, 1889.
Plutarch: Lives, translated by Stewart and Long. 4 v. Macmillan, 1880.
Appian: Roman History, translated by White. 2 v. Macmillan, 1899.
Sallust, Florus, and Velleius Paterculus, translated by Watson. Macmillan, 1887.
Cicero: Orations, translated by Yonge. 4 v. Macmillan, 1851–2.
Cicero: Letters, translated by Shuckburgh. 4 v. Macmillan, 1899.
Cæsar: Gallic War and Civil War. Macmillan, 1890.
Justin, Nepos, and Eutropius, translated by Watson. Macmillan.
Augustus: Deeds (Monumentum Ancyranum); in University of Pennsylvania. Translations and Reprints, vol. V. Philadelphia, 1898.
Suetonius: Lives of the Twelve Cæsars, translated by Thomas. Forester. Macmillan, 1898.
Tacitus: Annals, translated by Church and Brodribb. Macmillan, 1895.

Tacitus: History, translated by Church and Brodribb. Macmillan, 1894.
Tacitus: Germania, translated by Church and Brodribb. Macmillan, 1893.
Josephus: Antiquities and Wars of the Jews, translated by Whiston-Shilleto. 5 v. Macmillan, 1889–90.
Pliny the Younger: Letters, translated by Melmoth. Macmillan.
Marcus Aurelius: Meditations, translated by Long. Macmillan, 1887.
Ammianus Marcellinus: Roman History, translated by Yonge. Macmillan, 1894.
Julian the Emperor: Works, translated by King. Macmillan, 1888.
Eusebius: Ecclesiastical History and Life of Constantine, translated by McGiffert. Scribners, 1890.
Jerome: Works. Scribners, 1893.
Augustine: Works. 8 v. Scribners, 1886–8.
Munro: Source Book of Roman History. Heath, 1904.
Robinson: Readings in European History, Vol. I. Ginn. 1904.
Greenidge and Clay: Sources for Roman History, B. C. 133-70. Frowde, 1903.
Gwatkin: Selections from Early Christian Writers. Macmillan, 1893.

SOURCES IN PAMPHLET FORM—
Fling: "European History Studies." Ainsworth. 5c. each.
The Roman Constitution.
Roman Life in the Time of the First Punic War.
Roman Life in the Jugurthine Period.
Roman Life in the Early Empire.
Roman Law.
Indiana University "Extracts from the Sources." Bloomington, Ind. 3c.
Hannibal's Passage of the Alps.
Cicero's Oration against Verres.
Selections from the Satires of Juvenal.
Selections from the Letters of Pliny the Younger.
The Germania of Tacitus.
Laws of the Twelve Tables.
University of Pennsylvania. "Translations and Reprints from the Original Sources of European History." Philadelphia, or Longmans, New York.
The Early Christian Persecutions.
Monumentum Ancyranum.
The Early Germans.
Extracts from the Notitia Dignitatum.
The Canons of the First Four General Councils.
Cassell's National Library. Cassell, New York.
Plutarch translated in several volumes.

PERIODS OF ROMAN HISTORY—
Ihne: Early Rome. Scribners, 1893.
Allcroft and Mason: Struggle for Empire. Hinds & Noble, 1893.
Church: Carthage. Putnams, 1886.
Smith: Carthage and the Carthaginians. Longmans, 1890.
Smith: Rome and Carthage. Scribners, 1891.
Arnold: Second Punic War. Macmillan, 1849.
Dodge: Life of Hannibal. Houghton, Mifflin & Co., 1891.
Morris: Hannibal. Putnams, 1897.
How: Hannibal and the Great War between Rome and Carthage. London: Seeley, 1899.
Allcroft and Mason: Rome under the Oligarchs. Hinds & Noble, 1893.
Beesly: Gracchi, Marius, and Sulla. Scribners, 1893.
Allcroft and Mason: Decline of the Oligarchy. Hinds & Noble, 1893.
Oman: Seven Roman Statesmen. Longmans, 1902.
Beesly: Catiline, Clodius, and Tiberius. London: Chapman & Hall, 1898.
Strachan-Davidson: Cicero. Putnams, 1894.
Forsyth: Life of Cicero. 2 v. Scribners, 1877.
Boissier: Cicero and His Friends. Putnams, 1897.
Froude: Cæsar. Scribners, 1879.
Dodge: Cæsar. Houghton, Mifflin & Co., 1892.
Van Santvoord: House of Cæsar. Pafraets (Troy, N. Y.), 1902.
Fowler: Cæsar. Putnams, 1892.
Merivale: The Roman Triumvirates. Scribners, 1877.
Holmes: Cæsar's Conquest of Gaul. Macmillan, 1899.
Mahaffy: Greek World under Roman Sway. Macmillan, 1890.
Bossier: Roman Africa. Putnams, 1899.
Bossier: Rome and Pompeii. Putnams, 1896.
Hall: The Romans on the Riviera and the Rhone. Macmillan, 1898.
Bury: (Students') Roman Empire. American Book Co. 1893.
Capes: Early Roman Empire. Scribners, 1886.
Mommsen: Provinces of the Roman Empire. 2 v. Scribners, 1887.
Firth: Augustus Cæsar. Putnams, 1903.
Shuckburgh: Augustus. Unwin, 1903.
Tarver: Tiberius the Tyrant. Dutton, 1902.
Dill: Roman Society from Nero to Marcus Aurelius. Macmillan, 1904.
Gregorovius: The Emperor Hadrian. Macmillan, 1898.
Bryant: Reign of Antoninus. Macmillan, 1896.
Capes: Age of the Antonines. Scribners, 1887.
Watson: Marcus Aurelius Antoninus. Harpers, 1884.
Firth: Constantine the Great. Putnams, 1905.
Negri: Julian the Apostate. 2 v. Scribners, 1905.
Gardner: Julian. Putnams, 1895.

Glover: Life and Letters in the Fourth Century. Cambridge, 1901.
Dill: Roman Society in the Last Century of the Western Empire. Macmillan, 1899.
Kingsley: Roman and Teuton. Macmillan, 1889.
Hodgkin: Dynasty of Theodosius. Frowde, 1889.
Villari: Barbarian Invasions of Italy. 2 v. Scribners, 1902.
Hodgkin: Italy and Her Invaders. 8 v. Frowde, 1892–9.
Sheppard: Fall of Rome. Macmillan, 1861.
Bury: Later Roman Empire. 2 v. Macmillan, 1889.
Oman: Byzantine Empire. Putnams, 1892.

ROMAN ANTIQUITIES—
Ramsay-Lanciani: Manual of Roman Antiquities. Scribners, 1895.
Smith: Dictionary of Greek and Roman Antiquities. 2 v. London: Murray, 1890-1.
Seyffert: Dictionary of Classical Antiquities, edited by Nettleship and Sandys. Macmillan, 1895.
Schreiber: Atlas of Classical Antiquities. Macmillan, 1895.

ROMAN POLITICAL DEVELOPMENT—
Fowler: City-State of the Greeks and Romans. Macmillan, 1895.
Taylor: Constitutional and Political History of Rome. London: Methuen, 1899.
Greenidge: Roman Public Life. Macmillan, 1901.
Abbott: Roman Political Institutions. Ginn, 1901.
Arnold: Roman Provincial Administration. London: Macmillan, 1879. Out of print.
Mommsen: Provinces of the Roman Empire. 2 v. Scribners, 1887.
Seeley: Roman Imperialism. Little, Brown & Co., 1871.

SOCIAL LIFE OF THE ROMANS—
Guhl and Koner: Life of the Greeks and Romans. Scribners, 1889.
Church: Roman Life in the Days of Cicero. Macmillan, 1883.
Fowler: Roman Festivals. Macmillan, 1899.
Ingram: History of Slavery. Macmillan, 1895.
Rydberg: Roman Days. Putnams, 1879.
Thomas: Roman Life under the Cæsars. Putnams, 1899.
Johnston: Private Life of the Romans. Scott, Toresman & Co., 1903.
Inge: Society in Rome under the Cæsars. Scribners, 1888.
Pellison: Roman Life in Pliny's Time. Jacobs, 1896.
Lecky: History of European Morals. 2 v. Appleton, 1869.

ROMAN LITERATURE—
Mackail: Latin Literature. Scribners, 1898.
Cruttwell: History of Roman Literature. Scribners, 1878.
Simcox: History of Latin Literature. 2 v. Harpers, 1883.

Teuffel-Schwabe: History of Roman Literature. Macmillan, 1891.
Tyrrell: Latin Poetry. Houghton, Mifflin & Co., 1895.
Sellar: Roman Poets of the Republic. Oxford, 1881.
Sellar: Roman Poets of the Augustan Age. 2 v. Oxford, 1877.
See also translations of Roman authors mentioned under "Sources."

ROMAN ART—
Reber: History of Ancient Art. Harpers, 1882.
Burn: Roman Literature in Relation to Roman Art. Macmillan, 1890.
Wickoff: Roman Art. Macmillan, 1900.
Falke: Greece and Rome: Their Life and Art. Holt, 1885.
See under Greece for other histories of art.

ROMAN LAW—
Hadley: Introduction to Roman Law. Appleton, 1876.
Morey: Outlines of Roman Law. Putnams, 1893.
Muirhead: Historical Introduction to the Private Law of Rome. Macmillan, 1899.
Howe: Studies in the Civil Law. Little, Brown & Co., 1896.

ROMAN ARCHÆOLOGY—
Lanciani: Ancient Rome in the Light of Recent Discoveries. Houghton, Mifflin & Co., 1888.
Lanciani: Pagan and Christian Rome. Houghton, Mifflin & Co., 1896.
Lanciani: Ruins and Excavations of Ancient Rome. Houghton, Mifflin & Co., 1897.
Lanciani: Destruction of Ancient Rome. Macmillan, 1899.
Mau: Pompeii, translated by Kelsey. Macmillan, 1899.
Platner: Topography and Monuments of Ancient Rome. Allyn & Bacon, 1904.
Lovell: Stories in Stone upon the Roman Forum. Macmillan, 1902.
Burton-Brown: Recent Excavations in the Roman Forum. London: Scribners, 1905.

CHRISTIANITY—
General Church Histories:
Moeller: History of the Christian Church. 3 v. Macmillan, 1898–1900.
Gieseler: Church History. 5 v. Harpers, 1857–79.
Neander: History of the Christian Religion and Church. 5 v. Houghton, 1853–4.
Schaff: History of the Christian Church. 7 v. Scribners, 1884–92.
Alzog: Manual of Universal Church History. 3 v. Cincinnati: Clarke, 1874–8.
Kurtz: Church History. Lippincott, 1860.

Milman: History of Christianity. 3 v. Armstrong.
Milman: Latin Christianity. 8 v. in 4. Armstrong, 1881.
Allen: Outline of Christian History. Little, Brown & Co., 1886.
Allen: Christian Institutions. Scribners, 1897.
Fisher: History of the Christian Church. Scribners, 1887.

The Early Church:
Pressensé: Early Years of Christianity. 4 v. Methodist Book Concern, 1873.
Fisher: Beginnings of Christianity. Scribners, 1877.
Carr: Church and the Roman Empire. Longmans, 1902.
Spence: Early Christianity and Paganism. Dutton, 1902.
Ramsay: Church in the Roman Empire before 170. Putnams, 1893.
Gregg: Decian Persecution. Blackwood, 1898.
Healy: The Valerian Persecution. Houghton, 1905.
Mason: Persecution of Diocletian. London: Bell, 1876.
Renan: Influence of the Institutions, Thought, and Culture of Rome on Christianity. Scribners, 1898.
Hardy: Studies in Roman History. Macmillan, 1906.
Uhlhorn: Conflict of Christianity with Heathenism. Scribners, 1879.
Newman: Arians of the Fourth Century. Longmans, 1888.
Gwatkin: Arian Controversy. Longmans, 1889.
Cutts: St. Augustine. Young, 1881.
Stanley: Eastern Church. Scribners, 1884.
Smith-Wace: Dictionary of Christian Biography. 4 v. Little, Brown & Co., 1877–87.